Shakespeare's Bawdy

'Eric was a human lexicographer, like Samuel Johnson. He was a philologist rather than a linguist. He knew what Chomsky was doing and what had happened to phonology in Prague, but he eschewed the strict scientific approach. Linguistics is scared of semantics and prefers to concentrate on structures, leaving the study of the meaning of words to anthropologists – or, perhaps with misgivings, to Johnsonian word-lovers like Eric Partridge.'

Anthony Burgess

'*Shakespeare's Bawdy*'s status as a pioneering study remains unchallenged.'

Ralph Elliott

'Partridge remains the standard introduction on the subject.'

Reference Reviews

Eric
Partridge

Shakespeare's Bawdy

With a foreword by Stanley Wells

London and New York

First published 1957 by George Allen & Unwin

First published 1947
by Routledge & Kegan Paul
Second edition 1955
Third edition 1968

First published in Routledge Classics 2001
by Routledge
2 Park Square, Milton Park, Abingdon, Oxon, OX14 4RN
270 Madison Ave, New York, NY 10016

Reprinted 2007

Transferred to Digital Printing 2008

Routledge is an imprint of the Taylor & Francis Group, an informa business

© 1947, 1955, 1968, Eric Partridge

Typeset in Joanna by RefineCatch Limited, Bungay, Suffolk
Printed and bound in Great Britain by
TJI Digital, Padstow, Cornwall

British Library Cataloguing in Publication Data
A catalogue record for this book is available from the British Library

Library of Congress Cataloging in Publication Data
A catalog record for this book has been applied for

ISBN10: 0–415–25553–8 (hbk)
ISBN10: 0–415–25400–0 (pbk)

ISBN13: 978–0–415–25553–0 (hbk)
ISBN13: 978–0–415–25400–7 (pbk)

CONTENTS

FOREWORD   vii
PREFACE   xi

ESSAY   1

1 Introductory   1
2 Non-Sexual Bawdy   9
3 Homosexual   13
4 Sexual   19
5 General   53
6 Valedictory   59
Index to Essay   61

GLOSSARY   65

FOREWORD

When *Shakespeare's Bawdy* first appeared, in 1947, it was in an edition limited to 1,000 copies and selling at the high price of two guineas (at a time when forty-two Penguins could have been bought for this sum). Both the circumstances of its publication and certain features of the book itself aligned it with the category of erotic literature (or, in the vulgate, dirty books) such as might be perused with impunity by the wealthy and learned but should be placed and priced out of the reach of anyone else. Partridge follows the time-honoured custom of resorting to the sanitizing influence of Latin for certain expressions which English would have rendered offensive. So we read of a possible pun on '*penem in vaginam inmittere*'—to put the penis into the vagina (p. 89)—and of 'the innuendo being *digitae in vulvam inmissae* (or *impositae*)—or, at best, *vir sub indusio mulieris praetentans*, or not doing so', i.e. fingers put (or pushed) into the vulva, or the man pushing under the woman's clothes (p. 202). On occasion Partridge seems even to have coined Latinisms for sexual activity: the word penilingism (p. 92), apparently meaning 'tonguing the penis' is not recorded in the *Oxford English Dictionary* or its supplements.

Of course, Partridge was writing at a time when all editions of Shakespeare intended for use in schools were bowdlerized, when editors even of scholarly editions frequently shied away from sexual glosses, and when attitudes to expressions of sexuality were far less liberal than they were to become during the 1960s. He was a pioneer. Before his time studies had existed of what Hilda Hulme, in her *Explorations in Shakespeare's Language* (1962), was to call 'The Less Decent Language of the Time', notably the seven-volume *Dictionary of Slang and its Analogues* by John S. Farmer and W. E. Henley (New York, 1890–3). But the great *Oxford English Dictionary* (1888–1928) ignores many sexual words and expressions even though, for example, 'cunt', said by Partridge to be 'the most notorious term of all' for what he calls the *pudendum muliebre*, is, as he says, 'of impeccable "Aryan" origin, without any brutal or sadistic associations, undertones, or crescive overtones.' (Shakespeare does not use the word directly.) Both Alexander Schmidt's *Shakespeare-Lexicon* (2 vols, Berlin and London, 1874–5) and the *Shakespeare Glossary* (1911) prepared by C. T. Onions (one of the compilers of the *Dictionary*, of which the *Glossary* is an offshoot), are similarly restrictive. By contrast, *Shakespeare's Bawdy* helped to lead the way towards a new freedom and honesty in acknowledging and investigating the full extent of Shakespeare's linguistic range and in responding to the sexual resonances of a substantial section of his vocabulary. As attitudes relaxed, it appeared in a 'New Popular Edition' in 1955, was reprinted in 1956 and 1961, and was revised and enlarged by the author for a new edition (reprinted here with minor corrections) of 1968. Partridge died in 1979 at the age of 85.

Though the Glossary forms the bulk of *Shakespeare's Bawdy*, this is not simply a reference book. The opening Essay is valuable not least because it provides a helpful guide to the Glossary, alerting the reader to sexual significances in words and expressions that might otherwise appear to lack them. Partridge's interest is not primarily critical, but rather scholarly and to some degree biographical. Proclaiming himself 'neither pederast nor pedant', he counters suggestions made by Oscar Wilde, Samuel Butler, and others that Shakespeare may have been homosexual, while deducing that the dramatist's attitude to homosexuality, 'as that of every thinking person must be, was extremely tolerant' (p. 14). Needless to say, Partridge's own liberal attitude was, as he must have known, less universal even among 'thinking people' than he declares it should have been. There is more to be said on the subject, but Partridge's straightforward and sensible, if simplistic, treatment provides useful groundwork. He deduces not merely that Shakespeare was exclusively heterosexual but that he 'was an exceedingly knowledgeable amorist, a versatile connoisseur, and a highly artistic, and ingeniously skilful, practitioner of love-making, who could have taught Ovid rather more than that facile doctrinaire could have taught him; he evidently knew of, and probably he practised, an artifice accessible to few—one that I cannot becomingly mention here, though I felt it obligatory to touch on it, very briefly, in the Glossary' (p. 31). Here Partridge's customary frankness deserts him, and the reader is left to puzzle out the details of Shakespeare's connoisseurship for him- or herself. Partridge's Essay forms an eloquent, sometimes positively rhapsodic, appreciation of Shakespeare as 'the universal-spirited, the catholic-emotioned man he so dazzlingly, so movingly, was in life and in print' (p. 3).

The critical implications of Partridge's work have been carried forward in, notably, E. A. Colman's *The Dramatic Use of Bawdy in Shakespeare* (1974), which also includes a glossary; a later, more fanciful glossary with aims related to Partridge's is Frankie Rubinstein's *A Dictionary of Shakespeare's Sexual Puns and their Significance* (1984); but neither work supersedes Partridge. He has his limitations; for instance, he omits 'quean' (which can mean whore), fails to note the sexual significance of Dogberry's claim to be 'as

pretty a piece of flesh as any is in Messina', and (like both Colman and Rubinstein, who generally errs by excess), of 'bud'
(probably having as its secondary sense the glans of the penis in
Sonnet 1). Colman (pp. 12–13) rightly points to Partridge's
failure 'to provide explicit defence' for interpretations such as
the gloss 'To experience sexual emission' on 'come', but though
Colman may be correct in saying that this is not a demonstrably
Shakespearian usage, he himself provides a quotation from
Dekker showing that the sense was available to Shakespeare's
audience, which means that it should be included among potential contemporary meanings.

Reviewing the first edition of *Shakespeare's Bawdy*, Edward
Hubler remarked that 'The glossary will clarify passages which
have been but dimly understood even by Shakespeare scholars,
and the introductory essay will provide the reader with well-
founded generalizations on the range and nature of Shakespeare's usage' (*Journal of English and Germanic Philology* 47 (1948), p.
245). The tribute remains valid. *Shakespeare's Bawdy* is a classic of
Shakespeare scholarship well worthy of republication even—
perhaps particularly—for the more liberated readership of the
present time.

Stanley Wells

PREFACE

In the 18th Century, this book, or one like it, could have been published; in the Victorian period, not; up till (say) 1930, it would have been deprecated; nowadays, it will—as it should—be taken very much as a matter of course. (The apparently provocative title is merely a convenient abridgement of 'Sexuality, Homosexuality, and Bawdiness in the Works of William Shakespeare'.)

If Shakespearean criticism had not so largely been in the hands of academics and cranks, a study of Shakespeare's attitude towards sex and his use of the broad jest would probably have appeared at any time since 1918. 'Pederasts and pedants have been the curse of Shakespearean biography and criticism' (Hesketh Pearson, 1942): the academic critics (except Professors Dover Wilson and G. Wilson Knight) have, in the main and for most of the time, ignored the questions of homosexuality, sex, bawdiness: with one or two notable exceptions, they have been pitiably inadequate. The non-academic critics have done better on the homosexuality, but none of them has dealt fully, or even satisfactorily, with the normal sexuality and the bawdiness. As I am neither pederast nor pedant, I may be able to throw some light upon a neglected, yet very important, aspect of Shakespeare's character and art.

In order to avoid a too tedious catalogue-effect in the Essay, I have compiled a Glossary of such terms as fall 'within the meaning of the Act'. This Glossary will, I hope, have a value beyond that of a list, however comprehensive; even a value beyond that of the usual conscientious glossary.

The verse-numbering is that of The Shakespeare Head edition, which possesses the merit of presenting the plays in their chronological order.

Eric Partridge

1

INTRODUCTORY

Among the most generally interesting and particularly provocative books upon Shakespeare since (say) 1925 are Dover Wilson's magistral edition of Shakespeare's Works, H. Granville-Barker's brilliant Prefaces, G. Wilson Knight's profound studies, Hugh Kingsmill's thoughtful *The Return of William Shakespeare*, Chambers's authoritative *William Shakespeare*, and, in another order, Kenneth Muir & Sean O'Loughlin's *The Voyage to Illyria* and Hesketh Pearson's popular, wind-fresh *A Life of Shakespeare*. (This selection is not intended to belittle such important books as those by Edgar I. Fripp and Leslie Hotson.) None of them,[1] however, attempts a serious study of the main subject treated in the ensuing pages, whether in the sketch that is this essay or in the glossary, which, self-contained, deals with many themes that, even at this date, could not be handled in an essay designed to meet the needs of students of literature and of

---

[1] Several of those books do, inevitably, touch briefly upon Shakespeare's attitude towards sex and bawdiness: and in a notable manner. At the risk of appearing egotistic, I intend to set forth the views of only one person.

lovers of Shakespeare. This is not an *in camera* monograph for professional sexologists.

Little-minded men and women, [as *The Times Literary Supplement* said in a leader entitled 'Artist and Public' in its issue of August 17, 1940], write and paint their rubbish and the public laps it up, to the degradation of its taste. But the large-minded artist will always find within himself a great deal in common with the common people. *We have given up supposing that Shakespeare's sensational plots and bawdy jokes were only a high-brow's concessions to the groundlings.*[1] The modern consciousness of responsibility to the public in general will incline the large-minded artist to brave any exquisite sneers at the seductions of popularity, of royalties, of the box-office and so forth, and to make the most, not the least, of everything in him which is common to all men. It is no business of the artist, as artist, to educate the public. It is the very core of his business so to present his vision of truth that it can be shared and trusted by as many as possible when first he puts it forth, and by more and more as the public is trained in knowledge and judgment.

All this is almost what Shakespeare himself might have said for he knew what he was about in his plays and his poems; knew, too, that his work would survive. He sometimes regretted making himself 'a motley to the view' in his role of actor: he never expressed a doubt of posterity's opinion of his writings; he had good reason not to fret on that score.

No writer of even half the stature of Shakespeare could doubt that posterity would correctly appraise his worth; although perhaps only a second Shakespeare could adequately evaluate William Shakespeare. Much has been written about his 'universal mind'. But what of his universal soul, his universal sympathy, his universal manhood?

[1] The italics are mine.

I should not care to say that, during his life, Shakespeare was 'all things to all men',[1] for that stock-phrase has, in certain circles, come to have *une signification assez louche*, but he does seem to have been 'most things to all decent men'. Throughout his writings, as obviously in his life, Shakespeare reveals, occasionally in an explicit, generally in an implicit way, that in his spirit, his mind, his emotions, he strove to reconcile those opposites which, in fact (as sometimes he perceived), made him 'the myriad-minded', the universal-spirited, the catholic-emotioned man he so dazzlingly, so movingly, was in life and in print. In his general outlook and in his attitude towards sex and towards bawdiness, he shows that he was both an idealist and a realist; a romantic and a cynic; an ascetic and a hedonist; an etherealist and a brutalist; a philosopher and 'the average man'; a saint and a sinner; a kindly tolerator and a Juvenal-satirist; an Illuminate and a Worldly-Wise; a strict moralist and a *je-m'en-fichiste*; a glowing optimist ('How beauteous mankind is! O brave new world') and a Werther-cum-Hardy victim of *Weltschmerz*; a believer in a God-lovelied heaven and a pedestrian with feet scarce-lifting from earth all too earthy; the most lambently lyrical and dew-sweet of poets (*Romeo and Juliet*) and the most materialistically *terre à terre* of soured prose-writers (Pompey, Apemantus, the Porter in *Macbeth*); the most exacerbated libido-driven, yet expert, sensualist and—via *l'homme moyen sensuel*—the purest, most innocent novice; the subtlest thinker and the simplest emotionalist; an Ariel of the further empyrean and a Caliban of the nearest mud; a dialectical Portia and a love-living Juliet; a Cordelia and a Goneril; an Imogen and a Gertrude; a Cleopatra and a Miranda; an Antony and a Brutus; a Coriolanus and a tribune, a married man—a bachelor—a monk. He was in his life, as he is to us now, all these persons and many more, with all the intermediary types and

---

[1] 'I am made all things to all men', 1 *Corinthians*, ix 22. For the Greek original and the Vulgate rendering, see my *A Dictionary of Clichés*.

stages thrown in, with all their variations and nuances of character and temperament.

Not so strange, then, that Shakespeare's spirit, mind, and
body, as expressed in his life and his works, should have been
the arena on which was fought an almost continuous battle
between forces the highest and the lowest, the best and the
worst, the most spiritual and the most anti-spiritual; nor is it
strange that he should bitterly have resented that compromise
which he was obliged to make rather more often than was consonant with his deep-based contempt for compromise. Shakespeare was at the back of my mind when, in 1939, I wrote[1] a
passage elaborating this theme: the tragedies of unavoidable
compromise and of 'the world's slow stain'.

If ever there were a man filled with the joy and sap of life, it
was Shakespeare; and if ever there were a man compact of spiritual needs and loveliest and noblest aspirations, it was Shakespeare. He could muse and meditate with the most meditative,
also could he talk and do things with the best conversationalist
and the most energetic man of action. Thinker, yet not remote
from the stressful hurly-burly; dreamer, yet practical business-
man; deliberate sater of that desirous, sex-hungry body, yet
merciless contemner of his own yielding; condemning too his
dark mistress, yet continuing to love the woman she might have
been—and, for his happiness, should have been; never finding
the ideal love, yet forever seeking it, for he knew that such love
is, this side heaven, man's most abiding joy and content and
safety; expressing the physical aspect of love in its most intimate
details, either with frank joyousness and animal spirits or with a
self-reviling brutality and as if moved by an irresistible need to
cleanse, not merely his bosom but his entire system, of this most
perilous stuff, yet with his eyes upon a starry portal that might

---

[1] In a long essay on The Spectator, published in San Francisco by the Book Club of
California.

allow him, spirit-weary, mind-lorn, body-aching, to enter a house of tranquillity: complete and enduring union with such a woman as could joyously, unquestioningly, bring him the peace and the bliss of perfect understanding, unreservèd sympathy, and an unflawed understanding. He never found that woman, that home, that peace.

If the world blamed him for the frankness that spared nothing, he did not care: he might almost have been the epigrammatist that declared, 'A dirty mind is a constant joy', or the literary critic that, of a novel by Maupassant, had the courage to say, 'A book about cads, for cads; but jolly good reading'[1]: nevertheless, he deeply cared that, however often and however outspokenly he might describe the dirt, he should also praise that to which he aspired: the true, the beautiful, and the good.

Shakespeare was, physically, a pagan; also, he took a lively, very curious interest in sex. He was no mere 'instinctive' sensualist, but an intellectual voluptuary and a thinker keenly, shrewdly, penetratingly, sympathetically probing into sex, its mysteries, its mechanism, its exercise and expertise, and into its influence on life and character. And being the world's most supple as well as most majestic (he could out-play Milton on the verbal organ), subtlest as well as strongest writer, he expressed his views on love and passion and sex, with a power and pertinence unrivalled by other great general writers and with a picturesqueness unapproached by the professional amorist writers; the latter excel him only in technical details and in comprehensiveness, and then only because he was not concerned to write a *bréviaire divin de l'amour*, an *ars amoris*, a *Married Love*.

Before we pass to some account of the non-sexual bawdy, of homosexuality, and of sex in Shakespeare, let us obtain a prefatory idea of his approach to and treatment of sex by looking at

---

[1] I quote from memory and with conscious inaccuracy; that, however, is the true sense of the reviewer's verdict.

that system of imagery which he exhibited in English and which was imitated by the 17th Century amatory poets, the 18th Century amorists, and by such 19th Century writers as Meredith (a little), Swinburne (much), and Maurice Hewlett (continuing into the present century): the geography and topography of the female sexual features.[1]

Vaguely topographical is the passage at *Romeo and Juliet*, II i 17–33, but as it is insufficiently general and various for our present purpose, it must be omitted. Much superior is the passage at *Venus and Adonis*, verses 229–240, where Venus, passionately hugging Adonis, seeks thus to convert his reluctance to ardent desire and amorous deeds:

> 'Fondling,' she saith, 'since I have hemm'd thee here
> Within the circuit of this ivory pale,
> I'll be a park, and thou shalt be my deer;
> Feed where thou wilt, on mountain or in dale:
>   Graze on my lips; and if those hills be dry,
>   Stray lower, where the pleasant fountains lie
>
> 'Within this limit is relief enough,
> Sweet bottom-grass, and high delightful plain,
> Round rising hillocks, brakes obscure and rough,
> To shelter thee from the tempest and from rain:
>   Then be my deer, since I am such a park;
>   No dog shall rouse thee, though a thousand bark.'

The general sense is clear: clear, too, is most of the imagery. I do not care to insult anybody's knowledge or intelligence by offering a physiological paraphrase, nevertheless the inexpert

---

[1] That the same has, in English, never been done for men's is significant: social inhibitions, the restriction of women's emancipation to the spheres of politics and the professions, are the main causes: but a female 'geographer' will probably arise within the next twenty years.

reader would perhaps do well to consult the following terms in the glossary: **park, deer, feed, mountain, dale, fountain, bottom-grass, plain, hillock, brakes.**[1]

And, likewise 'in the order of their first appearance', the glossary will, at **country, Ireland, buttocks, bogs, heir, cliff** (sense 1), **Spain, Belgia, Netherlands, low**, prove not unuseful to those who, rightly or wrongly, have less than complete faith that the acuity of their perceptions will, in its full signification, elucidate every sexual reference in the famous passage at III i 110–136 of *The Comedy of Errors*, where Antipholus of Syracuse and Dromio of Syracuse discuss the monstrously fat kitchen-wench that is being considered by the latter as a bride:

Antipholus. Then she bears some breadth?
Dromio. No longer from head to foot than from hip to hip: she is spherical, like a globe; I could find out countries in her.
Antipholus. In what part of her body stands Ireland?
Dromio. Marry, sir, in her buttocks: I found it out by the bogs.
Antipholus. Where Scotland?
Dromio. I found it by the barrenness; hard in the palm of the hand.

[*With reference to agricultural infertility and to the legendary close-fistedness*]

Antipholus. Where France?
Dromio. In her forehead; arm'd and reverted, making war against her heir.
Antipholus. Where England?
Dromio. I look'd for the chalky cliffs, but I could find no whiteness in them; but I guessed it stood in her chin, by the salt rheum that ran between France and it.
Antipholus. Where Spain?
Dromio. Faith I saw it not; but I felt it hot in her breath.

[1] Heavy type in this Essay: words to be found in the Glossary.

Antipholus. Where America, the Indies? [I.e., *the West Indies.*]

Dromio. O, sir, upon her nose, all o'er embellish'd with rubies, carbuncles, sapphires, declining their rich aspect to the hot breath of Spain; who sent whole armadoes of caracks to be ballast at her nose.

Antipholus. Where stood Belgia, the Netherlands?

Dromio. O, sir, I did not look so low.

2

NON-SEXUAL BAWDY

To make of this a section, it is necessary to include the merely coarse and vulgar element, and even that element has to enlist several words and phrases that are vulgarisms only in the philological sense. Shakespeare was not a Rabelais: he took very little pleasure in the anatomical witticism and the functional joke unless they were either witty or sexual. Scatology he disdained, and non-sexual coprology he almost entirely avoided; if one may essay a fine, yet aesthetically important distinction, Shakespeare may have had a dirty mind, yet he certainly had not a filthy mind. But then Keats as well as Byron, Tennyson as well as Swinburne, had dirty minds, and I have yet to hear someone say that Keats, Byron, Tennyson, and Swinburne were the worse poets for having been dead neither above the ears nor below the waist. Dryden was no mealy-mouth; Pope had a sexually malicious mind (that of the frustrated weakling); the austere Milton could, in the Sin-Chaos-Night verses in Book II of *Paradise Lost*, emulate the Sycorax-Caliban material in *The Tempest*; the Poets' Poet, in *The Faerie Queen*, permitted himself some highly suggestive passages.

Even the author of *Songs of Innocence* was not so innocent as English men and women seem to expect their poets to be. Not all Scots have been tolerant towards Dunbar and Burns. More briefly: these poets were not so very dirty-minded, after all. They were men, not lay figures.

But to return to Shakespeare's non-sexual bawdy. What does it comprise? Nothing more than a few references to urination and chamber-pots; to defecation and close-stools; to flatulence; to podex and posteriors. Shakespeare was no coprophagist: most of the references are cursory: only three or four references show any tendency on Shakespeare's part to linger over them; where he does linger, it was for the pleasure of indulging such abundance of wit as few commentators and readers have fully[1] grasped.

The references to urine and urination are hardly worth mentioning,[2] except for two. Of that clay-footed piece of austerity, Angelo, somebody tartly remarks, 'When he makes water, his urine is congeal'd ice' (*Measure*, III ii 111–112). And in *Macbeth* the Porter, listing urine as one of the three things of which drink is 'a great provoker', ends his enumeration with the concise and witty words, 'In conclusion, [drink] equivocates him in a sleep, and giving him the lie, leaves him' (II iii 26–37), where *lie* means not only 'a falsehood' but also 'chamber-lie' (urine). To which we might perhaps add *Twelfth Night*, I iii 126.

As for defecation, Shakespeare barely touches on it as a bodily process except at **siege**: at **close-stool** twice, and twice at **jakes**, he refers to the equivalents of the commode and the privy. **Jakes**, however, does in the allusive shape **Ajax**, afford the dramatist the opportunity of making a neat though scabrous pun in *Love's Labour's Lost*, V ii 571–572: and a pun not at all scabrous in *Lear*, II

---

[1] A claim that I am far from being fatuous enough to make for myself; probably I have missed some of Shakespeare's wittiest scabrosities.

[2] Nevertheless, I suppose that I should be shirking my duty if I did not refer the curious to **chamber-lie**, **charged chambers**, **jordan**, **leak**, **make water**, **piss**, **stale** (noun, sense 2), and **urine**.

ii 125–126, 'None of these rogues and cowards But Ajax is their fool', which may fairly be described as 'rubbing their noses in the dirt'. Shakespeare had not that simple type of mind, so common among the 'hearties', which guffaws its delighted appreciation of long and tedious stories about being 'taken short'.

Flatulence was, in Shakespeare's day, the source and the target of humour and wit among all classes: nowadays, its popularity as a subject is, in the main, confined to the lower and lower-middle classes and to morons elsewhere. The days when, as at the end of the 17th Century, a pamphlet dealing with noisy venting and written by a pseudonymous Don Fartaudo could be published and enjoyed and when the ability to play tunes by skilfully regulating and controlling one's windy expressions was regarded as evidence of a most joyous and praiseworthy form of wit,—such days have 'gone with the wind'. At **break wind** there is a punning on *wind* = breath = words on the one hand, flatulence on the other: at **vent** there are two direct statements. In *Othello*, at III i 6–11, occurs a passage that contains at least four puns: one on *thereby hangs a tale*, one on **wind-instrument**, one on **tail**, a fourth on **tale**, thus:

> *Clown.* Are these, I pray you, wind-instruments?
> *First Musician.* Ay, marry, are they, sir.
> *Clown.* O, thereby hangs a tail.
> *First Musician.* Whereby hangs a tale, sir?
> *Clown.* Marry, sir, by many a wind-instrument that I know.

In *Hamlet* (II ii 396–401) we read:

> *Hamlet.* My lord, I have news to tell you. When Roscius was an actor in Rome,—
> *Polonius.* The actors are come hither, my lord.
> *Hamlet.* Buz, buz!
> *Polonius.* Upon mine honour,—
> *Hamlet.* Then came each actor on his ass.

Hamlet, already possessed of the news, as, referring to Roscius, he subtly shows the far from subtle Polonius, is irritated by the old busybody's stupidity: to indicate his irritation, he makes that 'rude noise', imitative of the breaking of wind, which, from probably even before Shakespeare's acting days, has been 'the gods' ' and the groundlings' means of showing their disapproval of bad acting, and thus repeats his intimation that he knew all about the arrival of the actors. When Polonius, thinking that this unexpectedly coarse 'raspberry' (or *razzer*, as the Cockney prefers to call it) signifies the prince's disbelief, solemnly avers, 'Upon mine honour', Hamlet puns on the word **honour** and impugns Polonius's conception of honour by saying, 'Then came each actor on his ass',[1] thus passing from wind-breaking to the source of the noise.

This bring us, therefore, to Shakespeare's allusions to the **butt** of the human body: the **bum**, **buttocks** or **holland** or **posteriors** or **tail** (sense 3) or **tale** (sense 2) or **rump** or, to adopt the deliberate perversion, **ass**. In addition to referring the reader to the Glossary entries at those terms, I need only remark that, in these passages, Shakespeare is never filthy: he is broad, ribald, healthily coarse, unsqueamishly natural, and unaffectedly humorous, with a humour that would have appealed to that old lady who, on being asked by a youth that had noticed she was squashing one of her parcels, 'Do you know what you're sitting on, mother?', replied, 'I *ought* to, young man: seeing that I've been using it for seventy years'. Shakespeare never exclaims 'Oh, shocking!', never sniggers: he fails—very naturally—to see that there is any occasion to be shocked: and to him the subject calls for a hearty laugh, not a prurient snigger.

---

[1] I owe the 'ass = fundament' explanation to the late Crompton Rhodes. (For further details, see *raspberry* in the 3rd edition of *Songs and Slang of the British Soldier*.)

3

HOMOSEXUAL

Like most other heterosexual persons, I believe the charge against Shakespeare; that he was a homosexual; to be, in the legal sense, 'trivial': at worst, 'the case is not proven'; at best—and in strict accordance with the so-called evidence, as I see it[1]—it is ludicrous.

The charge was first brought in 1889 by a homosexual (Oscar Wilde); it was renewed, exactly a decade later, by another; it was again renewed, at a second interval of ten years, by yet a third; and, roughly three decades later still, the subject—if we ignore several unimportant intermediate attempts—was, not very convincingly, re-opened. The theme has, since the world-war of 1914–1918, been touched on by several notable writers whose heterosexuality is not in doubt.

---

[1] To the counter-charge, 'But then you, perhaps, are blind', I answer: being as yet unimpaired with senility and having, for some thirty years, handled masses of evidence whether explicit or implicit, external or internal, and possessing an open mind, I think that I may, unconceitedly, claim to be a competent assessor and judge.

'With the publication of *The Portrait of Mr W. H.*, the Sonnets came into their own, and homosexuals were heartened to feel that there was no *prima facie* reason why they should not have written *Hamlet*' (Malcolm Muggeridge, *The Thirties*, 1940): they have persisted in thinking so. But as Oscar Wilde, though his *Portrait* provided excellent reading, egregiously failed to substantiate his charge; so too did Samuel Butler, in 1899, with *Shakespeare's Sonnets*, where the 'evidence' is childish; so too Frank Harris, in 1909, with *The Man Shakespeare*, where he dragged the dramatist down to his own level. A more temperately considered case was presented in that modern book to which I have already referred but which, for obvious reasons, I do not intend to particularize: yet, on the evidence presented even there, no jury of twelve good men and true (scholars) would hesitate to bring in a verdict of 'not guilty' and to add the rider, 'This charge should never have been laid'.

To re-examine the 'evidence' adduced by the homosexuals (as pathetically eager to prove that 'Shakespeare is one of *us*' as the Germans are to prove that he was a German) would be a waste of time; but I should like to refer my heterosexual readers—if they have not already consulted them—to Hugh Kingsmill's *The Return of William Shakespeare* and his friend Hesketh Pearson's 'Penguin', *A Life of Shakespeare*, where these two keen-witted, healthy-minded 'debunkers' (who love their Shakespeare) have some trenchant remarks[1] to make.

Shakespeare alludes to homosexuality very seldom and most cursorily. His attitude, as that of every thinking person must be, was extremely tolerant. He would, indeed, have subscribed in full to the sentiments expressed in the following brief passages from Kenneth Walker's excellent *The Physiology of Sex* (Pelican Books, 1940).

---

[1] Later in this section, I shall quote several of Hesketh Pearson's.

This new attitude to sex helps us not only to understand such comparatively rare anomalies as hermaphroditism, but also to effect certain necessary changes in our view of psychological homosexuality and the manner in which it expresses itself. If none of us can pride ourselves on being a hundred per cent man or a hundred per cent woman, what right have we to stigmatize as monstrous those in whom confusion is revealed more clearly than in us. Full sexual differentiation is comparatively rare. . . . There, in the unfortunate intersexual whose method of expressing his urge disgusts us, walk ourselves, but for the grace of a more satisfactory complement of hormones.

Modifying Havelock Ellis's definition of homosexuality, Kenneth Walker, whose little book should be possessed by all laymen and many doctors and every priest or clergyman, says that 'all sexual activities that are entirely and by preference outside the range in which procreation is possible may be deemed abnormal'; he adds that 'this would, of course, exclude from being considered normal all homosexual practices'.[1]

In the important chapter entitled 'Sexual Deviations', this medical man deals with the active (or virile) homosexuals and with the passive ones (or *pathics*, as the 18th Century called them); his *intersexual*, like the more general *invert*, applied to both men and women, whether active or passive participators.— Shakespeare, by the way, does not speak of Lesbians: Lesbianism was an extremely rare deviation in Shakespearean England.— The prevalent well-informed view is, on the one hand, that all female passives and all male actives are, respectively, exaggeratedly female and exaggeratedly male (the latter impelled by the perhaps sadistic appetence to possess *somebody*, the former by

[1] At this point he remarks that 'The word "deviation" has now [dis]placed "perversion" in scientific literature, since the latter term was used at a time when all sexual anomalies were regarded as deliberate sins'.

the perhaps masochistic libido to be possessed by somebody, even if it is only a woman); on the other, that the passive male homosexual is 'a man with an undue'—i.e., unduly large—'proportion of female elements in him' and the active female homosexual is 'a woman with an excessive contribution of the male'. Here it may be remarked that the term *male prostitutes* is nowadays understood to mean men that sell their bodies to men. (In low slang, the sellers are 'poofs'; but before the war of 1914–1918, *male prostitutes* equally often, or more often, designated men that sell their favours to women, the modern gigolos being examples of this type.)

Of feminoid males or, in everyday language, effeminates, whether they be actual or merely potential intersexuals or inverts, Shakespeare makes much the same sort of kindly-contemptuous or unmawkish-pitying remark as the averagely tolerant and understanding person of the present generation would make, as in Queen Margaret's fling at Prince Edward: 'Go, rate thy minions, proud insulting boy!' (3 *Henry VI*, II ii 84).

The definite references to male homosexuality are few. Perhaps the clearest-cut passages are these two:— '*Thersites*. Thou art thought to be Achilles' male varlet!—*Patroclus*. Male varlet, you rogue, what's that?—*Thersites*. Why, his masculine whore' (*Troilus and Cressida*, V i 14–16); and the Hostess, concerning Falstaff, 'In good faith, 'a cares not what mischief he doth, if his weapon be out: he will foin like any devil; he will spare neither man, woman, nor child' 2 *Henry IV*, II i 14–17). The indefinite references, not with any certainty to be taken as imputing homosexuality at all, are, apart from the *Sonnets*, exceedingly few. Perhaps the least vague are Beatrice's comment (*Much Ado*, II i 33–34) on 'a husband that hath no beard' and ''A came ever in the rearward[1] of the fashion' (2 *Henry IV*, III ii 326).

Only the *Sonnets* have seriously been adduced to indicate that

---

[1] See this term, and the second quotation at **mandrake**, in the Glossary.

Shakespeare either was or might have been a homosexual. On the subject of the flattery addressed to his patron, Hesketh Pearson has given us this 'no nonsense' pronouncement.

> Most of the Sonnets may be read as literary exercises, a number of variations on a theme. There was a craze for that sort of thing when Shakespeare wrote them. . . . They [the hundreds of Sonnets of this period] were not meant to be taken too seriously; the love-making in them was literary love-making; and the flattery of some young nobleman was part of the game; as in Richard Barnfield's *Certaine Sonnets*, where a youth of 'worship', who arouses the correct amount of jealousy in the poet, is addressed 'my love', 'Nature's fairest work', 'sweet boy' [cf *Sonnets*, 108, v. 5], whose lips drop honey, at whose beauty the world stands amazed, and all the rest of the nonsense [cf. both *Sonnet* 108 and *Sonnet* 126]. . . . Shakespeare knew many of his fellow sonneteers at the Inns of Court and could talk their jargon.

Further on in the same chapter ('Poet and Patron'), Hesketh Pearson writes thus trenchantly: 'Homosexualists have done their utmost to annex Shakespeare and use him as an advertisement of their own peculiarity. They have quoted sonnet 20 to prove that he was one of themselves. But sonnet 20 proves conclusively that he was sexually normal.' Here is the impugned sonnet:

> A woman's face, with Nature's own hand painted,
> Hast thou, the master-mistress of my passion;
> A woman's gentle heart, but not acquainted
> With shifting change, as is false women's fashion;
> An eye more bright than theirs, less false in rolling,
> Gilding the object whereupon it gazeth;
> A man in hew all *Hews* in his controlling,

> Which steals men's eyes, and women's souls amazeth.
> And for a woman wert thou first created;
> Till Nature, as she wrought thee, fell a-doting,
> And by addition me of thee defeated,
> By adding one thing to my purpose nothing.
> But since she prickt thee out for women's pleasure,
> Mine be thy love, and thy love's use their treasure.

As if that were not enough, what do the propagators of the 'Shakespeare was a homosexual' myth (though it is hardly old enough to be dignified with such a name) say to *Sonnet 144* with its antithetic man and woman, the comforting friend and the tormenting mistress?

> Two loves I have of comfort and despair,
> Which like two spirits do suggest me still:
> The better angel is a man right fair,
> The worser spirit a woman colour'd ill.
> To win me soon to hell, my female evil
> Tempteth my better angel from my side,
> And would corrupt my saint to be a devil,
> Wooing his purity with her foul pride.

'To call the evidence *bloody* would be fulsome flattery.'[1] The evidence is all in one sense, one direction: it can lead to only one conclusion. Had Shakespeare, so frank and so courageous, been a homosexual, he would have subtly yet irrefutably conveyed the fact. Had he even been much interested in the subject, he would have mentioned it far more often: as it is, he speaks of homosexuals in much the same way as he speaks of eunuchs.

---

[1] To adapt one of W. P. Ker's caustic pronouncements.

4

SEXUAL

We have got rid of the ridiculous notion[s] that sexuality is necessarily immoral, that because the female plays a more passive part in union she therefore has no erotic needs, and that it is neither respectable nor proper to write of sexual love as an art.—Kenneth Walker, Preface to *The Physiology of Sex*, 1940.

To avoid ... wide oscillations between puritanism and licence, a just and even balance must be held, and chastity be regarded as self-control within the sexual field. For to a 'normal man and woman sex contains no danger. In a normal human being sex harmonizes with all the other functions including the emotional and intellectual . . .' (Ouspensky).—Kenneth Walker, *ibid.*, p. 67.

Eunuchs, mentioned at the end of the preceding section, have been deprived of their birthright. (And the same would apply to a woman whose ovaries have—for any reason other than that of the most imperative necessity—been removed.) The allusions range from the figurative, as in 'Lord Say hath gelded the commonwealth, and made it an eunuch' (2 *Henry VI*, IV ii 161–163), and in *Twelfth Night*, I ii 62–63; through the literal-allusive, as in 'One that will do the deed, Though Argus were her eunuch and her guard' (*Love's Labour's Lost*, III i 195–196); to the direct, as in 'I would send them to the Turk, to make eunuchs of' (*All's Well*, II iii 88–89), and to the very frank, as in Cleopatra's 'I take no pleasure[1] In aught an eunuch has: 'tis well for thee, That, being unseminar'd, thy freer thoughts May not fly forth of Egypt' (I v 8–11); and finally to the recondite pun in 'The voice of unpaved eunuch' (*Cymbeline*, II iii 33), with reference to the fact that good alto singers were castrated in order that their voices should break much later or not at all, and with some such chain of association as 'unpaved: uncobbled: unstoned, hence stoneless: deprived of **stones**, hence without testicles'.

A man, or a woman, may be deprived of potency or fertility, not only by an operation but also by disease: and Shakespeare has much to say of venereal diseases and sores and blemishes, from buboes to syphilis, from venereally caused skin-diseases to gonorrhoea. Some idea of Shakespeare's objective and, to modern ears, sometimes brutal attitude may be gained by consulting the Glossary at such entries as **blain**, **bone-ache**, **itch**, **leprosy**, **malady of France**, **powdering-tub**, **tub-fast**, and from such passages as: '*Falstaff.* To serve bravely is to come halting off, you know: to come off the breach with his pike bent bravely, and to surgery bravely; to venture upon the charged chambers bravely.—*Doll Tearsheet.* Hang yourself, you muddy conger, hang yourself!' (2 *Henry IV*, II iv 49–54[2]) and the now embittered, misanthropic Timon's outburst:

---

[1] Cf. II v 5–6, (Cleopatra) 'As well a woman with an eunuch play'd As with a woman'.

[2] For the full flavour of this passage, the following terms should be consulted: **serve**, **breach**, **pike**, **surgery**, **charged chambers**, **muddy**, **conger**.

Lust and liberty,
Creep in the minds and marrows of our youth,
That 'gainst the stream of virtue they may strive,
And drown themselves in riot! itches, blains,
Sow all the Athenian bosoms; and their crop
Be general leprosy!

With this quotation may be compared passages in *Measure for Measure* and *Pericles* and, indeed, elsewhere; but to befoul yet further the already foul would be an unsavoury elaboration and an unprofitable. It would, however, be unforgivable to fail to mention that although, 'then [ca. 1590–1610], as now, actors had many female admirers, and it is clear enough from his words that he was prone to sensual indulgence' (Hesketh Pearson), Shakespeare appears never to have had a venereal disease: it is unlikely that he should have consorted, except conversationally, with prostitutes, for he possessed an exquisitely fastidious nature; he would, certainly from his male companions and probably from the lowly among his female companions (he being the sort of man in whom everyone would confide very freely), hear much about venereal disease, its incidence, its nature, its painful cures—and attempted cures. He is a trenchant and realistic recorder of, not a sermonizer upon, the theme of venereal diseases: his to observe; not to judge, or, rather, to condemn. This 'seeing eye' had an amused and tolerant glance for human foibles, although it was at the same time a very shrewd and penetrating glance: for pain, whether physical or mental, he had naught but pity, although he never fell into maudlin sentimentality, despite the far-seeing, wide-ranging nature of his profoundly humane sense of pity

Of Shakespeare's general attitude towards sex and love-making, something more will be said in the fifth section of this essay. It is an almost bewilderingly various attitude, both in its explicit statements and its implicit overtones and undertones: and always one must remember that Shakespeare-Proteus possessed an extraordinarily keen eye for character and an almost magical gift for making his personages speak in character. It is, therefore, safer and wiser to speak rather of his treatment of sex than of his attitude towards it; better, and wiser still, to speak of his remarks on and references to sex than of the treatment he accords it.

Let us then leave the generalities temporarily on one side and pass—*haud facilis descensus scribendi!*—to the particularities of the sexual organs and features of woman and man. A subject difficult to treat at once satisfactorily and aseptically.

Woman first. The male buttocks, as a sexual feature, do not interest Shakespeare at all (yet had he been a homosexual, they would have done so) and, as a physiological feature, only a little, as will be seen at the **bum**, **buttocks**, **rump** entries in the Glossary, unless it is to make a pun, as on **ass** (Glossary, and section 2 of this Essay) and on **posteriors**: but the female buttocks, despite the paucity of the references thereto, did undoubtedly attract his attention, as, for example, in Menenius Agrippa's 'I am known to be a humorous patrician, and one that loves a cup of hot wine . . .: hasty and tinder-like upon too trivial motion; one that converses more with the buttocks of the night'—cf. the 'latter end' pun in *Love's Labour's Lost*, v ii 621— 'than with the forehead of the morning', where *buttocks*, besides its ostensible meaning, is fairly to be taken as referring erotic- ally to women that he visited as lover or as wencher: and as also in the *Venus and Adonis* passage quoted near the end of section 1 and, as to 'buttocks', amplified at **hillock** in the Glossary, which should, in further amplification, be consulted at **mountain**.

The female breasts are dictionaried at such entries as **bosom**, **cliff**, **fountain**, **mammets**, **neck**, **throbbing breast**, **world**. Only three quotations need be given:

The breasts of Hecuba,
When she did suckle Hector, lookt not lovelier
Than Hector's forehead when it spit forth blood
                    Coriolanus, I iii 43–45;

On her left breast
A mole cinque-spotted, like the crimson drops
I' the bottom of a cowslip
                    Cymbeline, II ii 37–39;

His hand, as proud of such a dignity,
Smoking with pride, marcht on to take his stand
On her bare breast, the heart of all her land;
   Whose ranks of blue veins, as his hand did scale,
   Left their round turrets destitute and pale
                    Lucrece, 437–441:

whence it is not subtle to deduce that Shakespeare admired and revered the 'veiled twins' or 'twin lovelinesses' as certain Victorians called them and that his appreciation of *la belle gorge d'une belle femme* was at times amorous, aesthetic at other times; in which attitude he was exhibiting the healthy tendencies of a healthy, well-balanced male and mind.

Perhaps less aesthetic were his never unaesthetic references to the female **lap**, the *mons Veneris*, the pubic **hair**, the thighs. For Shakespeare, the word **lap** seems to have always borne a sexual connotation, as the reader may prove by consulting the Glossary: even

And in thy sight to die, what were it else
But like a perfect slumber in thy lap

is not, I fear, so lovely-innocent as it seems to be, and the normally innocent phrase, *to lay one's head in* (or *on*) *a woman's lap*, becomes the opposite of innocent in the well-known passage in

Hamlet (III ii 116–119) and the little-remembered urgency of Hotspur's 'Come, Kate, thou art perfect in lying down: come, quick, that I may lay my head in thy lap' (1 *Henry IV*, III, i 226–228). The physiological mount of Venus is alluded to at **mountain** and **Pillicock-hill**; and the pubic hair, certainly at **brakes** and perhaps also at **ling**. The female legs and thighs are hymned in

> By her fine foot, straight leg, and quivering thigh,
> And the demesnes that there adjacent lie
> > *Romeo and Juliet*, II i 17–20:

but that, after all, is from a man's point of view, and it is instructive to juxtapose a woman's, expounded in W. B. Maxwell's *This Is My Man*, 1933:

> He was a statue of white marble. No, a Greek god. . . . Yet till she knew him she had never felt there was any beauty in a man's frame. . . . Now she thought that women were clumsy in comparison. Too big round the hips, too bulging in front of the chest, with so much unnecessary roundness of contour, and the tapering of the leg with its too rapid transition from breadth to slenderness.

Of 'the demesnes that there adjacent lie', only one remains to be considered. The chief one. The *pudendum muliebre* or, to take the district rather than the principal town, the *genitalia muliebria* (the **secret things** of the Glossary). The district is, however, so much identified with the town—the **city** and its **fort**—that it hardly requires a separate treatment: witness the famous passage in *Hamlet* (II ii 231–238):

> *Guildenstern.* On Fortune's cap we are not the very button.
> *Hamlet.* Nor the soles of her shoe?
> *Rosencrantz.* Neither, my lord.

Hamlet. Then you live about her waist, or in the middle of her favours?

Guildenstern. Faith, her privates we.

Hamlet. In the secret parts of Fortune? O, most true; she is a strumpet.

The *pudendum muliebre* (hereinafter called 'the pudend') consists, 'as every schoolboy knows', of the *vulva*, the *vagina*, the *labia majora* and *labia minora*, the *clitoris*, and the *hymen*: those various components have received, from Shakespeare, only a slight individual treatment, but they do provide us with such terms as **glass of virginity**, **hymen**, **maidenhead**, **piled for a French velvet** and **velvet leaves**.

Much more important, however, is the pudend, considered as an entity. To judge by the number of synonyms, the pudend was, to Shakespeare, of considerably greater importance, and significance singly than all the rest of woman's sexual features collectively: it would appear to have been the one unfailing lodestar, the one sexual objective. This preoccupation with sex thus narrowly localized and thus unceasingly particularized is not peculiar to Shakespeare: it is not uncommon among fervent, poetic intellectual men, whose superior natures cause the pudend to become for them a mystic as well as a physical goal, something esoteric as well as material, both a haven for the weary mind and a harbour for their questing sexuality; not merely a conventional means to the conventional end of bodily and mental satisfaction, but also, between a man and a woman possessing mutual esteem and trust, the sure destroyer of that poignant inner loneliness which seeks the nirvana of a merging or a coalescence, however brief, with the body and mind and spirit of one's partner in the most intimate of all the usual expressions of sexual desire: for them, as indeed for certain others (not so intellectual, nor so spiritual, yet equally rich and perceptive emotionally), the pudend has become less a thing desired, however ardently, or a place sought, however eagerly, than a symbol, exalted by the needs of their sensuous as well as their sensual natures, and by their aesthetic cravings as well as by the aspirations of their secret minds and innermost souls.

That central fact must never be forgotten by those who are repelled by the myriad manifestations of Shakespeare's interest in women and their sexual features. It was part of his character and his temperament; nor did he wish to hide it; he did not even wish to represent it as other than it was. He neither pretended that he was a publicist nor cloaked his amatory sentiments and amorous nature with the hypocrisy of prurient-minded prudes and smug, clandestine voluptuaries. With that central fact borne in mind, the reader, if he so desires, may,—and, if he wishes to gain an adequate idea of the fertility and ingenuity of Shakespeare's amative fancy, he must,—ponder the puden-synonymy constituted by the following entries in the Glossary:

another thing, baldrick, belly (sense 3), **bird's nest, blackness, bosom** (sense 3), **box unseen, breach, buckles, case, charged chambers, chaste treasure, circle, city, clack-dish, cliff** (sense 2), **commodity, constable, corner, coun** (especially), the two **country** phrases, **crack, dearest bodily part, den, dial, et cetera, eye, flower, forfended place, gate, hole, hook, lap, ling, low countries, mark, medlar, naked seeing self, nest of spicery, Netherlands, O, peculiar river, (pick) the lock, Pillicock-hill, plum, pond, ring, rose, rudder, ruff, salmon's tail, scut, secret parts** and **secret things, Spain, sty, tail** (sense 1), **tale** (sense 3), **thing** (sense 1), **treasure** and **treasury, Venus' glove, vice, way, what, withered pear, wound.**

Of these terms, some, it will be noticed, are really, others apparently, euphemistic; some (e.g., **belly, bosom, lap**), are either spatially indefinite or euphemistic; some are poetical or 'literary' (**chaste treasure, flower, rose, treasury, Venus' glove**): some are geographical (**low countries, Netherlands,**

Spain), others topographical (**cliff**, **Pillicock-hill**, **pond**, **way**); a number are horticultural or agricultural; war and archery supply five or six; others, being based on shape-metaphors, are visual—vaguely, as in **circle** and **ring**, or definitely, as in **crack**, **corner**, **tale**, **wound**; and at least one (**et cetera**) is humorous. But the most notorious term of all is conveyed only by indirection: that firmly established Standard English word which, a vulgarism,[1] is omitted by *The O.E.D.* but is treated in John Brophy's masterly introduction to *Songs and Slang of the British Soldier* (edited by Brophy and myself), by Dr A. W. Read in a privately printed book and a publicly printed article, by myself in *A Dictionary of Slang*, and briefly in the Glossary. And yet the word is of impeccable 'Aryan' origin, without any brutal or sadistic associations, undertones, or crescive overtones. It lacks the ugliness of certain of the colloquial and slangy synonyms, and, more to the point, it lacks the brutality, or the deliberate materialism or cynicism, of such Shakespearean synonyms as **breach**, **clackdish**, **crack**, **hole**, **hook**, **medlar**, **scut**, and **withered pear**; even **thing**, which obviously is an euphemism, is also horribly materialistic.

Thing is both female, as in 1 *Henry IV*, III iii 20–24, and male, as in *Lear*, I v 51–52. This word, however convenient it may be to certain people that call a spade a 'garden implement', offends also because it is so ineptly vague a generality: such a degree of fuzziness or woolliness or deliberate generalization constitutes an insult to any intelligent person's sense of fitness.

From thing we pass to other words for the male generative organ, medically and culturally termed (quite satisfactorily too) the penis. The two most generally known synonyms—they have actually been accorded admittance to the sanctuary of *The O.E.D.*—are **cock** and **prick**, which appear in the following

---

[1] This and the ensuing remarks are equally applicable to the verb innuendo'd in **focative**.

SHAKESPEARE'S BAWDY

28

summary classification of the many synonyms (forty-five, as
against the sixty-eight in the *pudendum muliebre* list).

Warfare and jousting yield these:—**bugle, dart of love, lance,
pike, pistol, poll-axe, potent regiment, standard, sword** and
weapon.

Sport and the chase: **hook** and **horn**.

Gardening and farming: **carrot, holy-thistle, pizzle, poperin
pear, potato-finger, prick, root, stake, stalk, tail, thorn**.

Domestic: **bauble, cock** (probably short for *water-cock*), **codpiece, distaff, instrument, needle, organ, pen, pin, pipe,
stump, three-inch fool, tool, yard**.

Miscellaneous: **lag end, little finger, loins, nose, Pillicock,
R, Roger, tale, thing**.

Regarded from the semantic angle, this synonymy reveals that
the most potent idea in penis-terms is that of acuity, with the
idea of penetration reinforcing it, as in **dart, holy-thistle, hook,
horn** (sharp-pointed), **lance, needle, pen, pike, pin, prick,
stake** (sharp-pointed), **sword, thorn, tool**. Note, too, the
business-like, efficient, workmanlike air of such terms as
instrument, organ, tool, and **weapon**; and the 'visual' imagery
or shape-metaphors of **carrot, distaff, pipe, pistol, poperin
pear, potato-finger, root, stalk, stump**, and **tail** (in Latin, *penis*
means 'the male generative organ' and is also, in certain contexts, a synonym of *cauda*, 'tail'). Some few (e.g., **pike, poll-axe,
stake**) are—at the least, they seem to be—sadistic, and those
three and several others are certainly coarse and brutal (**hook;
sword** and **weapon; pizzle** and **potato-finger**). Certainly this
synonymy does not offer so large a proportion of poetic or
pleasing-picturesque terms as does the *pudendum muliebre* synonymy: although that is probably to be explained by the obvious,
yet too often unconsidered fact that Shakespeare was less likely to
idealize a man's than a woman's body. Individual terms of
particular etymological or semantic interest are these: **cock, codpiece, holy-thistle, pistol, prick, Roger, thorn, tool**, and **yard**.

Shakespeare does not hesitate to speak of **penis erectus** and even to play wittily upon the idea. Witness such Glossary entries as **edge** (with which compare **disedge**), **erection** and **source of erection**, **stand** and **stand to (it)**. The *spermata* do not deter him, as consultation of **bullets, germen, marrow, mettle,** and **stuff** will soon corroborate; nor does ejaculation, as will be seen by the entries at **bankrout beggar, bathe . . ., bereave, come, die, discharge, fading, get the upshoot, go** and **go off, loss, melt, mort o' the deer, offend in a dream, shoot** and **spend**.

Thence, by easy transition, we pass to the scrotum, which Shakespeare mentions as **bag** and **purse**, and the testicles, to which he vaguely alludes in **cullion**, punningly calls **baggage**, refers to in **bowl** and **billiards** and, the most wittily, **bawl**, poeticizes as **damsons**, correctly and literally names as **privates**[1]—an idea to which he reverts in **potent regiment**. That wittiest of all the references occurs in 2 *Henry IV*, ii ii 20–26: 'It is a low ebb of linen with thee . . . the rest of thy low countries have made a shift to eat up thy holland: and God knows whether those that bawl out of the ruins of thy linen shall inherit his kingdom'; for the full flavour of which it will be necessary to repair to the Glossary at **low countries, shift, holland,** and to notice that **those that bawl** not only contains a pun on *balls*, the commonest of all C. 18–20 slangisms or colloquialisms for the spermatozoa-secreting glands, but also puns on—and constitutes perhaps the earliest literary allusion to—the etymological significance of the word 'testicles', which, in the Latin *testiculi* (the hypocoristic form of *testes*), literally signifies 'the little witnesses' (to a man's virility); there is also, I think, a remote allusion to the phrase *clouds of witness* (or its equivalent). Moreover, *bawl* is further justified by the notorious fact that witnesses are often vociferous, noisy, clamant. Thus we see that an obscure Shakespearean phrase—there are half a dozen comparables—

---

[1] Cf. F. Manning's magnificent war-work, **Her Privates We**, 1930.

contains enough to furnish an Oscar Wilde or a Whistler with sufficient wit to justify his invitation to a stag-dinner.

Sexual organs or features, primary and secondary, evoke the idea of what is done with them: the needs and desires they subserve demand suitable instruments and agents, and they lead to certain amatory contacts, which in turn lead to definitely sexual actions. Kissing; clasping; caressing; copulation. There is no mystery, though much art, in a kiss: of the various relevant terms,[1] only one—if we exclude the lust-suggestive 'to mouth'— needs to be singled out. This is synonymous with Eric Mackay's 'kiss with cloven lips' or what is less euphemistically known as 'tongueing (a man or a woman)', an osculatory exercise that strikes all but the most ardent lovers as being more insanitary than amorous.

Clasping ranges from the almost meaningless waist-encirclement of the merely familiar to the passionate embraces of lovers: and in the Glossary entries at **arms**, **clasp**, **clip**, **embrace**, **hoop with embraces**, **hug**, **lay one's . . .**, and **strain** account for most of the nuances.

Caressing provides a richer synonymy, in which some of the terms are innocent enough, whereas several are either pro-foundly erotic or extremely sophisticated: **cherish** (cf. *The Book of Common Prayer*'s 'to love and to cherish'), **comfort**, **dally** and **dalliance**, **feed**, **handle**, **mutual entertainment**, **paddle**, **pas-times**, **penetrate**, **pinch**, **play** (n. and v.), **pranks**, **provoke** and **provocation**, **scratch**, **sport** (n. and v.), **stir** and **stir up**, **tickle**, **touch** (n. and v.), **wanton** (adj. and v.). All those refer to a man in the act of caressing a woman; several refer also to a woman engaged in caressing a man; but the ensuing terms refer to the woman caressing, or by caresses inciting, a man:—**Disedge** and **fondling**, **set on** and **raise up**.

The latter phrasal verb reminds us of the very odd fact that of

---

[1] **Kiss**, n. and v.; **kiss with inside lip**; **lip**, n. and v.; **mouth**, v.; **tilt with lips**.

the nine terms that in Shakespeare allude, or may be presumed to allude, to masturbation, only the third—and even that reverts most significantly to the woman-causer—alludes to a man's self-masturbation, none alludes to a woman's self-pollution, and only one (the second) alludes to a man so caressing a woman's *genitalia* that she is likely to experience an orgasm, whereas seven refer to a woman so caressing a man that, whether deliberately or unintentionally, she will probably cause him to have a sexual spasm and 'make love's quick pants'. These eight terms are **conjure it down, finger, go to bed, lay it, mar, rubbing, spin off, take down** and **take off**.

From the terms listed in the preceding paragraph, we—inevitably, I think—form the opinion that Shakespeare was an exceedingly knowledgeable amorist, a versatile connoisseur, and a highly artistic, an ingeniously skilful, practitioner of love-making, who could have taught Ovid rather more than that facile doctrinaire could have taught him; he evidently knew of, and probably he practised, an artifice accessible to few—one that I cannot becomingly mention here, though I felt it obligatory to touch on it, very briefly, in the Glossary.

That impression (should we not say, that conviction?) of Shakespeare's intimate knowledge of love-making is hardly lessened when we come to glance at the synonymies expressive both of copulation, the act, and of copulating, the action.

First the nouns, which, though sufficiently numerous, are overshadowed by the verbs.

Act, action, acture, adultery, amorous rite and **works,** [**amorously impleacht,**] **angling, assault,** [**between the sheets,**] **boarding, bout, business, conflict, conversation, copulation, custom, deed** itself and the **deed** phrases, **disport, downright way, effect of love, emballing, encounter, execution, foining, foot, fornication, game, getting-up, groping . . ., horsemanship, husbandry, incest, lechery** and the semantically comparable **luxury, making,** the **marriage** phrases, match, mirth, momentary trick, nose-painting, occupation, pricking, relief, rents and revenues, revels, rite, service and services, stair-work and trunkwork, taking, thrust, tick-tack, tillage and tilth, trading, traffic, trick, turn i' the bed, union, use and usury, work.

The verbs are so many that it is as well to divide them into those words or phrases which indicate the act seen from the man's point of view, these being much more numerous than the terms in the next two together; those words and phrases which present the act from the woman's viewpoint; and those which indicate the sentiments of both parties.

From the man's standpoint, first those terms which state or imply a man's deliberate siege of, or assault upon, a woman's powers of sexual resistance: **assail** (with corresponding **assault**), **assay**, **attempt** and **tempt**, **besiege** (cf. the noun **siege**, sense 1), **call to a reckoning**, **come to one's bed**, **entice**, **entreat**, **fall to**, **pervert**, **try**, **undermine**, which link naturally with the synonyms of the art and practice and deed of seduction: to **abuse** (someone's) **bed**, **betray**, **corrupt**, **dishonour**, **get a maidenhead**, **make defeat of virginity**, **pluck a sweet**, **seduce**, **thaw**, **undertake**, [**unseduced**,] **undo**, **woo**, **wrong**; and with those for rape and violation: [**adulterate**,] **break**, **conquer a maiden bed** (which equally belongs to the seduction sub-group), **constrain**, [**contaminate**,] **convince the honour of** (equally applicable to seduction), **crack** (v.), **defile**, **deflower**, **distain** and **stain**, **force** and **enforce**, **pollute**, **ransack**, **rape**, **ravish**, **spoil** (v.), **spot** (v.), **sully**, [**untrimmed and unviolated**,] **violate**, and **wrack** (cf. **wrack of maidenhood**).

Those three sub-groups have not only an intrinsic or absolute value but also an extrinsic or relative value: they show the ingenuity and wealth of Shakespeare's vocabulary; they also show that, if we consider them along with the main body of man-viewed coition, we can substantiate the frequently made eulogy, 'Shakespeare had a subtle mind that delighted in nice distinctions and in spiritually, intellectually, morally advisable grades and gradings'; furthermore, the wonderful appositeness of word to deed, of term to fact, the tone-value of the pregnant words and picturesque phrases, the sound-sense correspondence and harmony,—all these appear in the sum total of those sub-groups and this, the dominant corpus of the man-operative 'copulatory' verbs or verbal phrases,[1] which are either transitive or intransitive (or, in several instances, both transitive and intransitive):—To **achieve, bed, blow up** (cf. the agent, who is the **blower-up** or **underminer**), **board** (and **board a land carack**), **break the pale, broach** (as though a woman were a cask), **burden** and **burthen, carry, charge, clap, climb, colt** and **horse, come over** and **come to it, cope, couch, cover, do** (and the **do** phrases), **draw, ear, encounter, execute, fill a bottle with a tun-dish, fit** and **fit it, flesh one's will, foin, *foot** (corresponding to the already recorded noun), (see at) ***foca-tive,** several **go** phrases, **hang one's bugle in an invisible bal-dric, have, hick** and **hack, hit** and **hit it** and **hit lower, husband** and **husband her bed, joy, jump, *know** (and several combin-ations), **lay down, leap, lie** and **lie**-phrasal verbs, **lover** (cf. the originating noun), several **make** phrases, **man, manage** (and its engendering noun), **meddle with, mount, *occupy,** [on,] **pick the lock, please oneself upon, *plough, possess, prick out, put down** and **put to** (which is to be distinguished from **put-to**), **ram** (and its noun), **revel in, *ride, scale, serve, set up one's rest, sing, sink in, sluice, soil, stab, *strike, stuff, surfeit, take, *taste, throw** (cf. **thrown down**), **thrust to the wall, thump, tire on, top, tread, trim, tumble, *tup, use, vault, wanton, work.** Of the terms in that synonymy, some have been drawn from the farmyard and from farming in general, with one

---

[1] In the ensuing a-b-c-d, I have asterisked those words or phrases which are, as treated in the Glossary, the most important etymologically, semantically, or literarily.

or two from gardening: **colt, horse, ram, tup,** and **cover** and **tread,** as well as **leap, mount, vault,** all nine of which are equally—or more—applicable to the breeding of animals; **ear, plough,** and perhaps **husband,** from cultivation. From entertainment, games, sport, the chase, jousting, horsemanship, come these:—**break the pale, foin, jump** (to which we might perhaps add **leap, mount,** and **vault**), **make one's play, ride, set up one's rest,** and **sing.** Warfare, at sea and on land, supplies seven or eight terms, perhaps including **occupy,** which seems to have acquired an unenviable prominence in Shakespeare's day. But probably the most interesting fact about the list is the number of sadistic words: **clap, cope,** the verb alluded to in **focative, hick** and **hack, hit, strike,** and **thump,** all of which convey the idea of a blow, a hard punch or thrust; and the literal meaning of such expressions as **broach, charge, flesh one's will upon, put down, ram** (probably from a battering-ram), **throw, tire on,** does not suggest anything very gentle, nor does that of such verbs as **foin** and **stab, plough** and **thrust to the wall.** The sadism or, rather less cruelly, the brutality or, less brutally, the 'manly' roughness of so many male terms for 'to copulate (with)' is as noticeable as the submissiveness, or even the fatalism, of many of the female verbs.

The Shakespearean words for the woman's share in the primary sexual act are, or are implied in: **bear, buried with her face upwards, canvass,** [**carriage,**] **change the cod's head for the salmon's tail,** [**codding spirit,**] **conceive her tale, cuckold** (v.), **dance with one's heels, draw up, eat, exchange flesh, fall** and **fall backwards, give oneself, dishearten, keep down, let in, lie on one's back, lie under,** [**load,**] **mell with, put a man in one's belly, put to, shake a man's back, strive, stumble, take it, trip, turn to, wag one's tail, whore,** and **yield to** (etc.). In some of them we note the immemorial hypocrisy, the centuried fiction, that women *give* themselves or *yield* their bodies to men: a fiction extremely insulting to women, for it makes them poor, insentient creatures, the mere puppet-victims of men's lust. It must, however, be admitted that Shakespeare did not encourage—that, indeed, he did not believe in—this conventional picture of coy pre-nuptial reluctance and cold post-nuptial indifference.

Shakespeare, naturally enough, has certain words and phrases that convey mutual participation and the two angles of approach. These are **bolster more than their own, bosom** (v.), **commit, compound, contend, do it, do the deed of darkness** (etc.), **honey** (v.), **juggle, knot, lecher** (v.), **mingle bloods,** [**Mitigation,**] **sate,** and **wrestle**.

Such terms suggest certain others—terms expressive of procreation, especially from the male's point of view. Of these verbs, the chief are **beget** and **get, get the sun of** and **get with child, coin** and **stamp, father** and **make a son out of one's blood, gender, kindle,** [**procreant and procreation,**] and **propagate**.

Sexual dialogue between men is, no less in Shakespeare than in the smoking-room or -compartment, frank and often coarse: between members of the lower classes, both coarse and, often, brutal; between members of the middle class—well, we hear very little of that!; between aristocrats and other members of the upper and leisured class, it is still frank—it is frequently very frank indeed—but it is also witty.

In the first group, we may cite the Pompey-Abhorson dialogue in *Measure for Measure* and the Gregory-Sampson chit-chatting, back-chatting in *Romeo and Juliet* (i i 18–33). The latter runs thus:

Gregory. The quarrel is between our masters and their men.
Sampson. 'Tis all one, I will show myself a tyrant: when I have fought with the men, I will be cruel with the maids, and cut off their heads.
Gregory. The heads of the maids?
Sampson. Ay, the heads of the maids, or their maidenheads; take it in what sense thou wilt.

Gregory. They must take it in sense that feel it.

Sampson. Me they shall feel while I am able to stand: and 'tis known that I am a pretty piece of flesh.

Gregory. 'Tis well thou art not fish; if thou hadst, thou hadst been Poor-John.—Draw thy tool; here comes two of the house of the Montagues.

Sampson. My naked weapon is out: quarrel; I will back thee.

In the same play, at II i 17–39, we may examine a passage that is illustrative of high-born, courtier-like sexual wit. Mercutio's presence on the stage is equivalent to the play of storm-lightning in summer—and to saying that, whenever he speaks, we are likely to be exposed, as were his interlocutors, to the shafts of his wit, much as when, in another play, Beatrice appears, the standers-by, not excepting those dearest to her, did not know when they were safe: but perhaps both Beatrice's and Mercutio's friends knew that they were always unsafe in respect of the constant coruscations of an irrepressibly (and remarkably) brilliant mind.

To return to *Romeo and Juliet*. Wittier than the passage mentioned at the beginning of the paragraph before this one, is a passage in II iii 90–117.

Mercutio. Why, is not this better now than groaning for love? now art thou sociable, now art thou Romeo; now art thou what thou art, by art as well as by nature: for this drivelling love is like a great natural, that runs lolling up and down to hide his bauble in a hole.

Benvolio. Stop there, stop there.

Mercutio. Thou desirest me to stop in my tale against the hair?

Benvolio. Thou wouldst else have made thy tale large.

Mercutio. O, thou art deceived; I would have made it short: for I was come to the whole depth of my tale; and meant, indeed, to occupy the argument no longer.

Romeo. Here's goodly gear!

Enter NURSE *and her man* PETER.

Mercutio. A sail, a sail, a sail!
Benvolio. Two, two; a skirt and a smock.
Nurse. Peter!
Peter. Anon?
Nurse. My fan, Peter.
Mercutio. Good Peter, to hide her face; for her fan's the fairer face.
Nurse. God ye good morrow, gentlemen.
Mercutio. God ye good den, fair gentlewoman.
Nurse. Is it good den?
Mercutio. 'Tis no less. I tell you; for the bawdy hand of the dial is now upon the prick of noon.
Nurse. Out upon you! what a man are you!

For the full understanding of that passage, the reader should hie him (or her) to the Glossary and forthwith consult it at the following terms: **bauble**, **hole**, **tale** (senses 1 and 3), **hair**, **short**, **whole**, **occupy**, **smock**, **den**, **bawdy**, **dial**, and **prick**. If the reader accept my surmise that the second 'den' (*good den = good even*) contains an erotic pun, he will the more readily concur in my belief that Mercutio's 'the bawdy hand of the dial is upon the prick of noon' is not only one of the 'naughtiest' but also one of the three or four most scintillating of all Shakespeare's sexual witticisms; but its full subtlety and its profound eroticism will, even by the witty, be grasped only by reading and pondering the Glossary entries at **dial** and **prick** and by remembering the positional implication of clock-hands at noon and the *double entente* of 'prick' (the very stroke—cf. **strike** of the noon-chime or noon-ticking; the physiological sense both of the noun and of the verb). Verbal wit and witty eroticism can hardly be keener, go further, than in Mercutio's twelve-worded sentence. But then, Shakespeare is, beyond question, as indubitably the world's greatest wit as he is the world's greatest writer: to that wit, justice has never been adequately rendered. As a dramatic wit, he surpasses Etherege, Wycherley, Congreve[1] and the best French writers of comedy in the 18th Century: as an intellectual wit or a Society wit, he goes far beyond the powers of Lamb, Jerrold, Wilde, Shaw; as a comic wit (a wit in the widest, furthest-ranging implications of the word) he has never been approached. In him, erotic wit often becomes so penetrating, so profound, so brilliant that it would make us forget the eroticism, were it not that the eroticism itself is penetrating and profound; and certainly the degree of wit renders the eroticism aseptic and—except to prudes and prurients—innocuous.

But what of bawdy dialogue between two women or among three or four women? We have several good examples in *Romeo and Juliet* (passages in which the Nurse appears), in *As You Like It*, in *The Merchant of Venice*, in *Much Ado about Nothing*, and elsewhere. Some of the Shakespearean talk implied in Mercutio's 'That kind of fruit As maids call medlars, when they laugh alone' is as erotic as that between men. It is, however, less brutal and less direct, even in the following passage (*Much Ado*, III iv 23–74), the longest and wittiest[2] of the erotic interfeminine dialogues. It is that which, shortly before Hero's wedding, is spoken by Hero herself, her gentlewoman Margaret, and, though not at first, the witty Beatrice—though hardly wittier or more erotic than Margaret.

Hero. God give me joy to wear it! for my heart is exceeding heavy.

[1] To this theme I return: early in the next section.
[2] The Glossary should be consulted at **heavy**, **weight**, **on**, **honourable**, **light**, **burden**, **dance with one's heels**, **stuff** (v.), **maid**, **lay it to one's heart**, **prick** (v.), **thistle**, and **holy-thistle**.

Margaret. 'Twill be heavier soon by the weight of a man.

Hero. Fie upon thee! art not ashamed?

Margaret. Of what, lady? of speaking honourably? Is not marriage honourable in a beggar? Is not your lord honourable [—capable of getting on—] without marriage? I think you would have me say, 'saving your reverence, a husband'; an bad thinking do not wrest true speaking, I'll offend nobody: is there any harm in 'the heavier for a husband'? None, I think, an it be the right husband and the right wife; otherwise 'tis light, not heavy: ask my lady Beatrice else; here she comes.

Enter BEATRICE.

Hero. Good morrow, coz.

Beatrice. Good morrow, sweet Hero.

Hero. Why, how now? do you speak in the sick tune?

Beatrice. I am out of all other tune, methinks.

Margaret. Clap's into *Light o' love*; that goes without a burden: do you sing it, and I'll dance it.

Beatrice. Ye light o' love, with your heels!—then, if your husband have stables enough, you'll see he shall lack no barns.

Margaret. O illegitimate construction! [*The reference being to cuckoldry.*] I scorn that with my heels.

Beatrice. 'Tis almost five o'clock, cousin; 'tis time you were ready.—By my troth, I am exceeding ill:—heigh-ho!

Margaret. For a hawk, a horse, or a husband?

Beatrice. For the letter that begins them all. [*Cf.* **horse**, v.; **husband**, v.; and **horn**, sense 1.]

Margaret. Well, an you be not turn'd Turk, there's no more sailing by the star.

Beatrice. What means the fool, trow?

Margaret. Nothing I; but God send everyone their heart's desire!

Hero. These gloves the Count sent me; they are an excellent perfume.

Beatrice. I am stuft, cousin; I cannot smell.

Margaret. A maid, and stuft! there's goodly catching of cold.

Beatrice. O, God help me! God help me! how long have you profest apprehension?

Margaret. Ever since you left it. Doth not my wit become me rarely?

Beatrice. It is not seen enough; you should wear it in your cap.— By my truth, I am sick. [She may mean that she is having her period; she certainly means that Hero's marriage makes her wish that she were being married.]

Margaret. Get you some of this distill'd Carduus Benedictus, and lay it to your heart: it is the only thing for a qualm.

Hero. There thou prick'st her with a thistle.

Beatrice. Benedictus! why Benedictus? You have some moral in this Benedictus.

Margaret. Moral! no, by my troth, I have no moral meaning; I meant, plain holy-thistle.

And yet Hero and Beatrice and perhaps Margaret were virgins: Hero, a very modest one; Beatrice, proud in her self-regarding; and Margaret, despite Beatrice's fleering jape, no light-o'-love.

Men among men; women among women; and now, men and women conversing together on intimate subjects and making the most erotic innuendoes and the most doubtful puns.

Perdita, young and pure, speaks far from purely with men 'old enough to be her father'; Beatrice exchanges bawdy jests with her uncle; Lady Grey quibbles none too cleanly with her royal wooer; Anne Bullen shows to the 'merry gamester' (hinting 'joyous wencher'), Lord Sands, that she understands the two sexual meanings of **thing**; the chaste and patient Helena conducts a long discussion with the lewd Parolles on the subject of virginity. In *All's Well That Ends Well* (I ii 110–166) it is Parolles who broaches the subject and does most of the talking, but Helena encourages him to expatiate upon the subject of virginity in general and hers in particular. This is the Shakespearean *locus classicus*; and I hardly need to reproduce it here. Yet for the sake of the inexpert or the not-so-knowledgeable, I refer the reader to the following entries in the Glossary: **virginity, keep out, assail, sit down before, undermine** (and **underminer**), **blow up** (and **blower-up**), **breach, city, increase, virgin, principal, lying,** and **withered pear**.

Those who have read Hoby's *The Courtier*, translated from the Italian of Castiglione, will remember that this translation, much esteemed, served as a pattern for Elizabethan gentlemen. Now, *The Courtier* has not a little to say on the theme of verbal gallantry between men and women: and the general tenor of the remarks is that sensual conversation between the sexes is to be discountenanced. On the other hand, there is much evidence to show that in late-Elizabethan, in Jacobean, and in Caroline times, women spoke very freely of sex in the presence of men and that the men and women of those times conversed together, with considerable freedom, on the theme of fornication and 'wedding and bedding'. The comedies of Ben Jonson, the comedies and tragi-comedies of Beaumont & Fletcher, Heywood, Massinger, Middleton, offer many proofs of this freedom. Shakespeare and Beaumont & Fletcher were quite as 'free' as were Dryden, Etherege, Wycherley, Congreve. So was the Society of both of those periods; freer than that of the lax period of ca. 1920–1930, and 'protesting' far less than did the naughty 'twenties, which outwent the earlier periods only in the matter of discussions concerning homosexuality.

Among the sexual subjects discussed in mixed company, was that of cuckoldry—a man's plight, condition, emotions, jealousy, while his wife is being unfaithful to him. Some idea of the objectivity with which Shakespeare (and apparently many other Elizabethans and Jacobeans) regarded and treated this theme may be gained from a collocation of such passages as *Titus Andronicus*, II iii 66–71 and IV iii 69–75; *The Comedy of Errors*, II i

56–59; *Love's Labour's Lost*, IV i 110–117 and V i 61–65; *Midsummer Night's Dream*, V i 230–234; *King John*, II i 290–293; *2 Henry IV*, I ii 48–51; *Much Ado*, II i 25–27 (and 42–43) and V ii 38–39; *The Merry Wives*, I iv 47–49 and II i 117–122 and III iii 148–150 and V 67 and 145–148 and IV ii 21–22 and V v 24–27; *As You Like It*, III iii 46–59 and IV i 55–62; *Hamlet*, III i 139–141; *Troilus and Cressida*, I i 112–113 and IV v 45–46 and V i 52–54 and vii 9–12; *All's Well*, I iii 44–56 (the Clown's humorous defence and praise of cuckoldry; cf. his close-ensuing quatrain); *Othello*, I iii 372–373 and III iii 167–170; *Antony and Cleopatra*, I ii 4–5 and 76–78; *Coriolanus*, IV v 214–215; and *The Winter's Tale*, I ii 119, 146, 190–200, 267–268. The general impression given by these passages to the superficial is that Shakespeare is cynically indifferent to the cuckoldy fate of all the unfortunate husbands he knew and had read about, whereas that gained by the thoughtful is that he was profoundly philosophic (see especially *The Winter's Tale*, I ii 190–200) and not very philosophical on the subject.

Cuckoldry brings us to the allied subject of jealousy, over which we need linger only long enough to note that the psychological and spiritual aspects are treated by Shakespeare with deep understanding and unfailing sympathy, and to refer the reader to *The Winter's Tale*, I ii 108–120, for a jealous man's horrible suspicions and exaggerations of an imagined incipience of marital infidelity.

As for love, love in general: irrelevant here, it will be briefly touched on in section 5.

What, however, is urgently relevant at this point is some consideration of Shakespeare's sexual imagery; although it must relatively be inadequate by itself, yet, taken in conjunction with cursory remarks made earlier and later in this section, it will not, I trust, be absolutely inadequate. But, reluctant to allow the theme to run away with me and to get out of hand (and proportion), I must curtail my treatment of the sexual images, which are sufficiently varied to satisfy the most exigently fanciful of lewdery-lovers, the most imaginative students of physical love, and the most versatile and expert of lovers: they range from the starriest lyricism and idealism to the most brutal prose and materialism: they are culled from the totality of knowledge available to Shakespeare, who, moreover, has powerfully influenced all amatory writers since his death—including the translators of Rabelais, the 17th Century dramatists, poets and versifiers, the 18th Century novelists, and such 19th and 20th Century notables as Byron, Meredith, Swinburne, Hardy, Hewlett, Abercrombie, and many of the poets, novelists, dramatists that have become prominent since the war of 1914–1918.

To avoid excessive overlapping, I have made the following deliberately inexhaustive[1] classification: Musical; Religious; Trading and Commercial; Mechanical; Sport and Horsemanship and Hunting; Martial (including fencing and jousting); Nautical and Naval; Geographical and Topographical; Agricultural; Pastoral and Horticultural; Animal World; and Domestic and Social.

Among the musical metaphorical terms are **finger**, **pipe** (?), **virginalling**, **wind-instrument**.

Religion supplies **confessor**, **shrive** and **shriver**.

Trade and commerce yield such entries as **business**, **call to a reckoning**, **commodity**, **market-price** and **mart**, **rent** and **revenue**, **trade** and **trader** and **trading**, **traffic**, **usury**.

The mechanical words and phrases include **assay**, **coin** and **coiner**, **compound**, **counterfeit**, **disedge**, **instrument**, **pick the lock**, **print off**, **stamp**, **tool**, and **vice**.

Sports and games and manly pastimes account for many entries in the Glossary. Here are some of them.

Horsemanship: **horsemanship** itself, **manage**, **mount** and **vault**, **pace**, **ride** and **rider**.

Sport and games in general: **game**, **pastimes**, **play**, **sport**.

The chase (in its widest sense): **beagle**, **break the pale**, **buck**

---

[1] Nor do the category lists pretend to be exhaustive

and **stag** and **deer** and **doe**, **horn** and **horned herd**, **mort o' the deer**, and **winded in the forehead**.

Falconry provides us with **allure**.

From archery we get, for instance, **hit it**, **mark**, and perhaps **match**.

Fishing gives us **angling** and **fish** (v.), **groping . . .** and **hook**.

Athletics: **sensual race** and perhaps **leap** and **vault**.

And there are references to **billiards** and bowls (at **bowl**).

Warfare, individual combat, fencing and jousting form a large group. We may note **set up one's rest** from jousting; **foin**, **foining**, **thrust**, from fencing. Warfare, with several terms perhaps belonging rather to individual combat, constitutes the imagery-base of the following entries:—**assail** and **assault**; **bag and baggage**; **besiege** and **ram** and **siege** and **sit down before**; **buckler** and **defence**; **bullets**, **charged chambers**, **pistol** and **pistol-proof**; **charge** and **discharge**; **conquer . . .** and **make defeat . . .**; **fort** and **breach**; **dart**, **lance**, **pike**, **poll-axe**, **sword**, **weapon**; **hang one's bugle . . .**; **privates** and **soldier . . .**; **scale**; **ransack**, **sack** and **spoil**; **stab** and **strike**; **standard**; **undermine** and **underminer**, **blow up** and **blower-up**.

The sea and sea-fighting supply rather more numerous examples than these: **above deck** and **hatches**; **board** and **boarding**; **boat . . .**, **carack**; **leaky**, **poop** and **rudder**; and **put to sea**.

From Political and Physical Geography we draw the following: **Belgia**, **bogs**, **brakes**, **cliff**, **Corinth**, two **country** phrases, **dale**, **demesnes**, **fountain**, **globe** and **world**, **hill** and **hillock** and **mountain**, **holland**, **Ireland**, **low countries** and **Netherlands**, **plain**, **pond**, **road** and **way**, and **Spain**.

Agricultural, pastoral, horticultural entries include **bottom-grass**, **breed** and **breeder** and **breeding**; **bull** and **cow** and **heifer** and **calf** and **neat**; **yoke**; **geld**, **glib**, **splay**, **gib-cat** and **capon**; **horse**, **mare**, **colt**, **jade**, **hackney**, **hobby-horse**, **nag**; **sty**; **carrot** and **mandrake** and **potato-finger** and **plant** and **root** and **stalk**; **crop** and **uncropped**; **damson** and **plum** and

medlar and **poperin pear** and **withered pear** and, inevitably, **fruit** and **orchard**; **ear** and **plough** and **unear'd**; **germen** and **seed**; **holy-thistle** and **thistle**, **prick** and **thorn**; **velvet leaves**; **husbandry, tillage, tilth**; **raw** and **unripe**.

Thence we pass to such animal-kingdom terms as have not been included in the preceding paragraph: **beast, beastly, bestial**; **billing, bird's nest, cuckoo, guinea-hen, hen, quail, sparrows, strange fowl**; **bitch** and **make the beast with two backs**; these other copulatory verbs, **change the cod's head for the salmon's tail, cover, jump, leap, ram, serve, tread, tup**; **fish** (n.) and **mackerel**; **bull Jove**; **ram** and **Aries**; **goats** and **goatish**; **piss one's tallow** and **stale** (n., sense 2); **scut** and **tail**; **whale**.

And lastly the domestic (and social) entries: **apron, mountant**; **aunt**; **bathe in water** and **cock** and **sluice**; **bauble**; **beef** and **flesh** and **mutton** (cf. **laced mutton**); to **eat** and to **feed** (and **feeder**); **stomach**; **bolster . . ., buried . . ., down-bed, sheet**; **chamber-lie** and **jakes**; **bona roba, ruff, shift, smock**, and **unlace**; **placket** and **cod-piece**; **broach** and **fill a bottle . . .**; **burn** and **dish** (cf. **clack-dish**) and **relish** and **running banquet**; **malady** and **catching of cold** and **salve**; **dance . . .** ; **dial**; **ring** and **jewel**; **distaff** and **spin off**; **pen** and **pin**; **tool** and **yard**; **pipe** (?) and **tub**; **stair-work** and **trunk-work**.

An examination of every passage containing those examples of Shakespeare's sexual imagery would show, once and for all, how picturesque and arresting were his imagination and his fancy; how concise and pregnant and vivid the manner in which he expressed those mental faculties; how apt the use of the sexual metaphor in any given context; how wide the range of his knowledge (one feels that he knew things, not from books but at first hand, even when we know that, for instance in the warfare group, he could not have possessed a first-hand knowledge); how large and yet how exact his vocabulary; how rich his mind; his emotions how varied; how wide-scoped his aesthetic purpose, expressing itself in purest poetry or the most pedestrian prose and ranging from ethereal delicacy to the most cynical and brutal coarseness, with subtlety and wit applied sometimes to the most unlikely subjects.

But Shakespeare's objectivity and precision must not, even for a moment, obscure for us the fact that he could no less aptly employ the general abstraction than the particular fact, as we see in the following synonymy for lust (essenced in *Titus Andronicus*), amorous desire, dissoluteness: **affect** (which is not to be confused with the modern psychological sense of that noun) and **affection**, [**amorous**,] **appetite**, [**apt**,] **ardour**, [**bawdy** and] **bawdry**, **blood**, **desire**, [**glutton**,] **have a hot back** and all the other **hot** phrases (as well as **hot** itself), **hunger**, [**inclined**, **insatiate**,] **intemperance**, [**keen**, lascivious,] **lechery**, [**lewd**,] **liberty**, [**licentious**,] **liking**, **lust**, **luxury**, **passion**, [**prime**,] **prompture**, [**ribald**,] **riot**, [**salt**, **saucy**,] **satiety**, **sensuality**, [**sweating**, **ticklish**,] **variety**, **Venus** (cf. **Eros**), **voluptuousness**, **wantonness**, and **will**: nor is this list complete.

Very few of those terms are coarse. But that Shakespeare can be coarse, crude, brutal, has been shown or implied; perhaps sufficiently for most general readers and some scholars and students, although insufficiently, doubtless, for others. To those others, I offer these additions: many of the Falstaff scenes are coarse, and *Henry V*, II iii 23–28 is gruesome, macabre, horrible; the brothel-scene in *Pericles* (IV ii) is extremely coarse; so is *2 Henry IV* II iv, and there are others; many of the words for a prostitute and prostitution are coarse.

A prostitute is a: **beagle**, **callet**, **common customer**, **commoner**, **creature of sale**, **Doll Tearsheet**, **drab**, **guinea-hen**, **hare**, **harlot**, **heifer**, **Mistress Kate Keepdown**, **pagan**, **Phrynia**, **prostitute**, **punk**, **puzzel**, **stale**, **strumpet**, **trot**, **trull**, **whore**. (An amorous, self-indulgent woman, but not necessarily a whore, is a **bed-fellow** or **-mate**, or **-swerver** (this connotes infidelity), or a **play-fellow**; a **bitch** or **boggler**; a **concubine**, **fere**, **mistress**, **paramour**; a **dish**; an **encounterer** or **wanton**; a

fornicatress; a **hackney**, **hobby-horse**, or **nag**; a **hen**; a **minx** or a **siren**; a **slut**; a **wench**; a **wrestler**. Compare *Troilus and Cressida*, v ii 108–116.)

The frequenter of brothels is a **whoremaster**, **whoremonger**, or **fleshmonger**. A womanizer is a **bed-presser** or **chamberer**; a **blower-up** or **underminer**; a **bull** or **town-bull**; a **coiner**; a **copesmate** or **skains-mate**; a **diver**; a **doer**; a **feeder**; a **juggler**; a **lecher** or **libertine**; a **mandrake**; and a **mouse-hunt**.

A brothel keeper[1] is a **bad woman** (cf. **naughty house**), a **bawd** (much the commonest term, ca. 1580–1840) or a **parcel-bawd** (or 'part-timer'); specifically she is **Madame Mitigation** or **Mistress Overdone**.

A procurer or a pimp is a **broker** (or **broker-between**), a **mackerel**, or a **pandar**; the last is not necessarily—and, indeed, not usually—a professional.

Prostitution is **harlotry** or the **hold-door trade**. And a **brothel** is also a **bawd's house** (which hardly survived the 17th Century) or **bawdy-house**, still current as a literarism; a **common house** (cf. **common customer**, above), a **leaping house**, or a **naughty house**; it is also a **house of profession** or **resort** or **sale** (cf. **creature of sale**, above); especially, it is a **stew** or, more generally, **the stews**, with which compare the 18th Century–early 19th Century use of **bagnio**.

Yet, in all the coarsenesses, it must, I think, be admitted that Shakespeare knew what he intended to do—and did it. The word or phrase always suits either the speaker or the scene or the event: usually, it is consonant with all three factors. If it suits none of them, then the reader will find that it suits the psychological or moral or spiritual atmosphere, as in the speeches of Timon when fate has turned him into a misanthropist.

At the opposite extreme is delicacy. Now, delicacy can, on the verbal plane, consort with whores and wenchers and lovers only

[1] Shakespeare does not speak of a *procurer* or a *procuress*. He does, however, use the verb **procure**.

by throwing up a smoke-screen of euphemism[1]—or, as we shall see, in the paragraph next but one, of subtle or recondite wit. To cite every euphemism were as tedious as unnecessary. Here are a few euphemistic words and phrases: **the act—the act of shame—the act of sport**; **begin**; **capable** (or **able**) for 'sexually potent'—cf. **vigour**, 'sexual potency'; **do it—do the deed—do the deed of darkness—do the deed of kindness**; **et cetera**; **to exchange flesh**; **favours**; **forfended place**; **give oneself**; **know—know as a wife—know** (a person's) **body**; **offend in a dream**; **performance** (cf. **execution**); **to taste**; **yield one's body to shame—yield up one's body to** (another's) **will**.

Several of these phrases have a certain picturesqueness and beauty. Picturesqueness and poetry are not the qualities one would first think to look for in passages descriptive of, or allusive to, love-making and lust, yet Shakespeare, as Spenser had done before him and Milton and Meredith and Swinburne were to do after him, contrived to invest them with an occasional flash of lyricism, as in *Romeo and Juliet*, *The Winter's Tale*, *Venus and Adonis*, and elsewhere, and in such words and phrases as **deflower, flower** and **rose** and **pluck a sweet**; **get the sun of**; to **lover**; **mansion of love** (cf. the analogous use of **temple**); **jewel** and **treasure** and **virgin patent**. These expressions are illuminating, it is true; but much more illumination can be had from certain passages in *Romeo and Juliet*, *Venus and Adonis*, and even *Lucrece*.

In the four paragraphs preceding this, there are a few terms that exhibit Shakespeare's subtlety and wit in sexual contexts. In the Glossary, the reader will come upon some twenty or thirty examples: here I shall mention only six: **charged chambers, dial, eye** and **naked seeing self** (cf. **O**), **secretly open**, and **velvet leaves**. But no reader would wish me to explain the subtlety of *The Taming of the Shrew*, V ii 40–43, the pun-capping of

---

[1] For the general theme, see 'Euphemism and Euphemisms' in my *Here, There and Everywhere*, (Hamish Hamilton) 1950.

Henry V, III vii 46–49 and the 'overlapping' wit of v ii 300–320; Pandarus's innuendoes in Troilus and Cressida, IV ii 23–39, and Ulysses' brilliant sexual satire at IV v 55–63; Lucio's venomously witty bawdiness in Measure for Measure, III ii; the concentrated and elaborate synonymization of sexual provocation in the Porter scene of Macbeth (II iii 27–37); the pell-mell accumulation of copulation-images and epigrams of Lear, IV vi 111–134; the ardent-bitter sex-nausea of Timon, IV iii 133–148; Leonatus's outburst against women's sexuality in Cymbeline, II v; the not-so-simple simplicity of the Clown-Mopsa-Dorcas talk in The Winter's Tale, IV iii 244–259; the Sands-Lovell and Sands-Bullen repartees in Henry VIII I iv 10–18 and 44–50; that cornucopia of amorous phraseology, the first six hundred or so verses of Venus and Adonis, and its reminiscence, The Passionate Pilgrim.

In the last two examples, however, the wit lies only in the ingenuity displayed by Shakespeare in diversifying his terms and in that flashing intelligence which enables him to devise (not that he needs to cogitate: wet towels on the head and rackings within it were not for him) and to sustain, naturally and convincingly, an impressive and cumulative imagery. In all the other examples, however, even the Shakespearean scholars should, with very few exceptions, ask themselves, Do I perceive every nuance?—Sometimes, too, they should ask, Am I sufficiently versed in Shakespearean slang and cant[1] and colloquialism to know that a pun has been made or a double entente certainly or, at least, probably intended, for it has not even yet been fully appreciated that Shakespeare is the world's greatest wit, that he is extremely sexual (both intellectually and physically; by temperament, by observation, and by practice), and, above all, that he is never wittier, never more given to punning, than when, whether overtly or covertly, he is dealing with sexual matters or making a sexual allusion or intending his hearers and readers to

[1] Used in the low Falstaff scenes and by Autolycus in The Winter's Tale.

obtain an additional 'kick' by perceiving for themselves the witticism, the innuendo, the pun that he has in, or at the back of, his
mind and, in some cases, does not, directly, express at all,—
something that he knows will be detected only by a very alert
exercise of that faculty which enables us to surmise, then track
down, and finally work out the sense-associations resident not
merely in the words but in the words with their dramatic and
psychological contexts and implications super-added.

[1]But, after all, I should, perhaps—even at the risk of appearing
to arrogate to myself a non-existent superiority[1] substantiate
what I have just said by supplying at least one example. That
example is to be *Henry V*, III vii 46–69, which, though I shall not
subject it to an *explication française*, can perhaps be best understood
by being treated in parallel columns, with the significant words
and phrases indicated in heavy type and to be further consulted
in the Glossary.

Orleans. Your mistress bears
well.

Dauphin. Me well, which is
the prescript praise and perfection of a good and particular
mistress.

Constable. Ma foi, methought
yesterday your mistress shrewdly **shook your back**.

Dauphin. So, perhaps, did
yours.

As a horse bears or carries
its rider, so, in the sexual act, a
woman supports the **weight**
of the man lying upon her. (In
Shakespeare, the man is always
on top.)

Apparently a mistress whose
role is not confined to the passive: one who tosses, squirms,
wriggles.

---

[1] Professed Shakespearean scholars and competent lexicographers need not
read this section-ending. All other readers, however, might do worse than to
ponder it.
[2] I am no Shakespearean scholar; but merely a Shakespeare-lover, interested in
wit and in words.

Constable. Mine was not **bridled**.

Dauphin. O, then, belike she was old and gentle; and you **rode**, like a kern of Ireland, your French hose off, and in your strait strossers [*trousers*].

Constable. You have good judgement in **horsemanship**.

Dauphin. Be warned by me, then; they that ride so, and ride not warily, fall into foul **bogs**. I had rather have my horse to my mistress.

Constable. I had as lief have my mistress a **jade**.

Dauphin. I tell thee, constable, my mistress wears her own **hair**.

Constable. I could make as true a boast as that, if I had a sow to my mistress.

Dauphin. *Le chien est retourné à son propre vomissement, et la truie lavée au bourbier:* thou makest **use** of anything.

Nor, by implication, **mounted**.

Rode wildly, impetuously, uncouthly, and part-stripped for the sake of greater freedom of action.

You are a connoisseur in the expertise of copulation.

Be careful: they that ride thus impetuously incur the risk of missing the **mark** and of finding themselves in places less pleasant.

An old worn-out horse: therefore likely to have but a thin coat of hair.

My mistress, sir, has no need to wear either a wig or a merkin.

Even a sow could say as much.

In this French translation of the Vulgate *locus*, the word 'sow' is caught up; the rare rural vice of swine copulation.[1]

---

[1] Shakespeare very rarely refers to the male perversions of necrophily and intercourse with sows, bitches, cows; and he never refers to the female perversion of intercourse with dogs. But this is a grimy subject, best left to the professional writers on sexual deviations.

Constable. Yet do I not **use** my horse for my mistress; or any such proverb, so little kin to the purpose.

The same vice, with mare substituted for sow, is again implied. (I do not know the proverb referred to: but perhaps there isn't one.)

And that is not the smuttiest, nor is it the wittiest, sexual passage in Shakespeare.

5

GENERAL

How, in this matter of sex and bawdiness, does Shakespeare compare with other Elizabethan and Jacobean dramatists? With the Restoration playwrights? And with those who come later?

Of all the dramatists flourishing in the Elizabethan and Jacobean periods, Shakespeare is the wittiest, profoundest, most idealistic yet most cynical, and, proportionally to the *corpora operum*, the most abundant: Lyly, Marlowe, Kyd, Greene—Ben Jonson, Webster, Tourneur, Heywood, Dekker, Massinger, Middleton, Beaumont & Fletcher: all these men are inferior, in all those respects, to Shakespeare, and only Jonson in his comedies and Beaumont & Fletcher, whether in comedy or in tragicomedy, are as smutty; but unfortunately the smut of Ben Jonson, as of the collaborators, is less witty, Jonson's tending to be thought up and thought out, the collaborators' inclining to the shop-walkers' snigger ('I couldn't find those ribbons in your drawers, Miss Jones') and to the foppish courtiers' apparent inability to be other than innuendoish.

The Restoration dramatists, Dryden, Etherege, Wycherley,

Otway, Congreve, Farquhar, are, in their sexual repartees, often nearly as witty and almost as abundant, but never so profound, rarely so audaciously objective as Shakespeare; and only Wycherley is equally scabrous. And, by the way, it is odd that Charles Lamb, who intimately knew both his Shakespeare and his Restoration dramatists, should not have taken it upon himself to apply to the former the thesis he advanced so exquisite-airily and serious-eloquently about the 'immorality' of the latter: that theirs was a world of scintillating make-believe and coruscating wit, and therefore unamenable to, indeed unrestricted by, the humdrum norm and social decency of ordinary everyday life: Lamb, one surmises, felt that Shakespeare was too big to be thus diminished and too much an adult to be thus excused

As for the post-1720 dramatists in England, I need only say that none of them has been so **free**, so **liberal**, as Shakespeare; no, not even the most daring and self-expressive, even at their most **nasty** (for at least two of them are nasty, in a rather undergraduate and **unknown**[1]**-to-woman** way).

But what of love in general, what of lust, what of chastity in Shakespeare himself? Chastity and temperance,[2] themes on which he has much that is notable and unforgettable to say, are, by the terms of my self-imposed limitation of theme, outside the scope of this essay.

The general theme of love itself: this likewise falls outside my scope, and I must here[3] confine myself to referring the reader to the Glossary entries at **Eros**, **love**, **Venus**[4]; to the following

[1] Or, at least, insufficiently known.

[2] The curious reader may consult the Glossary at **bond of chastity**, **chaste**, **chastity**, **continency**, **temperance**, **virgin**, **virginity**—and elsewhere.

[3] Before very long, I hope, I shall bring out a book with some such title as *Love and Friendship in Shakespeare*, with chapters on love; passion and lust; jealousy; affection; friendship; with perhaps an excursus on Love in English Literature.

[4] Cf. the contents and implications of the entries at **bed** and **wedding-bed**, **nuptial**, **bride**, **bridegroom**, **groom**; **woo** and **wooer**.

Shakespearean passages, *The Two Gentlemen of Verona*, I i 1–52 and ii 56–58 and iii 141–150 (loving thoughts and bodies); *Love's Labour's Lost*, IV iii 324–346; *A Midsummer Night's Dream*, I i 232–245 and V i 1–22; *As You Like It*, IV i 132–152; *Troilus and Cressida*, III ii 8–28; and, for a cynical, fleshy, elaborated definition, *Othello*, I iii 319–365.

Lust, however, is relevant: 'The expense of spirit in a waste of shame Is lust in action' (*Sonnets*, 129, where the grammatical subject is 'lust in action', rhetorical emphasis being laid on the predicate): yet with the psychological, moral, spiritual aspects of lust I cannot relevantly concern myself. Of examples of the physical aspect and expression of 'lust in action', a sufficiency has already been quoted; in the preceding section, there is a synonymy of the words and phrases dealing with lust and amorous desire; and the reader may betake himself to the following *loci*: *Hamlet*, I v 42–57 and III iv 64–95 and 160–197; *Venus and Adonis*, vv. 787–804.

All passages cited hitherto have in common this implication: that at no period of his life was Shakespeare uninterested in sex, although there is one in which he suffered from sex-nausea: the period of *Hamlet*, *Troilus and Cressida*,[1] *All's Well That Ends Well*, *Measure for Measure*, *Othello*, *Macbeth*, *Lear*, *Antony and Cleopatra*, *Coriolanus*, *Timon*, *Pericles*, *Cymbeline*, and *The Winter's Tale* (earlier half): but his disgust did not make for reticence.

If we take the plays in the convenient division into Histories, Comedies, Tragedies, and Tragi-Comedies, we notice that, apart from the Falstaff scenes, the Histories are, sexually, much the 'purest'; then the Comedies; then, if we include *All's Well* the Tragi-Comedies; whereas the Tragedies, despite the comparative innocuousness of *Macbeth*, are, as a class, the most indelicate.

---

[1] 'Through [Thersites] Shakespeare got rid of much of his bile and a lot of sex-nausea that accompanied his phase of disgust with life in general', Hesketh Pearson, who is good on Shakespeare-and-sex, in *A Life of Shakespeare*, 1942.

Of the separate plays, taken in their probable chronological order, one may speak as follows:—

Henry VI: all three Parts are moderates—and much alike, one to another.

Richard III: on much the same level.

Titus Andronicus: not very rich in particularities; but the theme is that of tragedy ensuing from lust, rape, rapine, sexual and other cruelty. Parts are extremely sadistic; this play out-Kyds Kyd in crude sensationalism.

The Comedy of Errors: except for the 'female geography' passage, it is mild.

The Two Gentlemen of Verona: in particulars, it is roughly equal to *Titus*, but in general it is comparatively pleasant.

Love's Labour's Lost: same remarks, except that IV i 110–130 forms one of the most 'greasy' passages in the whole of Shakespeare.

Romeo and Juliet: Mercutio and the Nurse sex-spatter the most lyrically tragic of the plays.

A Midsummer Night's Dream: a pretty 'safe' play, hence a favourite in school examinations. (Cf. *Twelfth Night*.)

King John: closely comparable with the two earlier Histories.

The Taming of the Shrew: much the same remarks as for *The Two Gentlemen*.

Richard II: the cleanest play by Shakespeare and, by any standard whatsoever, a remarkably chaste one.[1]

The Merchant of Venice: dirtier than most teachers think; but, even so, it is reasonably clean.

Henry IV: Part I is much the 'milder' (hardly worse than *The*

---

[1] There is only one sexual reference worth the mention: 'My brain I'll prove the female to my soul, My soul the father: and these two beget A generation of still-breeding thoughts' (v v 6–8). This beats Tennyson's historical dramas for purity!

Merchant); Part II is, both in quality and in quantity, the 'stronger'.

Henry V: in quality, the obscenest of the Histories.[1]

Much Ado About Nothing: the sexual-worst of the Comedies, although

The Merry Wives of Windsor runs it close.

Julius Caesar: after Richard II, the cleanest historical play; and cleaner than even A Midsummer Night's Dream and The Tempest.

As You Like It: compare the remarks at The Merchant.

Twelfth Night: the cleanest comedy except A Midsummer Night's Dream.

Hamlet: though rather less bawdy than Othello, it is much bawdier than Macbeth and approximately as bawdy as Lear.

Troilus and Cressida: only slightly bawdier than Hamlet; yet, all in all, it leaves a nasty taste in the literary mouth.

All's Well That Ends Well: not a 'nice' play. Parolles can infallibly be depended on for dirt.

Measure for Measure and Othello are Shakespeare's most sexual, most bawdy plays; Othello, possessing a strength and a nobility absent in the other, is, on the physical plane, slightly the bawdier of the two, although quantitatively there is very little to choose between them.

Macbeth is the 'purest' of the Tragedies and, except for the Porter Scene, pure by any criterion.

King Lear: compare the remarks at Hamlet, than which it is, however, both less witty in its witty-sexual passages and less eloquent and impressive in its sexual invectives.

Antony and Cleopatra: Antony's world well lost for love of the riggish Egyptian reincarnation of Venus Aphrodite. (On much the same level of bawdiness as All's Well, Hamlet, and Lear).

Coriolanus: possesses a few more particularities than Macbeth, yet, in its general effect, even less 'objectionable'.

---

[1] Oddly, this term is applied only to the English historical plays.

Timon of Athens is, in III vi–the end, the most misanthropic of Shakespeare's plays, sexually as well as generally. Quantitatively comparable with *All's Well*, *Hamlet*, *Lear*.

Pericles: except for Marina, it is unsavoury. The brothel scene (IV ii) is perhaps the 'lowest' scene in Shakespeare; and, as a whole, this play outdoes *Timon* in bawdiness.

Cymbeline in many ways resembles *The Winter's Tale*, which is slightly the less bawdy but rather the more sexual. They are of much the same quantitative order as *All's Well*.

The Tempest: by far the purest of the Tragi-Comedies; slightly 'milder' than *Twelfth Night*.

Henry VIII: a little bawdier than the *Henry VI* trilogy and roughly equal to the First Part of *Henry IV*, than which, however, it makes a better general impression.

The periods of the first four plays and the last two would *seem* to be the least sex-interested in Shakespeare's theatre-life, although that of *A Midsummer Night's Dream*, *King John*, *The Taming* (much the smuttiest play in this group), *Richard II*, and *The Merchant of Venice* comes a good second. Another chronological division is this: 1 *Henry VI* to *The Comedy of Errors* (inclusive); from *The Two Gentlemen* to *Twelfth Night*; from *Hamlet* to *Pericles*, the bawdiest period of the four; and from *Cymbeline* to *Henry VIII*, a period of a bawdiness slightly more marked, quantitatively and qualitatively, than the first. The second period is the most uneven, for in it we have the 'purity' of *A Midsummer Night's Dream*, *King John*, *Richard II*, *Julius Caesar*, the comparative innocuousness of *The Merchant of Venice*, *As You Like It*, *Twelfth Night*, and the anything-but-innocence of *Romeo and Juliet*, *Henry IV*, *Henry V*, and *The Merry Wives of Windsor*.

6

VALEDICTORY

Of the influence of sex upon character, hence upon destiny, Shakespeare has said little that is explicit: and that little is mostly in the invectives of the bitter period. But, implicitly, he has said not a little especially in such plays as *Titus Andronicus*, *Romeo and Juliet*, *Hamlet*, *Troilus and Cressida*, *Othello*, *Antony and Cleopatra* ('Egypt, thou knew'st too well my heart was to thy rudder tied by the strings, and thou shouldst tow me after'), *Pericles*, *Cymbeline*, and *The Winter's Tale*; likewise in the *Sonnets*, where he is also at his most explicit, and in *Lucrece*.

In my study of Shakespeare's sexuality and bawdiness, I have come to feel that, from his plays and poems, there emerges something basic, significant, supremely important and most illuminatingly revelatory.

Although he never even hinted this, Shakespeare seems to have held, and to have consistently acted upon, the opinion; nay, the belief; that:—

To write is, in fact, to create; and to make love is potentially to create:

to write provides a means of releasing one's intellectual and spiritual energy, whereas to copulate is a means of releasing one's physical energy:

the desire to write is at least as urgent and powerful, intellectually and spiritually, as the desire to make love (especially, to copulate) is on the physical plane:

composition is superior to love-making as a means of satisfying the need for self-expression (or 'the creative urge'); almost equal to it as an anodyne to that loneliness with which all of us, but especially the literary and artistic and musical creators, are beset, and as a comfort and a solace:

moreover, to write of sex and love serves both to satisfy—and perhaps to justify—the intellectual and spiritual need to create and homoeopathically to assuage one's physical desires by that modified form of sublimation which consists in a not ignoble substitution.

A GENERAL INDEX TO THE ESSAY

Shakespeare's Plays and Poems; Other Authors and their Works; Sexual and Bawdy Themes; Tendencies and Characteristics; General Observations. (But not words and phrases, for the Glossary is alphabetical.)

Abercrombie, Lascelles: 43
All's Well: 20, 40, 57
amorists: 6, 31
amorous desire: *see* lust
animal world, terms from: 34, 44
Antony and Cleopatra: 20, 57, 59
archery terms: 27, 44
As You Like It: 55, 57

Barker, Granville: 1
Barnfield, Richard: 17
bawdiness: Preface; 9–12, 38, 59
bawds: 47
Beatrice: 16, 36
Beaumont & Fletcher: 41, 53
billiards: 44

Blake: 10
bowls, game of: 44
breasts, female: 22–23
Brophy, John: 27
brothels: 46–47, 58
brutality: 20, 35, 43
Burns: 10
Butler, Samuel: 14
Byron: 9, 43

caressing: 30
Chambers, Sir E. K.: 1
chase, terms from the: 28, 43–44
chastity: 54
coarseness: 9–12, 35, 46, 47
Comedies: 55–58

Comedy of Errors, The: 7–8, 56, 58
commerce: 43
Congreve: 38, 41, 54
coprology and scatology: 9
copulation: 31–35, 60
Coriolanus: 3, 23, 57
cuckoldry: 41–42
Cymbeline: 20, 23, 49, 58

defecation: 10–11
Dekker: 53
dialogue, sexual: 35–41
dirt or smut: 5, 43
domestic terms: 45
Dryden: 9, 41, 53
Dunbar: 10

Ellis, Havelock: 15
embraces: 30
emission, sexual: 29
Etherege: 38, 41, 53
eunuchs: 18–20
euphemism: 26, 48

falconry: 44
Falstaff: 16, 20, 46
farming metaphors: 28, 33–34, 44–45
Farquhar: 54
fencing, terms from: 44
flatulence: 11–12
frankness, sexual: 5, 35
Fripp, Edgar I.: 1

games: *see* sport
gardening metaphors: 28, 34, 44–45
genitals, female: 23–27
genitals, male: 27–30
geography and topography, meta-
    phors from: 6–8, 26–27, 44
Greene: 53

Hamlet: 12, 24–25, 55, 57, 58, 59

Hardy: 3, 43
Harris, Frank: 14
Henry IV: 16, 20, 24, 29, 56–57, 58
Henry V: 49, 50–52, 57, 58
Henry VI: 16, 20, 56, 58
Henry VIII: 49, 58
Hewlett, Maurice: 6, 43
Heywood, 41, 53
Histories, the: 55, 57, 58
Hoby: 41
homosexuality: Preface; 13–18, 41
horsemanship: 34, 43
Hotson, Leslie: 1
hymen, the: 25

idealism: 4, 5
imagery, sexual: 6–8, 42–48
intimacy (of detail): 4

jealousy: 42
Jerrold, Douglas: 38
Jonson, Ben: 41, 53
jousting: 28, 33, 44
Julius Caesar: 57, 48

Keats: 9
King John: 56, 58
Kingsmill, Hugh: 1, 14
kissing: 30
Knight, G. Wilson: xi, 1
Kyd: 53, 56

Lamb: 38, 54
lap, female: 23
Lear: 10–11, 49, 57
legs, female: 23
Lesbianism: 15
love: 4, 59–60
love-making: 21–22, 30–35, 60
Love's Labour's Lost: 10, 55, 56
Lucrece: 23, 59
lust: 35, 48, 55

Lyly: 53
lyricism: 43, 48

Macbeth: 3, 10, 49, 55, 57
Manning, F.: 30
Marlowe: 53
Massinger: 41, 53
masturbation: 31
Maupassant: 5
Maxwell, W. B.: 24
Measure for Measure: 10, 21, 35–36, 49, 57
mechanic arts and crafts, terms from: 43
Merchant of Venice, The: 3, 58
Mercutio: 36–38, 56
Meredith: 6, 43, 48
Merry Wives of Windsor, The: 57, 58
Middleton: 41, 53
Midsummer Night's Dream, The: 55, 56
military metaphors: 27, 28, 44
Milton: 5, 9
mons Veneris: 23
Much Ado: 16, 38–40
Muggeridge, Malcolm: 14
Muir, Kenneth: 1
musical terms: 43

nautical metaphors: 44
necrophily: 51
non-sexual bawdy: 9–12

Othello: 11, 55, 57, 59
Otway: 54
Ovid: 5, 31

pandars: 47
Passionate Pilgrim, The: 49
Pearson, Hesketh: xi, 1, 14–18, 55
penis erectus: 29
Pericles: 21, 58, 59

periods of sexuality, Shakespeare's: 55, 58–60
perversions: 13–18, 53
pimps: 47
podex: 10–12
poetic terms and metaphors: 45–46
Pope: 9
posteriors: 12, 22
procreation: 35
prostitutes and prostitution: 21, 46–47
prurience: 12, 38
pubic hair: 24
pudend, female and male: *see* genitals
puns and jokes, bawdy: 6–8, 49–50

Rabelais: 9, 43
Read, A. W.: 27
religious terms: 43
Rhodes, Crompton: 13
Richard II: 56, 58
Richard III: 56
Romeo and Juliet: 3, 6, 36–37, 56, 58

sadism: 28, 34, 55
scrotum: 29
semen: 29
sensuality, Shakespeare's: 3, 22
sex: 19, 59–60
Shakespeare, general characteristics: 1–6, 49–50, 60
shape metaphors: 27, 29
Shaw, G. B.: 38
smut: 53, 54
Sonnets: 16–18, 55, 59
Spenser: 9, 48
spiritual conflict: 4
sport and games: 28, 43
subtlety: 5, 32
Swinburne: 6, 9, 43, 48
synonymies: 23, 26–31

Taming of the Shrew, The: 48, 56, 58

Tempest, The: 3, 57, 58
Tennyson: 9, 56
testicles: 29
Times Literary Supplement, The: 2
Timon of Athens: 3, 20–21, 49, 58
Titus Andronicus: 46, 56
topography: *see* geography
Tourneur: 53
trade and commerce: 43
Tragedies, the: 55, 57
Tragi-Comedies, the: 55, 58
Troilus and Cressida: 16, 55, 57
Twelfth Night: 10, 20, 57, 58
Two Gentlemen of Verona: 55, 56

universality: 2–4
urination: 10

venereal disease: 20–21
Venus and Adonis: 6, 48, 55
virginity: 40–41

Walker, Kenneth: 14, 19
wantons: 46–47
warfare: *see* military
Webster: 53
wenchers: 47
Whistler: 30
Wilde, Oscar: 14–15, 30, 38
Wilson, Professor Dover: xi, 1
Winter's Tale, The: 42, 48, 58, 59
wit, Shakespeare's: 28, 38, 49–52
writer, Shakespeare as a: 5, 29
writing: 59–60
Wycherley: 38, 41, 53

GLOSSARY

AUTHOR'S NOTE, 1968

I have on p. 57 adjudged *Twelfth Night* to be 'the cleanest comedy except *A Midsummer Night's Dream*'. Mr Jonathan Benthall, a Cambridge scholar, has asked me to modify this statement by noting, both that Feste's closing song has little meaning unless it be taken to summarize his lifetime's sexual experience, and that, secondly, the Toby/Andrew dialogues show unequivocally—especially towards the end of Act I Scene 3—that the sexual polarity of the English residents is ill-established. (Though Sir Toby finally marries Maria quite cheerfully, he apparently, like Falstaff, 'cares not what mischief he doth'; and inversion seems to be the very essence of Sir Andrew.)

Another Cambridge scholar, but also a Princeton man, Dr George Steiner, has pointed out that I had done less than justice to *Measure for Measure*.

And I myself take this opportunity of mentioning a suspicion I had even in 1942, the year in which I wrote the first draft: that I had treated the *Sonnets* with an inexcusable perfunctoriness.

The *Sonnets* and *Measure for Measure* have now, I hope, been more adequately treated. Numerous other omissions have been made good and a few errors corrected.

Abhorson. A composite name, meaning 'son from (L. *ab*) a whore'. In C. 17–18, *son of a whore* was an abusive form of address comparable with the C. 19–20 *son of a bitch*. Abhorson is a minor character, the executioner, in *Measure for Measure*.
Cf. **whoreson,** q.v.

ability; able (cf. **capable**). Sexual potency; sexually potent. Following the quotation at **act:** 'They say all lovers swear more performance than they are able, and yet reserve an ability that they never perform', T. & C., III ii 84–86.
Ex Old Fr. *ableté*: L. *habilitas*, 'aptitude; ability': *habilis*, 'easy to control': *habere*, 'to have; to hold; to control'.

above deck. At a distance, in reference to keeping off an amorous man: see the quotation at **boarding,** which contains the related **hatches.**
Deck probably comes from the Middle Dutch *dek*, 'a cover'—hence, 'a deck', which covers the cavity of the ship: therefore, *above deck* implies 'outside the coverings (a woman's clothes)'.

abstemious; abstinence: in, and from, sexual intercourse. '. . . Flat treason 'gainst the kingly state of youth. Say, can you fast? your stomachs are too young: And abstinence engenders maladies', L.L.L., IV iii 290–292.—*Hamlet*, III iv 166–168, 'Refrain tonight; And that shall lend a kind of easiness To the next abstinence: the next more easy'.
From L. *abstinentia*, 'a holding (of oneself) away' from a thing, an act, etc.

abuse. To make a cuckold of; to wrong by infidelity. 'She's gone; I am abused; and my relief Must be to loathe her', *Othello*, III iii 267–268.—Perhaps cf. the quotation at **leave a pillow unprest.**
L. *abuti*, 'to misuse'; *a(b)* '(away) from' (the usual, the norm) + *uti*, 'to use'.—Cf. the proverb, *abusus non tollit usum*.

abuse someone's **bed.** To seduce someone's wife. 'See the hell of having a false woman! My bed shall be abused', *Merry Wives*, II ii 291–292.
Cf. preceding entry.

accost. '*Belch.* You mistake, knight: "accost" is [to] front her, board her, woo her, assail her. *Aguecheek.* By my troth, I would not undertake her in this company', *Twelfth Night*, I iii 57–60.

Literally, 'to come up to the side of (a person)'—'to approach familiarly': L. *accostare* (*ad*, to; *costa*, a rib).

achieve. To win, or to overcome, a woman sexually. 'A thousand deaths Would I propose to achieve her whom I love', *Titus Andronicus*, II i 80.—*The Taming*, I i 155, 'I burn, I pine, I perish, Tranio, if I achieve not this young modest girl'.—*Othello*, II i 61.

Cf. to *win* or *gain* a woman. Literally, 'to come to a head (with a person)': via French, ex Low Latin *ad caput venire* (hence, there is a parallel in **accost**).

act: the act; the act of shame; the act of sport. For *the act*, see **generation**, **work of;** cf. **hot deeds** and **bereave . . . ,** qq.v.— 'This is the monstrosity in love, lady,—that the will is infinite, and the execution confined; that the desire is boundless; and the act a slave to limit', *T. & C.*, III ii 80–83.—'When the blood is made dull with the act of sport, there should be—again to inflame it, and to give satiety a fresh appetite—loveliness in favour', *Othello*, II i 228–231.—*Ibid.*, v ii 210–212, 'Iago knows That she with Cassio hath the act of shame A thousand times committed'.—'. . . Where you did fulfil The loathsome act of lust', *Lucrece*, vv. 1635–1636. See also **action.**

act of darkness. See the *Lear* quotation at **deer.**

Actaeon. A typical cuckold. See the first quotation at **horn.**— 'Prevent, or go thou, Like Sir Actaeon he, with Ringwood at thy heels:—O, odious is the name!—What name, sir?—The horn, I say', *Merry Wives*, II i 117–120; ibid., III ii 40–41, 'A secure and wilful Actaeon'.

Actaeon, a famous huntsman, saw Artemis (Roman Diana) bathing: her prudery affronted, she changed him into a stag, in which form he was torn to pieces by his own dogs. Why *Actaeon*? Simply because a **stag** has magnificent antlers (**horns**).

action. Sexual intercourse. See quotation at **rotten** and cf. **acture.**

Act and *action* both come from L. *agere*, 'to set in motion; hence, to do': *act* ex L. *actus*, 'a moving, a movement'; *action* ex L. *actio*. The L. *agere* is cognate with Gr. *agein*, 'to lead, guide': cf. Sanskrit **ajati,** 'he goes or drives' (Wyld).

activity. Sexual activity—i.e., potency and virility. Pandarus, speaking to Troilus concerning Cressida, 'She'll bereave you o' th' deeds too, if she call your activity in question', *T. & C.*, III ii 56–58. Cf:—

acture is a collective, or a generalization, of **act:** i.e. *action*. 'Love made them not', in reference to a man's confessed copulations; 'with acture they may be, Where neither party is nor true nor kind', *A Lover's Complaint*, vv. 185–186.

For the -*ure* suffix cf. **prompture.**

adulterate, adj. Defiled, adulterous; defiling. 'I am possest with an adulterate blot', *Com. of Errors*, II ii 139.—'Swearing, unless I took all patiently, . . . never [should] be forgot in mighty Rome Th' adulterate death of Lucrece and her groom', *Lucrece*, vv. 1641–1645.

L. *adulterare*, which = *ad*, 'to' + *alterare*, 'to change, to something different (*alter*)'—hence, generally to something worse; hence, 'to worsen; to corrupt'.

adulterer; adultress. A married person fornicating illicitly.

'They call'd me foul adultress, Lascivious Goth, and all the bitterest terms', *Titus Andronicus*, II iii 109–110.—*Lear*, I ii 127 (*adulterer*).—*Lear*, II iv 132 (*adultress*).—*The W. Tale*, II i 77 (*adultress*).

The latter ex the former, which = L. *adulter* (see preceding entry) + agential -*er*.

adulterous. Given to, or guilty of, adultery. See quotation at **virgin-violator.**—Maecenas to Octavia, 'Th' adultrous Antony, most large In his abominations, turns you off', *A. & C.*, III vi 93–94.

Cf. **adulterate,** q.v.

adultery. Extra-marital sexual intercourse. See quotation at **cardinally.**—'I pardon that man's life.—What was thy cause?—Adultery? Thou shalt not die: die for adultery! No: The wren goes to't . . .', *Lear*, IV vi 111–115.—*Cymbeline*, III II I. *The W. Tale*, III ii 14.

L. *adulterium* (see etymological note at **adulterate**).

adultress. See **adulterer.**

affairs. Female pudend, as in *Sonnets*, 151, 'Proud of this pride, He is contented thy poor drudge to be, To stand in thy affairs, fall by thy side'. As a euphemism, now usually *affair*.

affect, n. Emotion, especially desire; amorous desire. 'I beg it not, To please the palate of my appetite; Not to comply with heat—the young affects In me defunct—and proper satisfaction' (my own—my selfish—satisfaction), *Othello*, I iii 262–265.

Ex past participle of L. *afficere*, 'to work upon, to influence'. Especially 'a being-strongly-worked-upon'.

affection. Love; passionate desire. *The Comedy of Errors*, V i 51 (see **stray . . .**).—'Now old desire doth in his death-bed lie, And young affection gapes to be his heir', *R. & J.*, II, Prologue.—See second quotation at **blood.**—*M. N. Dream*, I i 207.—'She loves him with a most enraged affection', *Much Ado*, II iii 105.—*Twelfth Night*, II iv 37.—*Hamlet*, I iii 34.—*T. & C.*, II ii 177.—'Nothing can affection's course control', *Lucrece*, v. 500. And elsewhere.

L. *affectio* (ex *afficere*: see preceding entry).

Ajax. A pun upon *a jakes* (see **jakes**): L.L.L., V ii 571–572, 'Your lion, that holds his poll-axe sitting upon a close-stool, will be given to Ajax'.—*Lear*, II ii 125–126, 'None of these rogues and cowards, But Ajax is their fool'.

See **jakes.**

allure, v. Addressing two prostitutes, Timon says, 'He whose pious breath seeks to convert you, . . . allure him, burn him up; Let your close fire predominate his smoke, And be no turncoats', IV iii 140–143.—'She showed him favours to allure his eye', *The Passionate Pilgrim*, 4, v. 6.

From Old Fr. *aleurrer*; *à*, '(in)to' + *leurre*, 'a bait, a lure'.

allurement. Sexual attractiveness deliberately exercised; enticement. 'An advertisement'—i.e., a warning—'to a proper maid in Florence . . . to take heed of the allurement of one Count Rousillon', *All's Well*, IV iii 212–215.

See preceding entry.

amorous; amorous on. Filled with or expressive of or inciting to (the execution of) lust or strongly desirous love. 'To court an amorous looking-glass', *Richard III*, I i 15.—'Fettered with amorous chains', *Titus Andronicus*, II i 15.—'Versing love To amorous Phyllida', *M.N. Dream*, II i 67–68.—*Much Ado*, I i 308, ibid., II i 149, 'My brother is amorous on Hero'.—*T. & C.*, III iii 233–234, 'The weak wanton Cupid Shall from your neck unloose his amorous fold'.— And elsewhere.

L. *amorosus*, in the same sense (*amor*, love).

amorous rites. The rites—the actions and words—of Eros or sexual love. 'Juliet. Spread thy close curtain, love-performing night, That runaway's eyes may wink, and Romeo Leap to these arms untalkt-of and unseen. Lovers can see to do their amorous rites By their own beauties', *R. & J.*, III ii 5–9.

Cf. **bed-rite, rite of love, marriage-rite.**

amorous view. Amorous intentions. Of Diomed, Ulysses says that he 'gives all gaze and bent of amorous view On the fair Cressid', *T. & C.*, IV v 128–283. Cf. *with a view to doing something.*

amorous works. See **work,** n.

amorously impleacht (= interwoven). 'These talents of their hair, With twisted metal amorously impleacht', *A Lover's Complaint*, vv. 204–205: symbolizing 'a penis encircled with pudend-hair'.

angling, in the quotation at **diver,** may = love-making; cf. **groping for trouts** and **hook.**

another thing. See **thing, another.**

appetite. Lust; lascivious desire. 'Bestial appetite in change of lust', *Richard III*, III v 80.—*Merry Wives*, I iii 62–64. 'She did so course o'er my exteriors with such a greedy intention, that the appetite of her eye did seem to scorch me up like a burning-glass!'—*Twelfth Night*, II iv 98.—*Hamlet*, I ii 142–144, 'She would hang on him, As if increase of appetite had grown by what it fed on'.—'Raging appetites', *T. & C.*, II ii 181.—See **sensual.**—See *Venus* quotation at **toy,** v.—And elsewhere.

Via Fr. ex L. *appetitus*: from *appetere*, 'to seek after', hence 'to desire eagerly'.

apron mountant. Phrynia and Timandra, 'Give us some gold, good Timon: has thou more?—*Timon*. Enough to make a whore forswear her trade, And to make whores, a bawd. Hold up, you sluts, Your aprons mountant', IV iii 132–135. The literal sense of the phrase is 'rising aprons': they rise—are raised—so readily that they might almost have a will of their own, when their wearers go about their business. Cf. **mount** and **climb.**

apt. Apt for love; nubile and love-desirous. 'Timon. Does she love him?—*Old Athenian*. She is young and apt: Our own precedent passions do instruct us What levity's in youth', I i 135–138.

L. *aptus*, fitted, suited; hence, fit or suitable.

ardour. The ardent passion of love; flaming lust. 'When the compulsive ardour gives the charge', *Hamlet*, III iv 87.—'The white-cold virgin snow upon my heart Abates the ardour of my liver', *The Tempest*, IV i 55–56.

Cf. **fire** and **heat.** Ex L. *ardere*, 'to burn' (via the n., *ardor*, and its Old Fr. derivative).

Aries, the Ram: allusively in *Titus Andronicus*, IV iii; cf. **ram.**

arms, in *Pericles*, II iii 97–98, contains an amorous pun: 'Loud music is too harsh for ladies' heads, Since they love men in arms as well as beds'.

arse. See:—

ass; riding on his ass. L.L.L., v ii 619–622 (in reference to a man playing the part of Judas), '*Boyet*. Therefore, as he is an ass let him go. And so, adieu, sweet Jude! nay, why dost thou stay?—*Dumaine*. For the latter end of his name.—*Berowne*. For the ass to the Jude; give it him:—Jud-as, away'.—*The Taming*, ii i 199.—*Hamlet*, ii ii 399 (see **buz**).—*Lear*, i iv 162–165, 'When thou . . . gavest away both parts, thou borest thine ass on thy back o'er the dirt' (excrement-vent); cf. vv 229–230.—*Cymbeline*, i 88 33.

Arse is a common-Teutonic word, cognate with Gr. *orrhos* (C.O.D.); *ass*, pronounced *ahss*.

assail. To attack, to aim at, the love or the virtue-yielding of a woman. 'She will not stay the siege of loving terms, Nor bide th' encounter of assailing eyes', *R. & J.*, i i 210–211.—See quotation at **accost**.— *All's Well*, i i 15.—'Beauteous thou art, therefore to be assailed', *Sonnets*, 41, v. 6.

Through Old Fr., ex L. *adsalire*, 'to leap at' (in attack).

assault. The onslaught of passion upon character, especially upon chastity and self-restraint. 'A savageness in unreclaimed blood, Of general assault', *Hamlet*, ii i 34–35, where a secondary sense appears: 'general tendency to assail the sexual contingency of a person (usually a woman)': cf. **assail,** q.v.— *Measure*, iii i 183.—See quotation at **unseduced**.—*Cymbeline*, iii ii 8.—*Lucrece*, v. 835.

The n. corresponding to **assail,** q.v.

assay. To try, attempt, in the way of love, especially in love-making. *Venus*, vv. 607–617, 'But all in vain; good Queen, it will not be: She hath assay'd as much as may be proved; Her pleading hath deserved a greater fee; She's Love, she loves, and yet she is not loved'.

Cf. **try** and **attempt**.—Ex L. *exagium*, 'a weighing'.

attempt; attemptable. To seek amorously to obtain; sexually approachable. 'This man of thine Attempts her love', *Timon*, i i 129–130.—*Cymbeline*, i iv 57–61. 'This gentleman . . .

vouching . . . his mistress to be . . . less attemptable, than any the rarest of our ladies in France'.

Attempt = to try (or, test vigorously); to handle.—L. *tem(p)tare*; cf. **tempt** and **try**.

aunt. A whore; a wanton; a paramour 'not of lofty origin, nor of good social standing'. 'The lark, that tirra-lirra chants, With hey! with hey! the thrust and the jay, Are summer songs for me and my aunts, While we lie tumbling in the hay', Autolycus in *The W. Tale*, IV ii 9–12.

A euphemism: an *aunt*, like a *cousin*, is a very convenient relation.

a-weary. Wearied by love-making. 'Cressida. Art thou a-weary of me?—*Troilus*. O Cressida! but that the busy day . . . hath roused the ribald crows, And dreaming night will hide our joys no longer, I would not from thee', IV i 7–11.

bachelor (and his children). 'Thou art a widow, and thou hast some children; And, by God's mother, I, being but a bachelor, Have other some', King Edward to Lady Grey, 3 *Henry VI*, III ii 102–104.

Cf. the first quotation at **beget**.

back, have a hot. To be lecherous or amorous. *Merry Wives*, V v 12–13, 'When gods have hot backs, what shall poor men do?'—Falstaff, amour-bent in reference to Jove, love-questing in the form of a bull.

See **hot** and cf. the implication of the low American 'That dame sure has hot pants'.

bad woman. A bawd. See the quotation at **hot-house**.

Cf. **naughty house**.

bag and baggage. See **let in**.

baldrick. See **hang one's bugle** . . .

balls. See **bawl**.

balm. See **salve**.

banish (a person) **one's bed.** To sever intimacy. 'I banish her my bed and company', 2 *Henry VI*, II i (near end).—1 *Henry IV*, II iii 43.—*Henry VIII*, III i 119.

bankrout beggar. (Cf. **bereave,** q.v.) 'Bankrupt beggar' in *Lucrece*, vv. 710–711 (Tarquin having sated himself upon Lucrece): 'Feeble Desire all recreant, poor, and meek, Like to a bankrout beggar wails his case', connotes that, in the rape, Tarquin lost more than honour, there being a considerable expenditure of semen: cf. vv. 692–693, 'Pure Chastity is rifled of her store, And Lust, the thief, far poorer than before' (with 'poor', 'poorer', cf. **lean**)—v. 730, 'A captive victor that hath lost in gain'—and vv. 734–735, 'She bears the load of lust he left behind, And he the burthen of a guilty mind'.

barren, in quotation at **ram,** v., = deprived of a man's love-making.

bashful. Sexually shy. 'Make bold her bashful years with your experience', *Richard III*, IV iv 227.

Basimecu. 'Monsieur Basimecu, the dauphin of France', 2 *Henry VI*, IV vii. In reference to the Dauphin's fawning manners, *Basimecu* constitutes a pun on *baise mon cul*, 'kiss my backside!' Cf. the low English catchphrase, '(Oh,) kiss my arse!', an impatiently jocular insult.

A modern reminiscent revival is *Bozzimacoo* in Oliver Onions's *Good Boy Seldom*, 1911.

bastard occurs, e.g., at 1 *Henry VI*, V iv 70, 'We'll have no bastards live, Especially since Charles must father it'; *Richard III*, V iii 334, 'these bastard Bretons'.—Also as adj. in *Com. of Errors*, III ii 19.—*Hamlet*, IV v 115.—'*Thersites*, I am a bastard too; I love bastards: I am a bastard begot, bastard instructed, bastard in mind, bastard in valour, in every thing illegitimate', *T. & C.*, V vii 16–18.—And elsewhere.

Semantically, *bastard* resembles *bantling* (bench-begotten), for *bastard* is composed of *bast* (used as a bed) + pejorative suffix *-ard*.

bastardizing. Illicit begetting. 'Fut, I should have been that I am, had the maidenliest star in the firmament twinkled on my bastardizing', *Lear*, I ii 135–137.

bastardy. Illegitimacy of birth. 'Born in bastardy', *2 Henry VI*, III ii 222.—*Richard III*, III v 74 and vii, 4 and 9.—*King John*, I i 74, 'Once he slander'd me with bastardy'.—*Lear*, I ii 10.—'Thy issue blurr'd with nameless bastardy', *Lucrece*, v. 522.

bathe in water, to. 'Never did passenger'—i.e., a traveller—'in summer's heat More thirst for drink than she for this good turn' (reciprocation of her passion). 'Her help she sees' (his genitals, uncovered by her), but help she cannot get' (he being 'frosty in desire'); 'She bathes in water, yet her fire must burn' (*Venus*, vv. 91–94): ostensibly, she is sweating freely; erotically, she experiences an orgasm—or, at the least, a flowing of the preliminary sexual secretions.

bauble. Penis. 'This drivelling love is like a great natural, that runs lolling up and down to hide his bauble in a hole' (see **hole**), R. & J., II iii 93–95.—See quotation at **service.**

M.E. *babel*, ex Old Fr. *baubel*, 'a toy, a plaything': cf. **play,** n., and **toy,** n.

bawcock. 'My bawcock', as address, = Cockney 'Old Cock'. *Twelfth Night*, III iv 113.

Fr. *beau coq*; with sexual overtone.

bawd. A procuress; occasionally, a pimp. R. & J., II iii 133 (former sense).—*Henry V*, III vi 62–63, 'Gower. Why, this [Pistol] is an arrant counterfeit rascal; I remember him now; a bawd, a cut-purse'.—Touchstone to a shepherd, 'To be bawd to a bell-weather', *As You Like It*, III ii 80–81.—'Breathing like sanctified and pious bawds, The better to beguile', *Hamlet*, I iii 130–131, and elsewhere.—T. & C. (see at **trader**).—In *Measure*: often.—*Lear*, II ii 20.—And elsewhere—e.g. *Sonnets*.

M.E. *baude*, 'a procurer or a pandar', directly ex Old French *baude*, which is probably cognate with **bold.**

bawd-born. (Cf. **Abhorson.**) 'Bawd is he doubtless, and of antiquity too; bawd-born', *Measure*, III ii 68–69.

bawdry. Unmarried cohabitation: *As You Like It*, III iii 91–92, 'Come, sweet Audrey; we must be married, or we must live on in bawdry'.

In *Hamlet*, II ii 508, however,—'A tale of bawdry',—it = bawdiness, as also in *The W. Tale*, IV iii 194.

bawd's house; bawdy-house. A brothel. 'Went to a bawdy-house not above once in a quarter—of an hour', 1 *Henry IV*, III iii 16–18 (and twice later in same act).—2 *Henry IV* (see **ruff**): *bawdy-house*.—*Henry V*, II i 33–37, 'We cannot lodge and board a dozen or fourteen gentlewomen that live honestly by the prick of their needles, but it will be thought we keep a bawdy-house straight', with a pun on *prick*.—*Measure*, II i 75 (see **naughty house**): *bawd's house*.—'I am for no more bawdy-houses', *Pericles*, IV iv 6.

Cf. **bawd** and **bawdy**.

bawdy. Immodest, indelicate, licentious; especially in sexual matters. R. & J.: see quotation at **prick**.—'A bawdy song', *Henry IV*, III iii 13.—'Bawdy villain', *Hamlet*, II ii 590.—Concerning Helen, 'In her bawdy veins', *T. & C.*, IV i 70.—'Bawdy talk', *Measure*, IV iii 178.—Elsewhere.

Suitable to, or characteristic of, a procuress or a pimp (see **bawd**).

bawdy-house. See **bawd's house.**

bawl, those that. Testicles; with a pun on *ball* (a testicle).

'It is a low ebb of linen with thee . . . the rest of thy low-countries have made a shift to eat up thy holland: and God knows whether those that bawl out of the ruins of thy linen shall inherit his kingdom', 2 *Henry IV*, II ii 20–26, where there is also a subtle, and a surprisingly early, literary reference to L. *testiculi*, 'testicles'—literally, 'little witnesses' to a man's virility.

(Treated more fully in the Essay, section 4.)

be out. Not to be engaged in sexual intercourse.

'*Orlando.* Who could be out, being before his beloved

mistress?—*Rosalind*. Marry, that should you, if I were your mistress; or I should think my honesty ranker than my wit', *As You Like It*, IV i 79–82.

beagle. 'The smallest English hound, used for hare hunting when field follows on foot' (*C.O.D.*). Aguecheek, concerning Maria, 'She's a good wench'; Sir Tony replied, 'She's a beagle, true-bred, and one that adores me': *Twelfth Night*, II iii 175–176.—*Timon*, IV iii 174–175, to Alcibiades, 'Get thee away, and take thy beagles with thee'. In the former quotation, probably it = a girl, a woman; in the latter, it = a whore (cf. **bitch**).

bear, v. To bear children; to bear, support, a superincumbent man. Both senses are implied in *The Taming*, II i 199–202, '*Petruchio*. . . . Come sit on me.—*Katharina*. Asses are made to bear, and so are you.—*Petruchio*. Women are made to bear, and so are you.—*Katharina*. No such jade as you, if me you mean.—*Petruchio*.—Alas, good Kate! I will not burthen thee!'—2 *Henry IV*, II iv 59.—*Henry V*, III vii 46–48.—*A. & C.*, III vii 8–9.—*Henry VIII*, II iii 99.

With the latter sense, cf. **burden, carriage, load.**

beard. In *Twelfth Night*, III i 46–54, Viola and the Clown pun, rather obscurely yet with obvious bawdiness, upon *beard* in its ordinary sense and upon *beard* as 'hair growing upon the *mons Veneris*', or, rather, 'pubic hair', especially in the words 'being kept together and put to use'.

beast. A god or a man, the former behaving like a sex-driven animal, the latter behaving with the sexual appetite of an animal: *Merry Wives*, V v 1–16 *passim*; and see **make the beast . . .**

2, A cuckold. Synonym: **monster.** See first quotation at **horned.**

beast with two backs. See **make the beast . . .**

beastly. Sexually beast-like; obscene. 'No grace? no womanhood? Ah, beastly creature! The blot and enemy to our general name!': thus Lavinia, about to be raped, to Tamora, inexorable mother of the ravishers (*Titus Andronicus*, II iii 182–183).— *Merry Wives*, V v 10.—*Measure*, II i 219.—And elsewhere.

beat love down, to. See **prick,** v.

bed, n. In Shakespeare, a bed evokes the vision of a bridal bed, or a bed of love-making. 'Widow to a woeful bed', *Richard III*, I ii 248; cf. IV iv 208, 'Slander myself as false to Edward's bed'.— *Ibid.*, IV iv 235, 'And lead thy daughter to a conqueror's bed' (Nietzsche: war is man's work, woman his relaxation).—'To her bed no homage do I owe', *Com. of Errors*, III ii 43.—*M.N. Dream*, II i 73.—See **fortunate bed.**—*As You Like It*, VI vi 92.— See **incestuous.**—It occurs elsewhere.

bed, v. To put (a woman) to bed as a bride or as a partner in sexual pleasure. 'Woo her, wed her, and bed her', *The Taming*, I i 144.—*All's Well*, II iii 272–273, 'Although before the solemn priest I have sworn, I will not bed her' (consummate the marriage); cf. III ii 22.

Cf. the modern literary phrase, *to wed and bed* (a woman).

bed-fellow; bed-mate. Especially in sexual intimacy. 'Happier the man whom favourable stars Allot thee for his lovely bed-fellow', *The Taming*, IV v 39–40.—*The M. of V.*, V i 233, 'Portia. I'll have that doctor for my bedfellow'.—*Bed-mate* in quotation at **lie long.**—*bed-fellow* in that at **play-fellow.**

With *bed-mate* cf. **copesmate.**

bed-presser. A fornicator; a whoremonger or womanizer. 'This bed-presser', Prince Henry of Falstaff in 1 *Henry IV*, II iv 246.

Cf. *carpet knight* and the Army-slang *poodle-faker.*

bed-rite. An action usual in such sexual intercourse as is regarded as something more than 'fun' or lust. (*Nuptial rites,* earliest occasions of sexual intercourse in marriage; *conjugal rites,* any sexual intercourse between man and wife.) 'No bed-rite shall be paid Till Hymen's torch be lighted', *The Tempest*, IV i 96–97.

Cf. **marriage-rite** and **love, rite of** and **amorous rites.**

bed-swerver. 'She's A bed-swerver, even as bad as those That vulgars give bold'st titles', Leontes concerning Hermione: *The W. Tale*, II i 91–93.

One who swerves from her duty to remain faithful to the marriage-bed or to her affianced.

Cf. Old Frisian *swerva*, 'to creep'.

beef. Women that, being prostitutes, serve as the flesh-food (see **flesh**) for the **satisfaction** of the **appetite** of **brothel**-frequenters. Pompey, referring to Mistress Overdone, a bawd, 'She hath eaten up all her beef, and she herself is in the tub', *Measure*, III ii 57–58.

Beef not *flesh*, because they have been prepared for consumption.

beg a child of. To seek sexual intercourse with (a woman). 'I think he means to beg a child of her', *3 Henry VI*, III ii 27.

beget. Usually of the father: to engender or procreate a child. 'I did beget her, all the parish knows: Her mother liveth yet, can testify She was the first fruit of my bachelorship', *1 Henry VI*, v iv 11–13.—'I will beget Mine issue of your blood upon your daughter', *Richard III*, IV iv 298–299.—*Two Gentlemen*, III i 290.—*King John*, I i 75.—*All's Well*, III ii 58.—*Measure*, v i 510, 'Whom he begot with child' = got with child: another nuance.—And elsewhere.

An intensive of **get,** q.v.

begetting, n. 'The . . . blood of your begetting', *Cymbeline*, v v 329–330. Cf. **getting**.

begin. To beget. 'If you could find out such a country where but women were that had received so much shame, you might begin an impudent nation', *All's Well*, IV iii 323–325.

Cf. **procreate.**

behind-door work. Casual coition, especially among servants. See the quotation at **stair-work** and cf. **work,** n., and **work of generation.**

Contrast **hold-door trade.**

belch, v. To eructate (Sir Toby Belch); to expel with an eructation. In *Othello*, III iv 115 (see quotation at **stomach**), it = to reject in sexual satiety, with appetite sated.

Perhaps cognate with *to bellow*.

Belgia. The belly; especially in its lower portion, the pelvic basin. '*Dromio of S.* She is spherical, like a globe; I could find out countries in her. . . . *Antipholus of S.* Where stood Belgia . . .? *Dromio of S.* O, sir, I did not look so low': *The Comedy of Errors*, III ii 112–131.

The semantics are partly explained by the entire passage (see the essay, near end of section 1) and partly by the obvious repetition of the sound *bell* in '*belly: Belgia*'.

belie. To lie by—at the side of; hence, to 'sleep with' (a woman). '*Othello.* Lie with her! lie on her!—We say lie on her, when they belie her.—Lie with her!': IV i 35–36.

belly. 1, Womb. See quotation at **quick.**

2, The female pelvic region, with especial reference to the genitals. See at **let in.**—'She sinketh down, still hanging by his neck, He on her belly falls, she on her back', *Venus*, vv. 593–594.

Belly is a doublet of *bellows*: they come from Old Teutonic *belgan*, 'to swell'.

3, Pudend: see **put a man in one's belly** and the quotation at **defend . . .**

bereave of the deeds. In 'Words pay no debts, give her deeds: but she'll bereave you o' th' deeds too, if she call your activity in question', T. & C., III ii 56–58, the deeds are **hot deeds,** and **bereave . . .** signifies 'deprive you of the power to commit further such deeds'—for the time being; see **activity.**

Cf. the quotations at **bankrout beggar.**

bestial, esp. of sexual passion. See first quotation at **appetite.**

Cf. **beastly,** of which it is the learned doublet.

besiege. To lay seduction-siege to a woman (or her maidenhead or virtue). *A Lover's Complaint*, vv. 176–177, 'Long upon these terms I held my city, Till thus he gan besiege me'.

Cf. **undermine, siege,** and **sit down before.**

betray. To seduce (a girl, a woman). L.L.L., III, i 23–24, 'These betray nice wenches,—that would be betrayed without these'.—See quotation at *pervert*, of which it is the almost exact etymological synonym: *be* = to the side; *tray*, via Old Fr., = L. *trahere*, 'to draw', although most authorities postulate its origin in *tradere*, 'to hand over'.

between a pair of sheets; between the sheet(s). In reference to bed-sheets and to the love-making that takes place between a pair of sheets. '*Falstaff*. I will toss the rogue in a blanket.—*Doll Tearsheet*. Do, an thou darest for thy heart: an thou dost, I'll canvass thee between a pair of sheets', 2 *Henry IV*, II iv 220–222.—*Much Ado*, II iii 140–141 ('between the sheet').

See **sheet.**

bewhore. To call a person **whore**. *Othello*, IV iii 115, Emilia, in reference to Desdemona, 'My lord hath so bewhored her, Thrown such despite and heavy terms upon her, As true hearts cannot bear'.

Cf. **strumpet,** v.

big; bigger. 'Nay, bigger; women grow by men': grow big with child: R. & J., I iii 97.—'Big-bellied', M.N. *Dream*, II i 129.— *Cymbeline*, I i 39.

Cf. **great.**

billiards, in *A. & C.*, II v 3–9, contains an amorous pun on the balls (innuendo'd to = testicles).

billing. (Cf. 'How she holds up the neb, the bill to him!', *The W. Tale*, I ii 183.) Kissing; cf. *billing and cooing* (like a pair of love-birds).

bird's nest. Pudend and pubic hair. R. & J., II iv 73–75, 'Nurse. I must another way, To fetch a ladder, By the which your love Must climb a bird's nest soon when it is dark'.

bitch. Opprobrious term for a woman; it connotes wantonness and a general lack of shame and decency (from a rutting bitch's attitude towards all sex-sniffing dogs). *Lear*, II ii 22,

Kent calls Oswald 'the son and heir of a mongrel bitch'.—
'*Painter.* Y'are a dog.—*Apemantus.* Thy mother's of my gener-
ation: what's she, if I be a dog?', Timon, I i 202–204.

Cf. *you son of a bitch!* (Etymologically, *bitch* is cognate with the
Old Norse equivalent; of obscure antecedents.)

blackness. '*Desdemona.* How if she be black and witty?—*Iago* . . .
She'll find a white that shall her blackness hit', Othello, II i 132–
134. See **hit;** there is the further pun: that the semen-bullet
shall hit her pudend. Shakespeare often employs the metaphor
of penis-pudend archery or fencing—not seldom in a brutally
frank and pertinent manner.

blain. '(Let our youth) drown themselves in riot! itches, blains,
Sow all the Athenian bosoms; and their crop to general
leprosy!', Timon, IV i 28–30.

A *blain* is a pustule—an inflamed sore on the skin: here,
obviously, blains caused by venereal disease. It comes from an
Aryan stem with basic sense of 'swell(ing)'.

blameful bed. In reference to adultery. 2 Henry VI, III ii 211.
(Contrast **fortunate bed.**)

blasted. Antony to Cleopatra (III xiii 105), 'You were half blasted
ere I knew you'—with connotation of causal knowledge (see
know): that is, she had half become a wanton before *he*
bedded with her.

Cf. the C. 18 slang *blasted brimstone*, 'a confirmed whore'; and
burn, sense 1.

Blast, v., ex the n., which = a sudden and violent movement
of wind; here, *blasted* probably refers to the blast of a furnace.

bliss. Extreme delight in sexual pleasure. Sonnets, 129, v. 12, (Of
lustful copulation) 'A bliss in proof, and proved, a very woe'
(in the experience, joyous; the experience over, its mere
memory is a woe).

Of common-Teutonic stock, it is probably cognate with
Gothic *milith*, 'honey' (therefore cf. **honey**), as Wyld has
pointed out, in support of another's proposed etymology.

blood. Hot blood; the blood as affected by sexual passion. 'The blood of youth burns not with such excess As gravity's revolt to wantonness', *L.L.L.*, v ii 28–29.—'Had she affections and warm youthful blood, She'ld be as swift in motion as a ball', *R. & J.*, II iv 12–13.—'When the blood burns, how prodigal the soul Lends the tongue vows: these blazes, daughter, . . . You must not take for fire', *Hamlet*, I iii 116–120; *ibid.*, III iv 72.—Elsewhere.

Connected with 'humours' (cf. *choler*) and heredity (cf. *blue blood*).

blow. Sexual stroke or thrust: see quotation at **swell.** Semantically cf. **hit** and **strike.**

blow up; blower-up. To explode, and thus inject semen into; one who does this. *All's Well*, I i 118–121, 'Parolles. Man, sitting down before you [= woman regarded as a place besieged], will undermine you, and blow you up.—Cf. I i. 124–126) 'In blowing him down again, with the breach yourselves made, you lose your city'.

Part of Shakespeare's warfare-imagery; cf. **fort** and **siege.**

board, v. To accost as a preliminary to wooing or to love-making; (Of a man) to coït with. *Much Ado*, II i 134–135, 'Beatrice. I am sure he is in the fleet: I would he had boarded me'.—*Merry Wives*, II i 88 and 90.—See quotation at **accost.**—'Certain it is I liked her, And boarded her i' the wanton way of youth', *All's Well*, v iii 209–210.

Lit., to go aboard (a ship): therefore, cf.:

board a land carack. To coït with (a woman): *Othello*, I ii 51.

See preceding entry and **carrack.**

boarding. The vbl. n. of **board,** q.v. 'Mistress Page. He would never have boarded me in this fury.—*Mistress Ford.* Boarding, call you it? It'll be sure to keep him above deck.—*Mistress Page.* So will I: if he come under my hatches, I'll never to sea again', *Merry Wives*, II i 88–93.

boat hath a leak, her. To Edgar's 'Come o'er the bourne, Bessy, to me', the Fool adds, 'Her boat hath a leak And she must not speak Why she dares not come over to thee' (*Lear*, III vi 25–28). Perhaps, 'she is having her period', but probably 'she is suffering from gonorrhoea'. (Cf. **leaky**.)

The *boat* may be the female body (cf. **carrack**), a rich prize that a man is ready to **board;** or it may, by a shape-allusion, be the female pudend.

body. In *Romeo and Juliet*, II iv 40–42, 'Though his face be better than any man's, yet his leg excels all men's; and for a hand, and a foot, and a body, though they be not to be talkt on, yet they are past compare'—words spoken by the bawdy Nurse—it perhaps signifies 'penis', as a notable scholar has suggested, or 'genitals', as I prefer.

boggler. Lit., 'a fumbler'; hence, a fornicatress, or perhaps a strumpet, in Antony's 'You have been a boggler ever', addressed to Cleopatra (III xiii 110): cf. the quotations at **blasted** and **leave a pillow unprest.**

Ex *boggle* in its transferred senses, 'to equivocate, to fumble': this verb comes *ex bogle*, 'a phantom or goblin'.

bogs. 'In what part of her body stands Ireland?—Marry, sir, in the buttocks: I found it out by the bogs', *Com. of Errors*, III ii 114–116; *by* is used in the two senses, 'by the side of; near' and 'by means of; because of': Ireland is famous for the wetness of its climate (see **Ireland**) and the partly resultant frequency of its bogs. But *the bogs* may, already in Shakespeare's day, have been a slang synonym of a latrine.—*Henry V*, III vii 57–58, where the innuendo is to the anus.

bold; boldness. Lacking or lack of, or free(dom) from, the restraints of female modesty. 'How she holds up the neb, the bill to him! And arms her with the boldness of a wife To her allowing husband!', *The W. Tale*, I ii 183–184.—'Youth is hot and bold', *The Passionate Pilgrim*, 12, v. 7. Cf. **saucy.**

bolster more than their own. To coït illicitly. Iago to Othello,

'Damn them, then, if ever mortal eyes do see them bolster
More than their own', III iii 398–400.

The verb *bolster* appositely applies only to the man: cf. the
synonym (and semantic parallel), '**to stuff**'. Etymologically, a
bolster probably = 'the puffy, swelled, thing' (Wyld).

bona roba. A well, though flashily, dressed prostitute or uneasy-
virtued girl (or woman). 'We knew where the bona-robas were,
and had the best of them all at commandment', *2 Henry IV*, III ii
24–26.—*Ibid.*, v. 202, a bona-roba is made to bear the happy
name of Jane Nightwork (cf. the *Othello* quotation at **work,** v.).

Literally, 'fine dress' (Italian *buona roba*).

bond of chastity. A woman's vow of conjugal fidelity. 'He could
not But think her bond of chastity quite crackt', *Cymbeline*, v v
206–207.

Cf. **chaste treasure** and **virgin patent.**

bone-ache. See **Neapolitan . . .**

bosom, n. 1, The area of the breasts; 2, The female lap, as in 'So I
might live one hour in your sweet bosom', *Richard III*, I ii 124
(Gloster to Lady Anne).—'Poor wounded name! my bosom,
as a bed, shall lodge thee, till thy wound be thoroughly
heal'd', *Two Gentlemen*, I ii 114–115.—'The milk-white bosom
of thy love', *ibid.*, III i 250.—'Her excellent white bosom',
Hamlet, II ii 112.—*Lear*, IV v 26.—*A. & C.*, II iii 2.—And
elsewhere.

3, The sexual parts of man and woman: see the quotation at
blain.

An O.E. word, of common-Teutonic origin; perhaps cognate with O.E. *bog*, 'shoulder; arm'—hence breast (covered
with folded arms).

bosom, v. To be bosom to bosom, to be lap-joined (see the n.,
second sense). 'I am doubtful [= I suspect] that you have been
conjunct And bosom'd with her, as far as we call hers', *Lear*, v i
12–13: cf. the catch-phrase, *married like the monkeys—only about the
middle.*

bottom-grass. In 'I'll be a park, and thou wilt be my deer; Feed where thou wilt. . . . Within this limit is relief enough, Sweet bottom-grass, and high delightful plain' (Venus to Adonis, vv. 231–236), there is obviously a *double entente*, for 'bottom-grass' = *bottom growth*, 'thick, short grass in meadows, below the longer and comparatively sparse growth' (Wyld), also (*bottom* = the human posterior) 'the hair growing in and about the crutch'; cf. **brakes,** q.v., which connotes a rougher growth than that of 'sweet bottom-grass'; and **beard.**

bout. A bout, **turn,** occasion of physical love. 'Damsel, I'll have a bout with you again', Talbot in 1 *Henry VI*, III ii 56.

Lit., 'a spell of activity of any kind'; perhaps, as Wyld remarks, it = obsolete *bought* (cf. geographical *bight*), 'a bend': to bend one's back in hard work: to '*get down to it*' (see **downright . . .**).

bowl. See the quotation at **rubbing:** the game of bowls is played with balls (cf. entry at **bawl**). Perhaps relevant is 'If it be not too rough for some [*girls, mind you, not men*] that know little but bowling' (*The W. Tale*, IV iii 332–333).

box unseen, a. A pudend—see quotation at **kicky-wicky.** Cf. **chaste treasure** and **secret parts.**

brach. Bitch-hound; hence, a term of abuse, as in Ben Jonson, 1610, and esp. 'a pathic', as in *Troilus & Cressida*, II i 126–127, 'I will hold my peace when Achilles' brach bids me, will I?'

brakes, 'thickets; clumps of brushwood', is, in *Venus*, v. 237, allusive to the pubic and vulval hair; cf. **bottom-grass** and **tree.**

brat occurs several times in the sense 'an illegitimate child'; e.g., *Com. of Errors*, IV iv 37.

breach, n. In 2 *Henry IV*, II iv 51 (see quotation at **charged chambers**), the *breach* (cf. **hole** and **wound**) is the pudend; so too in *All's Well*, I i 125, and in *Lucrece*, v. 469.

Cf. **gate** and **wound** and:—

break, v.t. To devirginate; to **defile** or **violate** sexually. 'The broken bosoms'—see **bosom** in its second nuance of 'lap'— 'that to me belong Have emptied all their fountains in my well' (of lust): *A Lover's Complaint*, vv. 254–255.

Etymologically parallel is to **corrupt.**

break the pale. To stray amorously from the marriage-fold. 'Too unruly deer, he breaks the pale, And feeds from home; poor I am but his stale', *Com. of Errors*, ii i 100–101.

Lit., to break through the pale or fence of the deer-park.

break wind. To relieve flatulence the anus way. 'A man may break a word with you, sir; and words are but wind; Ay, and break it in your face, so he break it not behind', *Com. of Errors*, iii i 75–76.

breast. 1, The female bosom as a whole; hence, also bosom and lap (see quotation at **throbbing breast**). 2, either of what the dictionaries term 'the milk-secreting organs', as in 'Come to my woman's breasts, And take my milk for gall, you murd'ring ministers', Lady Macbeth: i v 48–49.—'The breasts of Hecuba, When she did suckle Hector, lookt not lovelier Than Hector's forehead when it spit forth blood', *Coriolanus*, i iii 43–45.—See quotation at **pick the lock.**—See **world.**— 'Her bare breast, heart of all her land; Whose ranks of blue veins, as his hand did scale, Left their round turrets destitute and pale', *Lucrece*, vv. 439–441.—*Sonnets*, 130, v. 3.

Etymologically, *breast* may come ex a Sanskrit word meaning 'spike' and therefore it may = 'the pointed, projecting, swelling part of the body' (Wyld).

breed, v. 1, To give birth to. 'Yet every mother breeds not sons alike', *Titus Andronicus*, ii iii 146.—Several times in *Troilus and Cressida*. And elsewhere (e.g., *Sonnets*, 12 vv. 13–14).

2, To beget children (by: upon) a woman. 'No more . . . I would wish This youth should say, 'twere well, and only therefore Desire to breed by me', *The W. Tale*, iv iii 101–103.— *Venus*, v. 172.

Breed is of common-Teutonic stock (from a n. signifying 'warmth') and is cognate with *brood*.

breeder. A female creature, especially a woman capable of child-bearing. 'You love the breeder better than [you love] the male', 3 *Henry VI*, II i 42.—'Get thee to a nunnery: why wouldn't thou be a breeder of sinners?', *Hamlet*, III i 121–122.—(Of a mare) 'The fair breeder', *Venus*, v. 282.

See **breed.**

breeding, adj. and n. 'His breeding, sir, hath been at my charge: I have so often blusht to acknowledge him, that now I am brazed to it', *Lear*, I i 9–11.—'O blessed breeding sun', *Timon*, IV iii 1.—'A breeding jennet', a small Spanish horse (here, a mare)—'lusty, young and proud' (*Venus*, v. 260).

See **breed.**

bride usually summons to Shakespeare's mind the idea of the bridal bed and 'honeymoon' bliss, as in 'Henry, surfeiting in joys of love, with his new bride', 2 *Henry VI*, I i 251–252. *Bride-bed* occurs in *M.N. Dream*, v i 391.—And elsewhere.

bridegroom. (Cf. preceding entry.) 'Those dulcet sounds in break of day That creep into the dreaming bridegroom's ear, And summon him to marriage', *The M. of V.*, III ii 51–53.— 'With a bridegroom's fresh alacrity', *T. & C.*, IV iv 146.—See *Lear* quotation at **die.**— *A. & C.*, IV xiv 100–101.

bridle, v. To 'put a bridle on one's mistress' is obviously synonymous with 'to prepare her for a **bout** and then to **ride** her': *Henry V*, III vii 52. There may even be a pun on 'to put the bridal-bit in her mouth': *penem in vaginam inmittere*.

broach. To broach a woman—as one broaches a cask; sexually it constitutes a pun on *broach* in the specific nuance, 'to open and then begin to use'. Enobarbus to Antony, 'The business you have broached here cannot be without you; especially that of Cleopatra's, which depends wholly upon your abode.— *Antony.* No more light answers' (I ii 176–179), where *wholly* should be compared with **holy** (q.v.) and *abode* connotes sexual immanence.

broad awake. 'Somewhat too early for new-married ladies.— *Bassianus.* Lavinia, how say you?—*Lavinia.* I say no; I have been broad awake two hours and more', *Titus Andronicus*, II ii 17.

Ostensibly synonymous with *wide-awake*, it is physiologically allusive to sexual intercourse.

broad goose, in *Romeo & Juliet*, II iii 89, seems to have a sexual connotation.

broke. To act as a broker; to barter for a woman. 'I have broke with her father, and, his good will obtained, name the day of marriage', *Much Ado*, II i 289–291.

broker. A go-between (in a love-affair); a flesh-broker, a procurer, a pimp. 'Now, by my modesty, a goodly broker!', *Two Gentlemen*, I ii (Julia to her maid, Lucetta, bringer of a love-letter).

Lit., 'a middleman'—from an Old Fr. word *brocour* (originally, 'a broacher of casks': *broacher* is a doublet of *broker*).

broker-between. An agent in love-affairs especially in furtive or illicit love-affairs; a pandar. See second quotation at **pandar,** n.

Cf. **broker,** q.v.

broker-lackey. One who, to the qualities of a flesh-**broker**, joins those of a lackey: *T. & C.*, v. x 33–34, Troilus to Pandarus: 'Hence, broker-lackey! ignomy and shame Pursue thy life, and live aye with thy name'.

brothel; brothel-house. An establishment that has prostitutes available on the premises. *Much Ado*, I i 234–238, '*Benedick.* Prove that ever I lose more blood with love than I will get again with drinking, . . . hang me up at the door of a brothel-house for the sign of blind Cupid'.—'Epicurism and lust Makes it more like a tavern or a brothel Than a graced palace', *Lear*, I iv 249–251; cf. IV iv 97.—'Maid, to thy master's bed,— Thy mistress is o' the brothel!', *Timon*, IV i 12–13.—*Pericles*, V Prologue, 1.

Brothel owes its present sense to a confusion of O.E. *brothen*, 'ruined (man)', and *bordel*, 'hut' (It. *bordello*); cognate with *board*.

brow; brows. In reference to cuckoldry horns (see **horn**) planted there. E.g. *L.L.L.*, IV i 117.—See quotations at **mort o' the deer** and **hardening.**

Cf. **forehead.**

brutish. Brutally carnal; crudely sensual: see quotation at **libertine:** cf. **beastly** and **bestial.**

buck. A cuckold (cf. **stag,** q.v.). 'Buck!—I would I could wash myself of the buck!—Buck, buck, buck! Ay, buck; I warrant you, buck; and of the season too, it shall appear', *Merry Wives*, III ii 148–150.

Cf **horned beef, q.v.** (*Buck* is the male of deer in general.)

buckler. See **swords and bucklers.**

bugle. See **hang one's bugle . . .**

bull. A man regarded as an habitual copulator: a bull serves the cows and heifers (see **heifer**). Allusively as 'the Bull' in *Titus Andronicus*, IV iii.—See **town bull.**

Etymologically, *bull* may = 'the impregnator' and be derived from, or cognate with, an Aryan word meaning 'to swell'.

bull Jove. Amorous Jove in the form of a bull—one of his many convenient transformations. 'From a god to a bull? a heavy descension! it was Jove's case', *2 Henry IV*, II ii 174–175.— *Much Ado*, V iv 44–51, 'We'll tip thy horns with gold, And all Europe shall rejoice at thee; as once Europe did at lusty Jove, When he would play the noble beast in love'.—'*Benedick* [*in reply to Claudio*]. Bull Jove, sir, had an amiable cow; And some such strange bull leapt your father's cow, And got a calf in that same noble feat Much like to you, for you have just his bleat', *Merry Wives*, V v 2–4.

bullets. '*Falstaff* [*to Pistol*]. Do you discharge upon mine hostess.—*Pistol*. I will discharge upon her, Sir John, with two bullets.—*Falstaff* She is pistol-proof, sir. . . . *Hostess.* Come, I'll drink no proofs nor no bullets.' Ostensible or primary allusion: *balls* is a synonym for bullets, but also for testicles; secondary or hidden allusion is to semen. The Hostess's complete speech would seem to glance at penilingism.

bull's pizzle. See **pizzle.**

bum. Posterior. 'Puck. The wisest aunt, telling the saddest tale, Sometimes for three-foot stool mistaketh me; Then slip I from her bum, down topples she', *M.N. Dream*, ii i 51–53.—'Your bum is the greatest thing about you', *Measure*, ii i 218–219.— *Timon*, i ii 240.

Echoic: that which *booms*. (Grose puns *arse* as *ars musica*.)

bung. When Doll Tearsheet cries, 'Away, you cut-purse rascal! you filthy bung, away!' (*2 King Henry IV*, ii iv 126–127), she is, I think, using *bung* in the sense 'bung-nipper' or cut-purse. Yet it is just possible that she is using it in the slang sense 'bung-hole' or anus, as Mr Eric P. Newman of St Louis, Missouri, maintains. For *bung* (and *bung-nipper*) in cant, see either the *O.E.D.* or my *Underworld*.

burden, n. and v. To weigh down, press upon, a woman in sexual intercourse; the weight of a man's body during intercourse. Several times in R. & J.: e.g., at ii iv 77.—*Henry VIII*, ii iii 43 (see **load**).

Cf. **bear** and **heavier** and **buried . . .**

2, Synonymous with **load** (n.), sense 2. 'Bearing the wanton burden of the prime', *Sonnets*, 97, v. 7.

buried with her face upwards. '[She] dies [of love] for him.— *Pedro.* She shall be buried with her face upwards', *Much Ado*, iii ii 63–64: concerning Beatrice, to be well-nigh smothered by love-superincumbent Benedick.

burn, v. 1, (Of a woman) to infect with venereal disease. Concerning 'light wenches': 'They appear to men as angels of light: light is an effect of fire, and fire will burn; *ergo*, light wenches will burn. Come not near her', *Com. of Errors*, iv iii

54–57. Lit., 'to cause to burn': the burning sensations of certain venereal diseases. The Aryan base means 'to bubble—also, to glow—with heat'.

2, To inflame (a person) with love; be love-inflamed: *Two Gentlemen*, II v 47–48 (former nuance); see at **blood** (latter nuance).—*M.N. Dream*, I i 173, 'That fire which burn'd the Carthage queen'.—See **achieve.**

burn out. To exhaust—to reduce to ashes in the flames of excessive physical love. 'She burnt out love, as soon as straw out burneth', *The Passionate Pilgrim*, v. 14 (cf. the quotation at **burn with love,** q.v.).

burn up is an intensive form of **burn,** v., sense 1: see quotation at **allure**.

burn with love. 'She burnt with love, as straw with fire flameth', *The Passionate Pilgrim*, 7, v. 13.

See **burn**, sense 2, and cf.:—

burning, adj. Ardent; aflame with love, or with lust. 'Burning youth', *Measure*, I iii 6.—'Phoebus' burning kisses', *Coriolanus*, II i 219. Cf:—

burning eye. Amorous eye; passionate glances. 'And Titan, tired in the mid-day heat, With burning eye did hotly overlook them; Wishing Adonis had his team to guide So he were like him, and by Venus' side', *Venus*, vv. 117–180.—*Lucrece*, v. 35, 'His drumming heart cheers up his burning eye'.

Perhaps cf. **O.**

burthen, v. For the sense, see **burden.** '*Petruchio*. Alas, good Kate! I will not burthen thee!', *The Taming*, II i 202.

business. Sexual intercourse; sexual intimacy. See quotation at **broach**. Cf. the euphemistic modern *to have (something) to do with a woman* and the Shakespearean **do naught with.**

Ex *busy.*

butt, n. The **buttocks** (see next entry). In T. & C., v i 26–28, '*Thersites.* Do I curse thee?—*Patroclus.* Why, no, you ruinous butt; you whoreson indistinguishable cur, no', there may possibly be an allusion to *butt*, 'a two-hogshead cask for ale or wine', though I think not. Here, *butt* is probably a Shakespearean adumbration of the modern-slang *shit* (an objectionable fellow).

Butt seems to have originally been applied to the thick end of a weapon or tool.

buttock; buttocks. 'In what part of her body stands Ireland?—Marry, sir, in the buttocks: I found it out by the bogs', *Com. of Errors*, III ii 114–116.—*All's Well*, II ii 15–19, 'Countess. Marry, that's a bountiful answer that fits all questions.—Clown. It is like a barber's chair, that fits all buttocks—the pin-buttock, the quatch-buttock, the brawn-buttock, or any buttock'.—The singular occurs in *Coriolanus*, II i 52 (with an erotic pun).—And elsewhere.

Butt, 'end', + *-ock*, diminutive suffix: 'little end' (cf. humorous **latter end**).

buz! or **buzz!** 'Should be! should—buzz!', Petruchio to Katharina, *The Taming*, II i 206.—'Polonius. The actors are come hither, my lord.—Hamlet. Buz, buz!—Polonius. Upon mine honour.—Hamlet. Then came each actor on his ass.' (Puns: 'honour' and 'ass', which is pronounced *arse*.)

This is the Elizabethan convention—Shakespeare's, anyway—for that 'rude noise' (an anal emission of wind) which, in theatrical slang, is known as a *raspberry*, as the late Crompton Rhodes pointed out to me in 1931.

calf. Leontes (jealous of Polixenes) says to his son, Mamillus, 'How now, you wanton [= playful] calf! Art thou my calf?', *The Winter's Tale*, I ii 126–127: i.e., 'Art thou offspring to me, the bull, from my wife?'

Cf. **cow**, q.v.

call to a reckoning. To summon (a woman) to a bout of love-making: *1 Henry IV*, I ii 52–53.

Ex an alehouse reckoning.

callet. A low prostitute. 'Base-born callet as she is', 2 *Henry VI*, I
iii 80.—'This shameless callet', 3 *Henry VI*, II ii 145.—'He
called her whore: a beggar in his drink Could not have laid
such terms upon his callet', *Othello*, IV ii 120–121.—*The W. Tale*,
II iii 90.

Origin obscure; the most probable cognate, if not origin, is
Erse and Gaelic *cail(l)e*, 'a girl'; 'a hussy'.

calm. '*Falstaff* How now, Mistress Doll!—*Hostess*. Sick of a calm;
yea, good faith.—*Falstaff* So is all her sect; an they be once in a
calm, they are sick.—*Hostess*. You muddy rascal, is that all the
comfort you give me?', 2 *Henry IV*, II iv 35–40.

Either menstruation or a disease-enforced abstinence from
prostitution.

canvass. To solicit; hence, to make much of (a person): see
quotation at **between a pair of sheets.**

capable. Sexually capable; nubile. See quotation at **put to** and cf.
capable.

capon, in 'You are cock and capon too' (*Cymbeline*, II i 23), the
imputation is that Cloten, though a cock (i.e., potent),
behaves like a capon (or castrated cock)—hence, timorously,
like a **eunuch**.

carack. See **carrack.**

cardinally; carnal strings; carnally. The first is a malapropism
for *carnally*: the second, the ties and tuggings of sexual desire.
'. . . My wife; who, if she had been a woman cardinally given,
might have been accused in fornication, adultery, and all
uncleanliness', *Measure*, II i 78–80.—*Ibid.*, v i 211–212,
'*Duke*. Know you this woman?—*Lucio*. Carnally, she says.'—
Othello, I iii 333–334, 'Our raging motions, our carnal stings
[= prickings of lust; letches], our unbitted lusts'.

Carnal, 'fleshly', hence 'sexual'.

carrack or **carack.** Shakespeare uses the latter spelling; and by
the word (literally, 'a large merchant ship') he intends us to
understand a woman that can be hailed and 'boarded' (see

board), as is clear in the phrase **board a land carack** and in the quotation at **Spain:** i.e. a whore or a wanton.

Cf. **boat . . .,** q.v.

carriage. See the quotation at **lie on one's back**, where *carriage* seems to bear two senses: the way in which women carry themselves, and their ability to *bear* men easily during sexual intercourse.

Cf. **burden** and **load.**

carrot. Penis—in the punning Latinism, *caret* (it is missing): see the passage quoted at **fuck.** In certain country districts, *beet-root* is used in the same sense: cf. **root.**

carry. To carry a woman by storm, as one would a fortress; to gain sexual mastery or possession of a woman. See second quotation at **siege.**—*A. & C.,* II vi 68–70.

'In the various meanings of the word in English, the senses of mooring and supporting the weight of something . . . appear always to lurk, whether in the literal or figurative uses', Wyld: cf. **carriage,** q.v.

case. Pudend. *Merry Wives,* VI i 49–54, 'Sir Hugh Evans. What is your genitive case plural, William?—*William Page.* Genitive case!—*Evans.* Ay.—*William.* Genitivo,—horum, harum, horum.—*Mistress Quickly.* Vengeance on Jenny's case! fie on her!—never name her, child, if she be a whore.—*Evans.* For shame, 'oman': *horum* recalls **whore;** *harum* recalls **hair** and **hare.** In line 58, Mistress Quickly refers to *horum* as *whorum.* The same *case* pun occurs in *All's Well,* I iii 21–23.

Case because it sheathes a sword (see **swords and bucklers**).

catastrophe. See **tickle one's catastrophe.**

catching of cold. In *Much Ado,* III iv 59–60, '*Beatrice.* I am stuft; I cannot smell.—*Margaret.* A maid, and stuft! there's goodly catching of cold', Beatrice means that her nose is stuffed-up with mucus, but Margaret alludes to **stuff,** v., and says, 'That's a fine way of catching cold!' Margaret certainly hints that

Beatrice has been too much uncovered and perhaps glances at that equivocal word **occupy;** there is, very probably, an implication that, as the nasal, so the vaginal passage may be blocked (cf. low-slang *to block a woman*).

chain, v. To embrace as with a chain. Cleopatra to Antony, 'Chain mine arm'd neck', IV viii 15. (Cf. **hoop with embraces.**)

chalky cliffs. See **cliff.**

chamber. See **charged chambers** and:

chamber-lie. Urine: see quotation at **jordan.** Usual spelling: *lye* (perhaps ex Fr. *l'eau*, 'water'). In *Macbeth*, II iii 36, *lie* puns 'urine' and the desire to **lie** with a woman (or perhaps the detumescence of *penis erectus*).

chamberer. A carpet-knight, or any other man, addicted to sexual indulgence: who frequents the bed-rooms (*chambers*) of ladies. 'I am black, And have not those soft parts of conversation That chamberers have', *Othello*, III iii 263–265.

'Let us walk honestly, as in the day; not in rioting and drunkenness, not in chambering and wantonness, not in strife and envying', *Romans*, xiii 13; *chambering* = 'habitual illicit copulation'; for a fuller treatment, see *A New Testament Word-Book*.

change eyes. To exchange loving glances. Prospero, concerning Ferdinand and Miranda, 'At the first sight They have changed eyes', *The Tempest*, I ii 441–442.

change the cod's head for the salmon's tail. *Othello*, II i 155–156, 'She that in wisdom never was so frail To change the cod's head for the salmon's tail': a difficult phrase, even when we remember that *cod's head* probably refers to *codpiece* and that probably it therefore = penis (the head of the *cod* or scrotum), and that *salmon's tail* probably = pudend (cf. **fish,** q.v., and see **tail,** 1). A woman does not change, i.e. exchange, the former for the latter; she exchanges the latter for the former: the pun demands that *change . . . for* = 'put . . . in the place of', hence 'put . . . in'.—Occasionally it is almost impossible to

determine the exact sense of Shakespeare's sexual witticisms:
but, the subtlety and highly developed nature of his sexuality
being incontrovertible, we should be ignorant—and stupid—
to think that there is no sexual witticism.

charge, v. To assail sexually; to coït with (a woman). 'Pistol. Then
to you, Mistress Dorothy; I will charge you.—Doll *Tearsheet*.
Charge me! I scorn you', 2 *Henry IV* II iv 120–121.

Cf. **assail** (and **assault**); *charge*, however, may bear the additional connotation, 'to load with semen'.

charged chambers. In 'To serve bravely is to come halting off
the breach with his pike bent bravely, and to surgery bravely;
and to venture upon the charged chambers bravely' (2 *Henry
IV*, II iv 49–53), there may be a triple allusion: to pike = penis
(see **pistol**); to female pudend; and to the charged chambers
of a mine, or a countermine, attacking the outer defences of a
fortress, and, therefore, testicles.

charms. *The Passionate Pilgrim*, II vv. 5–8, ' "Even this," quoth she,
"the warlike god embraced me," And there she clipt Adonis
in her arms; "Even thus," quoth she, "the warlike god unlaced
me," As if the boy should use like loving charms': actions
(caresses, kisses, unlacing) occultly potent in amorous
eloquence and for love-making.

Charm: via Fr. *charme*, ex L. *carmen*, 'song' or, rather, 'chant or
incantation'.

chaste. Abstaining from sexual intercourse and caresses, especially if unlawful or illicit. In 1 *Henry VI*, at V iv 49–51, Joan la
Pucelle declares, 'Joan of Arc hath been A virgin from her
tender infancy, Chaste and immaculate in very thought'.—See
quotation at **virtuous.**—'Lucrece was not more chaste Than
this Lavinia', *Titus Andronicus*, II i 108.—R. & J., I i 215.—'I will
find you twenty lascivious turtles, ere one chaste man', *Merry
Wives*, II i 79–81.—T. & C., I iii 300.—*Measure*, II iv 184.—And
elsewhere, esp. in *Lucrece*.

Through Fr., ex L. *castus*, which, says Wyld, is prob. related to '. . . *castigare*, "cleanse, punish", *castrare*, "to cut, castrate", and *carere*, "to be without, lack" '.

chaste treasure. Chastity embodied in the pudend-casket, which is hymen-locked. 'Weigh what loss your honour may sustain, If . . . you . . . your chaste treasure open To his unmaster'd importunity', *Hamlet*, I iii 29–32.

  Cf. 'the treasure of her honour' (at **pick the lock**)—**bond of chastity**—**virgin patent.**

chastity. Faithfulness in marriage; moderation in love-making; in a virgin, abstention from coïtion; hence, purity. *Much Ado*, IV i 97.—*As You Like It*, III iv 16.—*Measure*, II iv 185.—And elsewhere. Cf. **chaste.**

  A certain modern newspaper-editor's dictum was, 'Avoid the word *chastity*: it's so damned suggestive!'

cheapen. To bargain for (a woman) in marriage; to woo: 'Virtuous, or I'll never cheapen her; fair, or I'll never look on her', *Much Ado*, II iii 32–33. There may, however, be a pun on 'deflower'. Cf. **mart,** q.v.

cherish and **cherisher,** in *All's Well*, I iii 46–49, have a sexual undertone: an early sense of *cherish* is 'to keep warm'. Cf. **comfort,** q.v.

child, with. Pregnant. 'The holy maid with child!', 1 *Henry VI*, v iv 65.—*All's Well*;, v iii 311.

circle. (Cf. **ring,** q.v.) Pudend. ''Twould anger him To raise a spirit in his mistress' circle Of some strange nature, letting it there stand Till she had laid it and conjured it down', *R. & J.*, II i 23–27.—Remotely innuendoed in *Henry V*, v ii 302.

  Magic circle and—physiologically inaccurate—sexual circle.

city. See quotation at **besiege** and cf. **fort.**

clack-dish. A beggar's bowl for the reception of alms. In the quotation it is used metaphorically for pudend. 'Not the duke? Yes, your beggar of fifty; and his use was to put a ducat in her clack-dish: the duke had crotchets in him', *Measure*, III ii 127–129.

Clack is echoic of the sound of coins falling into the bowl; and a beggar, to attract attention, would tap it smartly.

clap, v. 'Within a while All the best men are ours; for 'tis ill hap If they hold'—i.e., refrain—'when their ladies bid them clap', *Henry VIII*, last two verses. There is a pun on *clap one's hands (in approval)* and on the basic sense, 'to strike sharply together' (see **strike**) hence, 'to coït'.

clasp, n.; **clasping.** An embrace (close and sexual). (Desdemona) 'Transported . . . To the gross clasps of a lascivious Moor', *Othello*, I i 126–128.—'Your untimely claspings with your child', *Pericles*, I i 128.

The v. comes ex the n., which, with variant *clapse*, is of dubious etymology: the word does not appear before M.E.

cleave the pin. To cause emission in a male: L.L.L., IV i 136, 'Then will she get the upshoot by cleaving the pin'.

cliff. 1, A female breast (either of the two breasts). Only by punning allusion in *Com. of Errors*, III ii, in the female-geography passage, thus, 'Where England?—I look'd for the chalky cliffs, but I could find no whiteness in them' (cf. *Sonnets*, 130, v. 3. 'If snow be white, why then her breasts are dun').

2, Pudend: T. & C., v ii 11–12 (see at **sing**). Cf. *mons Veneris*, the mount (or mound) of Venus: the pubic area in a woman,—whence derives the sense in palmistry.

climb, v.; vbl. n., **climbing.** Both occur in 2 *Henry VI*, II i, in a passage excerpted at **plum**, q.v.—See quotation at **bird's nest.**

To climb a woman's legs (as though they were the limbs of a tree) and then **enjoy** her.—Cf. **mount** and **scale.**

clip, v.t. To embrace closely, whether affectionately or amorously. 'Enter the town, clip your wives', *A. & C.*. IV viii 8.—*Coriolanus*, I vi 29.—*Cymbeline*, v v 451–452.—*The W. Tale*, v ii 55.—'To clip Elysium, and to lack her joy', *Venus*, v. 600.—*The Passionate Pilgrim*, II vv. 6 and 14.

Ex O.E. *clyppan*, 'to embrace'.

close-stool. A chamber-pot stool-mounted and covered (hence *close*). 'Your lion, that holds his poll-axe sitting on a close-stool, will be given to Ajax', L.L.L., v ii 571–572.—'A paper from Fortune's close-stool to give to a nobleman!', *All's Well*, v ii 17–18.

cloy, v.t.; **cloyless.** To satiate; unsatisfying, rendering insatiable. *A. & C.*, ii i 125 (*cloyless:* see **libertine**).—*Ibid.*, ii ii 240–242, (of Cleopatra) 'Other women cloy The appetites they feed; but she makes hunger Where most she satisfies'.

Ex obsolete *accloy*, 'to choke' (literally, 'to put a nail'—L. *clavus*—'into'). C.O.D.

coasting welcome, in *Troilus & Cressida*, iv v 59, clearly means 'an accosting welcome'.

cock. Penis, *The Taming*, ii i 224 (see quotation at **hen**).—Pistol's cock is up, And flashing fire will follow', *Henry V* ii i 54–55—cf. the entry at **pistol.**—See the punning quotation (from *The Passionate Pilgrim*) at **trick.**

L. *coccus*, the male domestic fowl: probably echoic of its cry (cf. **cuckoo**). Hence applied to 'objects supposed to represent cock's head and comb: *watercock*, &c.', especially cock (short for *watercock*) and tap: hence, *cock* = 'penis', not only from the shape but also from the fact that the penis emits water (as does a tap) and sperm (Gr. *sperma*, seed).

cock!, by; cock's passion! Here, *cock* is a euphemism for *God*. 'Cock's passion, silence!', *The Taming*, iv i 112.—'Young men will do't, if they come to 't; By cock, they are to blame', *Hamlet*, iv v 60–61.

See **cock.**

cod is present in the next three entries; cf. **eel** and **fish.**

codding spirit. 'Indeed, I was their tutor to instruct them: That codding spirit had they from their mother', Aaron in reference to Tamora and her raping sons (*Titus Andronicus*, v i 99). There is an equivoque, for 'codding spirit' = 'tendency to jest' and 'tendency to play with a **codpiece';** Shakespeare, bearing in mind *cod*, 'to hoax', was paying yet more attention to the 'cod' of:—

codpiece. That bag-like flap which, in front of breeches (etc.), covers the penis and scrotum; hence, the penis itself and sometimes the testicles too. 'A round hose, madam, now's not worth a pin, Unless you have a codpiece to stick pins on', *Two Gentlemen*, II vii 55–56.—In L.L.L., III i 181, Cupid is called 'king of codpieces'.—*Much Ado*, III iii 133–135, '. . . The shaven Hercules in the smircht worm-eaten tapestry, where his codpiece seems as massy as his club'.—*Measure*, III ii 115–117, 'Why, what a ruthless thing is this in him, for the rebellion of a codpiece to take away the life of a man!'—*Lear*, III ii 27 and 40.—*The W. Tale*, IV iii 616.

O.E. *codd*, 'bag', hence M.E. *cod*(*de*), 'pod; hence, scrotum'; of common-Teutonic stock.

cod's head. See **change the cod's head . . .**

coin, v. To 'coin' a child; to engender one; to create one as one mints a coin. See quotation at **saucy sweetness.**

Cf. **stamp,** q.v., and **coiner**, and the fact that *matrix* is both the womb and a mould.

coiner. A man regarded as a coin-stamper in the mint of sexual intercourse. 'That most venerable man . . . my father, was I know not where When I was stampt; some coiner with his tools Made me a counterfeit', *Cymbeline*, II v 3–6.

Cf. **coin** and **stamp,** qq.v.

cold, adj. Chaste; sexually frigid; sexually distant. See quotation at **hot dreams;** that from *A Lover's Complaint* at **luxury.**

Contrast **hot,** q.v., and cf. **frosty.**

colt, v.t. (Of a man) to coït with (a woman). Posthumus, concerning Imogen and Iachimo, 'She hath been colted by him'; *Cymbeline*, II iv 133.

Synonymous with **horse,** v.; cf. also **hackney** and **nag, mount** and **ride.**

come. To experience a sexual emission. (Following the quotation at **vice,** is this:) '*Margaret*. Well, I will call Beatrice to you, who I think hath legs.—*Benedick*. And therefore will come?'—

Perhaps in *Twelfth Night*, III iv 31–32, '*Olivia*. Wilt thou go to bed, Malvolio?—M. To bed! aye, sweet-heart; and I'll come to thee'.—See second quotation in next entry.

The Aryan base of *come* 'expressed the related, but different, ideas "go" and "come"'' (Wyld): cf., therefore, **go.**

come into my chamber; come to one's bed. To seek sexually in bed or bed-room. 'Quoth she, before you tumbled me, You promised me to wed . . . So would I ha' done, by yonder sun, An thou hadst not come to my bed', *Hamlet*, IV v 62–66.—Cressida to Troilus, after a love-filled night, 'My lord, come you again into my chamber: You smile and mock me, as if I meant naughtily.—*Troilus*. Ha, ha!': IV ii 36–38, where there is probably a pun on male orgasm and almost certainly a sexual invitation.

come over To coït with (a woman). Concerning a sonnet: 'In so high a style, Margaret, that no man shall come over it' (better it). '*Margaret*. To have no man come over me! why, shall I always keep below stairs?', *Much Ado*, V ii 6–10.

For semantics, cf. **mount** and **lay knife aboard.**

come to it. See quotation at **cock!, by.**

To come to it—to the sexual act; cf. **it.**

comfort, v. To soothe and solace with love's caresses and with yet greater intimacy. '*Nurse*. Hie to your chamber: I'll find Romeo To comfort you', R. & J., III ii 138–139.—*Julius Caesar*, II i 283–285, Portia to Brutus, 'Am I yourself But, as it were, in sort or limitation, To keep with you at meals, comfort your bed, And talk to you sometimes'.—*All's Well*, I iii 46–47.

L. *confortare*, 'to make strong' (*fortis*).

coming-in, 'revenue', is punned-on to mean '(a man's) sexual ingression': *The M. of V.*, II ii 160–161, 'Eleven widows and nine maids is a simple coming-in for one man': cf. the Biblical *go in unto* and the entry above at come.

commission. See **performance** (at end) and cf.:—

commit, v.i. To commit adultery. 'Commit not with man's sworn spouse', *Lear*, III iv 81–82.

Cf. **mutually committed.** Perhaps Shakespeare was punning on the etymological sense of L. *committere*, 'to send together; hence, to *join* together'.

commodious. In 'The parrot will not do more for an almond than he'—Patroclus—'for a commodious drab' (*T. & C.*, v ii 194–195), there are three senses: 1, roomy, spacious (cf. **broad awake** and **secretly open**); 2, handy or convenient or suitable; 3, amorous, or sexually oncoming—with an oblique reference to:—

commodity. Pudend, particular and generic. *2 Henry VI*, IV vii (near end), 'When shall we go to Cheapside, and take up commodities upon our bills?', with pun on bill-hooks (hence, penises: cf. **pike**) and commercial bills.—In the famous *King John* passage (II i 567 ff.) on Commodity, the word is elaborately and subtly punned-on in its sexual (the derivative) and in its commercial (the original) sense—'trade; gain': 'Commodity, the bias of the world . . . this Commodity, this bawd, this broker, this all-changing word'.—Pandar, in *Pericles*, IV ii 29–30, to the Bawd's 'Is it a shame to get when we are old?', replies, 'O, our credit comes not in like the commodity, not the commodity wages not with the danger', where there is a similar pun.

Commodity being 'something adapted for use and convenience' (Wyld), the sexual sense may spring from the ordinary man's tendency to regard a woman as a sexual convenience (cf. the old slang *convenient*, 'a mistress') reserved for his private use.

common. (Of a prostitute or a loose woman) available to all men; the temporary property of every chance-comer: see quotation at **road;** and cf. the next three entries.

common customer. A common whore. 'I think thee now some common customer', *All's Well*, v iii 284.

Cf. preceding entry, and the two following this one; cf. also **trader** and the L. *femina publica*, 'a public woman'—a woman available to the public; a prostitute.

common house. A brothel. 'If these be good people in a common-weal that do nothing but use their abuses in common houses, I know no law', *Measure*, II i 41–43.

Cf. the two preceding entries, and:—

commoner. A common whore. 'Barrack hack' is the sense in *All's Well*, v iii 190, 'A commoner o' the camp'.—'O thou public commoner!', *Othello*, IV ii 73.

Cf. the three entries preceding this one.

compound, v. To colt; semantically, to 'mingle'; to procreate by mingling'. 'My father compounded with my mother under the dragon's tail'—with pun on **tail,** 1 or 3—'and my nativity was under *ursa major*; so that it follows, I am rough and lecherous', *Lear*, I ii 132–135.—*Timon*, IV iii 273 (see **stuff,** n.).

Lit., 'to mix' (ingredients: potent semen with fertile ovaries).

compulsive. Compelling; (almost) irresistible. See quotation at **ardour.**

conceive. 'The slip, the slip; can you not conceive?' R. & J., II iii 47.—*The Taming*, v ii 22–24, 'Widow. Thus I conceive by him.—*Petruchio*. Conceives by me!—How likes Hortensio that?—*Hortensio*. My widow says, thus she conceives her tale'.—See **hang one's bugle**—and elsewhere.

conception. A becoming pregnant. 'Conception is a blessing; but not as your daughter may conceive', *Hamlet*, II ii 194–195.—*Timon*, I ii 110.—*Pericles*, I i 8.—And elsewhere.

L. *conceptio*: ex *capere*, 'to take': when a woman conceives, she is, by some, said to *take*.

conceptions. Conceptive; capable of conceiving (offspring). 'Ensear'—i.e., inwardly cauterize—'thy fertile and conceptious womb, Let it not more bring out ingrateful man!', *Timon*, IV iii 187–188.

Ex **conception.**

conceive her tale. See second quotation at **conceive.** The pun is on **tail,** 1.

concubine. An unmarried woman (or a widow) living with a man as his mistress. 'I know I am too mean to be your queen, And yet too good to be your concubine', Lady Grey to King Edward, 3 *Henry VI*, III ii 97–98.

L. **concubere,** 'to **lie with', concubina** being a woman that habitually lies with a man.

concupiscible. Lewd, lascivious. 'He would not, but by gift of my chaste body To his concupiscible intemperate lust, Release my brother', *Measure*, v i 97–99.

For the more usual *concupiscent*, 'eagerly desirous' (L. *cupere*, to desire).

concupy. Troilus, inveighing against the absent Diomedes (who has taken Cressida from him), invites this aside from the ill-natured, filthy-minded Thesites, who, ostensibly, refers to Troilus's sword: 'He'll tickle it for his concupy' (v ii 178). There seems to be an allusion to lustful desire (cf. preceding entry) and, secondarily, to **concubine;** perhaps the word is a blend of **concubine** and **occupy.**

confessor. '*Lovell.* O, that your lordship were but now confessor To one or two of these!' ('These' are fair ladies.) '*Sands.* I would I were; They should find easy penance . . . As easy as a down-bed would afford it', *Henry VIII*, I iv 15–18. Shakespeare makes this *confession-penance* pun elsewhere: see **shift.**

Cf. **shrive,** q.v.

conflict. Amorous 'struggle'. 'Conflict such as was supposed The wandering prince and Dido once enjoy'd When with a happy storm they were surprised', *Titus Andronicus*, II iii 21–22.

Cf. **wrestle** and **contend.**

conger, 'a large sea-eel', is, in 2 *Henry IV*, II iv 54, remotely yet definitely allusive to the sense of **eel,** q.v.

conjunct. Joined amorously; physically entwined. See **bosom,** v.

conjure it down. See **circle** and **lay it.**

conquer a maiden bed. Helena (disguised) to Bertram, 'When you have conquer'd my yet maiden bed, Remain there but an hour, nor to speak to me', *All's Well*, IV ii 57–58.

Cf. **make defeat of virginity** and **convince the honour of** and the third quotation at **touch**.

conscience. 'Love is too young to know what conscience is' (*Sonnet* 151) contains, like **constable,** below, and like **country matters,** on p. 110, a characteristically Shakespeare *double entente* on the pudend.

constable. There is probably an innuendo of *cunt* in 'I tell thee, constable, my mistress wears her own hair' (see **hair**): *Henry V*, III vii 61–62.—*All's Well*, II ii 29–34, 'Countess. Have you . . . an answer of such fitness for all questions?—Clown. From below your duke to beneath your constable, it will fit any question.—Countess. It must be an answer of most monstrous size that must fit all demands.'

Grose speaks of a lady that would never use the word—it had such an ill sound!

constrain. To violate (a woman; or figuratively). 'Her spotless chastity . . . you constrain'd and forced', *Titus Andronicus*, V ii 177–178.

Cf. **strain,** q.v., and **force.**

contaminate; contaminated. Defiled. 'This body, consecrate to thee, By ruffian lust should be contaminate', *Com. of Errors*, II ii 131–132.—*Henry V*, IV v 13–16, 'Let him . . ., Like a base pandar, hold the chamber door Whilst by a slave, no gentler than my dog, His fairest daughter is contaminate'.—'A contaminated stale', *Much Ado*, II ii 24.

Contaminate (L. *contaminare*) is 'to bring into (undesirable) contact (*tangere*, to touch)'.

contend. To 'struggle' amorously: *Two Gentlemen*, I ii 129 (see at **embrace,** v.).

Cf. **strive, wrestle,** and also **conflict.** Contend = L. *contendere*, 'to strive': ex *tendere*, 'to stretch'.

continency; continent. (Concerning Petruchio and his bride)

'In her chamber, Making a sermon of continency to her', *The Taming*, IV i 173–174.—*Measure*, III ii 177 (see **ungenitured**).

L. *continere*, 'to hold (*tenere*) together; hence, to repress (one's vagrant desires)'.

conversation. Sexual intimacy (cf. the legal phrase, *criminal conversation*). 'His conversation with Shore's wife', *Richard III*, III v 30.

Ex. L. *conversari* 'to keep company with'.

convince the honour of. To seduce; to lead sexually astray. 'Posthumus. Your Italy contains none so accomplisht a courtier to convince the honour of my mistress', *Cymbeline*, I iv 94–95.

Cf. **conquer a maiden's bed,** q.v.

cool, v. To cool the sexual heat, the amorous ardour, of (a person). On the night of the storm, the Fool in *Lear* says, 'This is a brave night to cool a courtezan', III ii 79.—'His'—Antony's— 'captain's heart . . . is become the bellows and the fan To cool a gipsy's lust', *A. & C.*, I i 6–10.

Cf. the often humorous 'That will damp his ardour!' and 'His love has cooled'. *Cool*, adj., is from the same radical as **cold.**

cope, v. To deal satisfactorily—indeed, successfully—with; in the quotation, it = to coït with (a woman). Iago to Othello (IV i 86–87), 'Where, how, how oft, how long ago, and when He hath, and is again to cope with your wife'.

Long obsolete in English. But in Scottish low slang, it survives in the forms *coup* and *cowp*. From Fr. *couper*, 'to strike', it is yet another of those sadistic verbs of copulation: cf. **hit, strike, thump, and fuck** itself.

copesmate. A paramour; a partner in sexual intercourse, especially in lustful copulation. 'Mis-shapen Time, copesmate of ugly Night, . . . Eater of youth, false slave to false delight, Base watch of woes, sin's pack-horse, virtue's snare', *Lucrece*, vv. 925–928.

Cf. preceding entry.

copulation. Sexual intercourse—sexual congress—coïtion.

Touchstone to Corin, 'That is another simple sin in you; to bring the ewes and the rams together, and to offer to get your living by the copulation of cattle', *As You Like It*, III ii 78–80.— 'The wren goes to 't, and the small gilded fly Does lecher in my sight. Let copulation thrive', *Lear*, IV vi 115–117.

Ex L. *copulare*, 'to bind or fasten together' (*copula*, anything that fastens or binds one thing to another): 'and the two [man and woman] shall be one flesh'. *Copulare = co-apulare*; *apulare* being a diminutive form of the presumed v. *apere*, 'to fasten', with that stem *-ap* which occurs also in *apt*.

Corinth, as city-type of (especially, sexual) licentiousness: *Timon*, II ii 71.

corner. Pudend; cf. Fr. *petit coin*. Othello, doubting Desdemona's chastity, 'I had rather be a toad . . . Than keep a corner in the thing I love For others' uses', III iii 270–273.

Old Fr. *cornier*, ex L. *cornu*, 'horn' (with stress on its point?).

cornuto. Italian (ex L. *cornu*, a horn) for 'horned' (see **horned**); hence, a man fitted with the **horns** of cuckoldry; a cuckold. 'The peaking cornuto her husband', *Merry Wives*, III v 67–68.

corrupt, v.; **corruption.** To seduce and defile a virgin; to induce a married woman to become unfaithful to her husband.— Sexual indulgence carried to excess or operating in unpleasant ways. See quotation at **enseamed bed.**—*All's Well*, III v 73 (see **unlawful**).—*Measure*, III i 159–160, 'Angelo had never the purpose to corrupt her'.—*Othello*, IV ii 187–188.—*Coriolanus*, IV iii 33–34.—*Lucrece*, v. 1172.

L. *corrumpere*, 'to destroy': *rumpere*, 'to break' (the honesty of): cf. the more brutal **break.**

couch, v. To lie down, especially in sexual intercourse. '*Gratiano.* I should wish it dark, That I were couching with the doctor's clerk', *The M. of V.*, v i 304–305.—*Othello*, IV iii 56.

Fr. *coucher*, ex L. *collocare*, 'to dispose' (oneself: for sleep, etc.).

coun. Princess Katharine's pronunciation (after Alice's) of the English *gown*: *Henry V*, III iv 47–53, '*Katharine. Comment*

appelez-vous le pied et la robe?—Alice. De foot, madame; et de coun.—
Katharine. De foot et de coun! *O Seigneur Dieu! ce sont mots de son
mauvais, corruptible, gros, et impudique: je ne voudrais prononcer ces mots
devant les seigneurs de France pour tout le monde. Foh! le foot et le coun!*'
Coun and *foot*, being approximations to French *con* (pudend)
and *foutre* (a vigorous vulgarism, comparable with its equivalent 'to fuck'), are indeed, as French words, 'bad, corrupt,
gross, and indelicate'.

Con, unlike English *cunt*, derives from L. *cunnus*, which may,
by a crude shape-metaphor, have been suggested by L. *cuneus*,
'a wedge' (the origin of Fr. *coin*; 'corner', whence the euphemistic *petit coin*, 'cunt'; English *coign*); perhaps from that Aryan
radical denoting 'femininity, femaleness' which is present in
quean, Lowland Sc. *quin*, 'girl'; *cow*, and Greek *guné*, 'woman'.
(See, too, *A Dictionary of Slang*, ed. 3 at *cunt*.) In **confessor** and
constable, either the French *con* or the English word may well
be 'undertoned' in the passages quoted in these entries.

See also **piss** below.

counterfeit, adj. Virtuous-seeming but actually lewd or wanton.
'Strike me the counterfeit matron,—It is her habit only that is
honest, Herself's a bawd', *Timon*, IV iii 112–114.

Ex Fr. *contrefait*: L. *contra*, 'against' + *facere*, 'to make': '(something) made against the rule'.

counterfeit, n. See quotation at **stamp,** where *counterfeit* = a bastard. Ex the adj.

country. See next two entries and perhaps 'I could find out
countries in her' (*Comedy*, III ii 112–113): pudend and
adjacencies.

country matters, or, in Quarto 1, 'contrary matters', where,
clearly, the same pun is intended. Immediately after the *Hamlet*
quotation at **lap:** 'Do you think I meant country matters?—
Ophelia. I think nothing, my lord': III ii 120–121.

The adjacent *lap* makes it clear that Hamlet meant, 'Do you
think that I was referring to sexual matters?': matters

concerned with cunt; the first pronouncing-element of country is **coun**. Ex Old Fr. cuntré (a fact not irrelevant): L. (terra) contrata.

country mistresses. In 'Each of us fell in praise of our country mistresses' (Cymbeline, I iv 56–57), the surface-sense, the ostensible sense, the primary sense, is 'the mistresses—belovèd women—of our own countries', but the ulterior, the secondary sense is 'our mistresses regarded as bed-fellows': cf. **country matters,** q.v.

courtezan. A prostitute (in C. 18–20, generally a better-class whore). In 1 Henry VI, at III ii 45, Burgundy calls Joan la Pucelle a 'shameless courtezan'.—'Dallying with a brace of courtezans', Richard III, III vii 74.—A minor character in Com. of Errors, IV iii.—See quotation at **cool**.—Cymbeline, III iv 124.

Ex It. cortigiana, lit. 'a kind woman': cf. the euphemistic be kind to a man and do a girl a kindness.

cover, v. To mount and then impregnate the female—mostly of the larger animals. The M. of V., III v 50–53, 'Lorenzo. Bid them prepare dinner.—Launcelot. That is done too, sir; only "cover" is the word.—Lorenzo. Will you cover, then, sir?—Launcelot. Not so, sir, neither; I know my duty.'—Othello, I i 112–113, 'You'll have your daughter cover'd with a Barbary horse'.

Cf. **tup,** q.v.

cow. See second quotation at **Bull Jove.**

coy, 'reluctant, or very shy, in love-making'; Venus, v. 96.—Lucrece, v. 669.

crack, n. A rupture of chastity; whether directly or by indirection, the vulva. With dramatic irony in Camillo's 'I cannot Believe this crack to be in my dread mistress', addressed to Leontes: The W. Tale, I ii 319–320.

crack, v. 'Boult, take her away; use her at thy pleasure: crack the glass of her virginity,'—the membrane constituting her maidenhead—'and make the rest malleable', Pericles, IV v 142–144.—See quotation at **bond of chastity.**

An echoic word, cognate with creak.

crackt within the ring. Devirginated. Allusively in Hamlet's remark to an actor that is to play a woman's part, 'Pray God, your voice, like a piece of uncurrent gold, be not crackt within the ring' (II ii 434–435).

See **crack,** v. (and cf. the n.), the **ring.**

creation. Procreation. See quotation at **downright way.**

creature of sale. (Cf. **house of sale.**) A harlot in a brothel. 'Bawd. We were never so much out of creatures', *Pericles*, IV ii 6.— Lysimachus to Marina, 'Why, the house you dwell in proclaims you to be a creature of sale', *Pericles*, IV v 77–78.

Cressid or **Cressida.** Type of flighty, highly sexed girl: *Henry V*, II i 79.—*Twelfth Night*, III i 54.—*T. & C.*, III ii 199–200. In the first of these passages, plain 'whore' is intended.

crop, n. and v. 1. Children—harvest of marriage; to bear a crop of children. *All's Well*, I iii 44–45, 'He that ears my land spares my team, and gives me leave to in'—i.e., to get in, to gather— 'the crop.—'He plough'd her, and she cropt', *A. & C.*, II ii, 242.

For the semantics, cf. **tillage** and **tilth.** The v. ex the n., which has basic sense 'protuberance'—hence growth above ground.

cuckold, n. A married man to whom his wife is unfaithful. 'A gig of a cuckold's horn', *L.L.L.*, V i 64–65.—*The M. of V.*, V i 265, 'What, are we cuckolds ere we have deserved it?'—*Much Ado*, II i 42–43, 'There the devil will meet me, like an old cuckold, with horns on his head'.—'Cuckold! wittol!— Cuckold! the devil himself hath not such a name', *Merry Wives*, II ii 299–300; 314, 'Fie, fie, fie! cuckold! cuckold!'; and elsewhere in the play.—*Hamlet*, IV v 116.—*T. & C.*, V i 52–54, 'The goodly transformation of Jupiter there, his brother, the bull,—the primitive statue, and oblique memorial of cuckolds'.—And elsewhere.

M.E. *cokewold,* = Old Fr. *cucault,* 'cuckoo; cuckold' (Mod. Fr. *coucou,* and *cocu,* respectively). The cuckoo deposits its eggs in the nests of smaller birds: so does not the cuckold. Cf. **cuckoo(-bird),** q.v.

cuckold, v. To be marriage-unfaithful to (a man); (of a man) to seduce the wife of. 'Master Brook, you shall cuckold Ford', *Merry Wives,* III v 134–135.—*Othello,* I iii 327, and IV i 201.

From the noun.

cuckold-mad. Angry almost to madness at having been betrayed by one's wife: see the quotation at **horn-mad.**

cuckold-maker. One who causes another to be a **cuckold.** T. & C., V vii 9, Thersites, in reference to Menelaus and Paris, who are fighting, 'The cuckold and the cuckold-maker are at it'.— *Henry VIII,* V iii 124.

cuckoldry. The state of being a cuckold; the practice of cuckoldmaking.

cuckoldy. Wife-betrayed. Ford, masquerading as one Brook, to Falstaff, 'Do you know Ford, sir?—*Falstaff,* Hang him, poor cuckoldy knave!', *Merry Wives,* II ii 268–270.

cuckoo; cuckoo-bird. A cuckold (French *cocu*: hence the easy transition; cf. 'you silly cuckoo!'). 'The cuckoo then on every tree Mocks married men', *L.L.L.,* V ii 891–892.—*M.N. Dream,* III 130–135 (**cuckoo**).—*Merry Wives,* II i 122 (**cuckoo-bird**).—*All's Well,* I iii 63–64.

For origin, see **cuckold,** n.

culled—see **posteriors.** 'The word is well culled' contains a pun on the French *cul*, the backside. In the same passage, 'chose' is perhaps the French euphemism *chose*, ('women's *thing*'); and the repetition of 'assure' probably puns on *ass*, for *arse*.

cullion; cullionly. A low fellow; low. 'Away, base cuilions!', 2 *Henry VI,* I iii 38.—'You whoreson cullionly barbermonger', *Lear,* II ii 33.

Ex Old Fr. *coillon, couillon,* 'testicles' and a coarse term of abuse: cf. that legendary rascal, 'Bollicky [properly: Ballocky] Bill, the sailor', often euphemistically 'Barnacle Bill'.

cunt. See **coun.**

Cupid. L. *Cupido*, the god of love in its aspect of physical desire (L. *cupere*, 'to desire'). 'Methinks I should outswear Cupid', *L.L.L.*, I ii 61–62.—*Ibid.*, III i 176–183, 'This wimpled, whining, purblind, wayward boy; This signior-junior, giant-dwarf, Dan Cupid; Regent of love-rimes, lord of folded arms, Th' anointed sovereign of sighs and groans, Liege of all loiterers and malcontents, Dread prince of plackets, king of codpieces, Sole impersonator and great general Of trotting paritors'; iv iii 56, 'O, rimes are guards on Wanton Cupid's hose'; IV iii 363, 'Saint Cupid, then! and, soldiers, to the field!—*R. & J.*, *passim.*— See **hare-finder;** frequently elsewhere in *Much Ado.*—And, in other plays.

custom, 'sexual intercourse as a habit or an unquestioned custom': *Hamlet*, III iv 162, 'That monster, custom, who all sense [?—sensuality, or rather, the senses] doth eat'.

customer. In *Measure*, IV iii 4 (see at **house. . .**), it = a male frequenter of brothels. In *Othello*, IV i 120, 'I marry her!—what, a customer!', it is short for **common customer.**

For the semantics, cf. **trade** and **trader.**

cut loaf, steal a shive of a. See **steal a shive . . .**

Cytherea. See **Venus,** end of first paragraph.

dale. Venus, inciting (and trying to excite) Adonis to roam in that **park** which is her fair body, says, 'Feed where thou wilt, on mountain or in dale' (v. 232)—on the eminences or in the valleys: the valley between her breasts; the vulva-valley; and perhaps the rearward ravine.

dalliance; dally. Leisurely love-play; to play, leisurely-amorous, with a member of the opposite sex. 'Wanton dalliance with a paramour', *1 Henry VI*, v i 23.— *Richard III*, III vii 74 (sec **courtezan**): the verb.—'The primrose path of dalliance', *Hamlet*, I iii 50; cf. III ii 266 (quoted at **edge**).—'Do not give dalliance too much rein; the strongest oaths are straw To the fire i' the blood', *The Tempest*, IV i 51–53.—See quotation at **sport, v.**

Ex Old Fr. *dalier*, 'to chat', and therefore parallel to **conversation**. Cf. **toy** and **sport** and **play**.

damson. See **plum.**

Dan Cupid. See **Cupid,** second quotation.

dance with one's heels. Much Ado, III iv 41–45, '*Margaret.* Clap's into *Light o' love*; that goes without a burden: do you sing it, and I'll dance it.—*Beatrice.* Ye light o' love, with your heels!—then, if your husband have stables enough, you'll see he shall lack no barns' (perhaps with pun on *bairns*, as well as on cuckoldry). (Of the woman) to beat the bed with one's heels during the rhythmic motion of the sexual act.

darkness. See **do it.**

dart of love. See **dribbling . . .**

daughters of the game. See **game . . .**

day-bed. See **lewd,** second quotation.

dead men's fingers. 'Garlands . . . Of crow-flowers, nettles, daisies, and long purples That liberal shepherds give a grosser name, But our cold maids do dead men's fingers call them', *Hamlet*, IV vii 168–171. Lyte's *Herbal*, 1578, shows that 'the long purple' is the Orchis, especially the variety 'Priest's Pintle'.

Cf. **carrot** and **little finger** and especially the entry at **liberal.**

dearest bodily part. The pudend. '*Iachimo.* If I bring you no sufficient testimony that I have enjoy'd the dearest bodily part of your mistress, my ten thousand ducats are yours', *Cymbeline*, I iv 149–152.

Cf. **chaste treasure, jewel, treasury.**

deed of darkness, the; the deed of kind. See **do it** and cf **act.** See also **bereave** and **hot deeds.**

deer, f. and m. Figuratively used of man and woman in reference to sexual activities. In *The Comedy of Errors*, at II i 100–101 (see **break the pale**), it is a man. In *The Taming*, V ii 56, it is a woman.—*Merry Wives*, V v 17–18, '*Mistress Ford.* Sir John, art thou there, my deer? my male deer?—*Falstaff.* My doe with the black scut!'—Cf. 'A servingman . . . that, . . . served the lust of my mistress' heart, and did the act of darkness with her', *Lear*, III iv 85–88.—Venus to Adonis, 'I'll be a park, and thou shalt be my deer' (v. 231).

Possibly influenced by the homophone, (one's) *dear*, or darling.

defeat of virginity, make. See **make defeat.**

defence. A woman's defence against seduction. 'Thou art the issue of my dear offence, Which was so strongly urged, past my defence', *King John*, I i 257–258.—*All's Well*, I i 115–116, 'But [man] assails; and our virginity, though valiant in the defence, yet is weak'. Cf.:—

defend one's belly. '*Pandarus.* You are such a woman! One knows not at what ward you lie.—*Cressida.* Upon my back, to defend my belly', *T. & C.*, I ii 261–263.

L. *defendere*, to ward off: cf., therefore **keep out.** (See **belly,** senses 2 and 3.)

defile. To pollute or violate (a woman). 'Pitch that defiles: defile! a foul word', *L.L.L.*, IV iii 3.—*Merry Wives*, I iii 94–96, '*Falstaff.* . . . His dove will prove . . . And his soft couch defile', where 'dove' is Ford's pretty wife.—'My bed he hath defiled', *All's Well*, V iii 298.—*Lucrece*, v. 787.

Ex M.E. *defilen*, 'to make foul'.

defiler. A man that pollutes a woman; hence, metaphorically, 'Thou bright defiler Of Hymen's purest bed!', *Timon*, IV iii 384–385.

defiling, n. Sexual defilement or pollution. 'She an eater of her mother's flesh By the defiling of her parent's bed', *Pericles*, I i 30–131.

deflower. To devirginate; to rape (a married woman). 'Let my spleenful sons this trull deflower', *Titus Andronicus*, II iii 191 and IV 26 (see *Tereus*) and V iii 38 (see **enforce**).—*R. & J.*, IV v 37.—'A deflower'd maid!', *Measure*, IV iv 22.—*Lucrece*, v. 348.

To deprive a girl (or a woman) of the **flower** of her chastity—properly, of her virginity (cf. **rose**).

degenerate. Effeminately unmanly. See first quotation at **loose.**

Lit., 'having lost the qualities of one's race; hence, having forfeited one's good qualities'. Contrast the etymological sense of *generous*: 'well-born'.

delight, n. and v. To afford sexual pleasure to; sexual pleasure. *Hamlet*: 'Man delights not me; no, nor woman neither, though by your smiling you seem to say so', II ii 314–316. (Only homosexuals could understand this passage as an implication that Hamlet was a homosexual.)—'Paris, you speak like one besotted on your sweet delights. You have the honey still, but these the gall', T. & C., II ii 142–144.—See quotation at **naked bed.**—'The shame that follows sweet delight', *Lucrece*, v. 357.—*Sonnets*, 36, v. 8.

Via Fr., ex L. *delectare*, 'to please considerably'.

demesnes. Cf. **park** and see the quotation at **thigh,** where *demesnes*, would seem to comprise the lap and *mons Veneris*, the pudend and the buttocks.

Demesne: Old Fr. *demeine*: L. (*terra*) *dominica*, the land belonging to a *dominus*, or lord.

den. Vaguely allusive to pudend (cf. **hole**) in the R. & J. quotation at **prick.**

desire, n. Amorous desire. '*Theseus*. Now, fair Hippolyta, our nuptial hour Draws on apace; four happy days bring in Another moon: but, O, methinks, how slow This old moon wanes! she lingers my desires Like to a step-dame', *M.N. Dream*, I i 1–5.— See quotation at **performance.**—See at **sinful fantasy.**— 'Keep you in the rear of your affection, Out of the shot and danger of desire', *Hamlet*, I iii 34–35.—T. & C., III ii 82.—*All's Well*, IV ii 34–35, 'Stand no more off, But give thyself to my sick desires'.—And elsewhere.

Ex the v., which, via Fr., comes from L. *desiderare*, 'to feel the lack of; to long for'.

desire, v. To desire (a person) sexually. 'Dost thou desire her foully for those things That make her good?', *Measure*, II ii 174–175.

devest. To unclothe (oneself). 'In terms like bride and groom Devesting them for bed', *Othello*, II iii 176–177.

dial. A clock's dial, or a sundial, is at least twice in Shakespeare the vehicle of a metaphor for the pudend. See the R. & J. quotation at **prick** and consider 'Dials the signs of leaping-houses' (1 *Henry IV*, I ii 9): in the former, 'the bawdy hand of the dial' is directly allusive to the lustful hand of the woman, and indirectly allusive to the penis, that, *erectus* at noon, is to be *inmissus*, in 'the dial'.

Dian. Poetic for *Diana*, 'chaste Dian', the huntress and goddess of the Romans; cf. next entry. 'She'll not be hit with Cupid's arrow,—she hath Dian's wit; And, in strong proof of chastity well arm'd, From love's weak childish bow she lives unharm'd', R. & J., I i 206–209.—M.N. *Dream*, IV i 74.— Allusively: *As You Like It*, III ii 1–4.—*All's well*, I iii 213.—*Coriolanus*, V iii 67.—'Thou ever young, fresh, loved, and delicate wooer, Whose blush doth thaw the consecrated snow That lies on Dian's lap', *Timon*, IV iii 386–388.—And elsewhere.

'Her name contains the same root as *dies* [day]', E. H. Blakeney: for further details, see my *Name This Child*.

Diana; Diana's priest. See **Dian.** 'If I live to be as old as Sibylla, I will die as chaste as Diana, unless I be obtained by the manner of my father's will', *The M. of V.*, I ii 107–109.—*Pericles*, II v 10 and v ii 17.—*Cymbeline*, I vi 131–132, 'Should he make me live like Diana's priest, betwixt cold sheets'. *Ibid.*, II iii 73.

die; die in a woman's lap. To experience a sexual orgasm. 'Benedick [to Beatrice]. I will live in thy heart, die in thy lap, and be buried in thy eyes', *Much Ado*, V ii 99–101.—Cf. quotation at **buried.**—'I will die bravely, like a smug bridegroom', *Lear*, IV vi 201.

Cf. the first quotation at **lap.**

dildo. A servant says that Autolycus is selling 'the prettiest love-songs for maids; so without bawdry, which is strange; with such delicate burdens of "dildos" and "fadings", 'jump her and thump her"' (*The W. Tale*, IV iii 193–196).

Ostensibiy, a meaningless word; but almost certainly with reference to the erotic sense, 'an artificial phallus'.

Webster suggests origin in *diddle-o*, with ultimate origin in O.E. *dyderian*, 'to deceive, to cheat'.

discharge. To effect a seminal ejaculation: 2 *Henry IV*, II iv 112–115, '*Falstaff*. Do you discharge upon mine hostess.—*Pistol*. I will discharge upon her, Sir John, with two bullets'; by a pun on *Pistol's* name. Perhaps also in T. & C., III ii 87.

Lit., to unload oneself upon.

disease, n. 1, Venereal disease. See **make the diseases** and the quotation at **Mitigation.**—*Henry VIII*, I iii 35–36.

2, A being cuckolded. Leontes, 'Many thousand on's Have the disease, and feel't not', *The W. Tale*, I iii 206–207.

Old Fr. *desaise*; with *ease*, cf. It. *agio*.

disedge. To take the **edge** off a man's sexual appetite. Imogen, apostrophizing her absent husband: 'I grieve myself To think, when thou shalt be disedged by her That now thou tirest on, how thy memory Will then be pang'd by me', *Cymbeline*, III iv 93–96.

dish; dish for the gods. (Cf. Pompey's 'Your fine Egyptian cookery Shall have the fame, I have heard that Julius Caesar Grew fat with feasting there', *A. & C.*, II vi 63–65.) Enobarbus, speaking of Antony in connexion with Cleopatra, 'He will to his Egyptian dish again': II vi 124; cf. Antony to Cleopatra, 'I found you as a morsel'—cf. the modern *tasty morsel*—'cold upon dead Caesar's trencher' III xiii 116–117.—*Ibid.*, V ii 274–275, 'A woman is a dish for the gods, if the devil dress her not'.—See at **way of women kind.**

For the semantics, cf. **eat, feed, stomach,** and the modern slang use of *dish* itself for 'an attractive girl'.

dishearten. See **hearten.**

dishonour, n. and v. Sexual dishonour; violation; seduction.—
To seduce or ravish; to seduce the wife of. 'Not palating the
taste of her dishonour', *T. & C.*, IV i 60.—'You have holp . . . To
see your wives dishonour'd to your noses', *Coriolanus*, IV vi
82–84.—*The W. Tale*, I ii 453–455, 'He does conceive He is
dishonour'd by a man which ever Profest to him'.—*Lucrece*,
vv. 1184–1185.

Contrast **honour,** q.v.

disport, n. Amorous play. See quotation at **toy,** n.

Ex the v. *disport* (for origin, see **sport,** v.).

distaff. see the quotation at **spin off,** where *distaff* almost certainly = the penis. Properly, a distaff is a cleft stick (generally
some three feet long) upon which either flax or wool used to
be wound for hand-spinning.

distain. To pollute sexually. 'Were Tarquin Night, as he is but
Night's child, The silver-shining queen he would distain',
Lucrece, vv. 785–786.

Cf. **stain;** also **defile** and **pollute.**

distempered blood. Blood detrimentally affected by lust or
ardent love. 'The hot passion of distemper'd blood', *T. & C.*, II
ii 169.

Distemper = 'to upset the right proportions of', *temperare*,
being 'to combine in due proportion': contrast **temperance,
temperate;** and see **blood.**

ditch-delivered. *Macbeth*, IV i 30–31, 'Finger of birth-strangled
babe Ditch-deliver'd by a drab': a whore's (or a beggar's
female companion's) child, born in a ditch.

diver. (Cf. **groping for trouts . . .**) A man regarded as a
diver into the pudend-pond of a woman. Charmian to
Cleopatra, in reference to Antony, ''Twas merry when You
wagered on your angling; when your diver Did hang a
salt-fish on his hook which he With fervency drew up' (II vv.
15–18).

do. (Of a man) to copulate with. 'I have done thy mother', *Titus Andronicus*, IV ii.—'What has he done?—A woman', *Measure*, I ii 84–85.

do it; do the deed; do the deed of darkness; do the deed of kind. To have sexual intercourse. 'Or if you like elsewhere, do it by stealth; Muffle your false love with some show of blindness,' *Com. of Errors*, III ii 7–8.—L.L.L., III i 195 ("do the deed": see quotation at **eye**).—*Ibid.*, v ii 24, 'Look, what you do, you do it still i' th' dark'.—*The M. of V.*, I iii 84, (of ewes and rams) 'In the doing of the deed of kind'.—*Hamlet*, IV v 60 (*do't*: see quotation at **cock!, by**).—*Timon*, IV i 8, 'Do't in your parents' eyes' (= sight).—*Pericles*, IV v 27–29, '*Bawd.* We have one here, sir, if she would—but there never came her like in Mitylene.— *Lysimachus.* If she'd do the deed of darkness, thou wouldst say.'

Cf. the nouns **act** and **performance.**

do naught with. To have sexual intercourse with (a woman). *Richard III*, I i 99–100, 'He that doth naught with her, excepting one [= the husband], Were best to do it secretly, alone'.

Cf. **business,** q.v.

do one's office. To render to a woman the sexual duty or service due from another man. "Twixt my sheets Has done my office', *Othello*, I iii 389–390.

Cf. **do it,** etc.

do the deed. See **do it.**

doe. A girl or a young woman. 'Single you thither, then, this dainty doe' (Lavinia), *Titus Andronicus*, II i 117.—Falstaff calls Mistress Ford his 'doe with the black scut': *Merry Wives*, V v 17.

Contrast and compare **deer.**

doer. A whoremonger, a fornicator. *Measure*, IV iii 20, Pompey, 'All great doers in our trade'. See **do.**

Doll Tearsheet. See **Tearsheet.**

dote. To love with an idolizing, passionate fondness. *Othello*, III iii 170.

Cf. Middle Dutch *doten* and Old Fr. *redoter*, (Mod. Fr. *radoter*).

dove. Girl or woman soft, gentle, loving and attractive: see second quotation at **defile.**

In *Hamlet*, IV v 166, Ophelia calls Hamlet her *dove.*

down. See quotation at **standard.**

down-bed. *Henry VIII*, I iv 18 (quoted at **confessor**). The pun is on 'a bed with a mattress stuffed with *down*', and 'a bed on which the compliant ladies would be asked to recline in order to give effect to their **penance**'. Also cf. **perfect in lying down** and:—

downright way. In 'They say this Angelo was not made by man and woman, after the downright way of creation', *Measure*, III ii 105–106, the phrase = reclining in order to coït: cf. the modern colloquialism, *get down to it*, 'to (lie down, in order to) coït'.

doxy. In Shakespeare's day, usually a beggar's woman or girl: but also, a paramour in general, or even a wanton. Autolycus, an itinerant rogue, sings, 'When daffodils begin to peer, With hey! the doxy over the dale', *The W. Tale*, IV ii 1–2.

'Origin uncertain', Webster. The *O.E.D.* proposes obsolete *dock*, 'a person's buttocks'; ex *dock*, 'an animal's tail' (cf. *tail*, senses 1 and 3): which is more than merely plausible, for cf., further, **wagtail.**

drab, n. A prostitute, especially one plying her trade in poverty. 'Dost thou deny thy father, cursed drab?', *1 Henry VI*, V iv 32.—*2 Henry VI*, II i.—'Must, like a whore, unpack my heart with words, And fall a-cursing, like a very drab, A scullion!': *Hamlet*, II ii 596–598.—*T & C.*, V i 99.—*Measure*, II i 236.— 'With die [= dicing) and drab [or rather, her earnings] I purchased this caparison', *The W. Tale*, IV ii 26–27.

Either ex or cognate with Erse *drabog*, and/or Gaelic *drabag*, 'slattern; prostitute'. Whence:—

drabbing, n. Wenching, womanizing, especially with drabs. 'Such wanton, wild, and usual slips As are companions noted and most known to youth and liberty.—*Reynaldo*. As gaming, my lord.—*Polonius*. Ay, or drinking, fencing, swearing, Quarrelliug, drabbing', *Hamlet*, II i 22–26.

draw, v. (Of a man) to expose (his sexual organ) by bringing it out, as if sword from scabbard: see quotation at **tool.**—The quotation at **pleasure.**

Of common-Teutonic origin; in several old Teutonic lauguages, *draw* = not only 'to pull, drag', but also 'to carry'.

draw up. (Of a woman) to receive, to incept (a man). Cleopatra, 'I will betray Tawny finn'd fishes; my bended hook shall pierce Their slimy jaws; and, as I draw them up, I'll think them every one an Antony, And say, "Ah, ha! y'are caught"' (II v 11–15).— In the quotation at **diver,** there may be a reference to male ingression or, rather, inmission.

dribbling dart of love. 'Believe not that the dribbling dart of love Can pierce a complete bosom', *Measure*, I iii 2–3. Ostensibly, the arrow shot by sentimental Cupid; ulteriorly there is a reference to the sexual sting of amorous passion. In euphemism, **dart of love** = penis; *dribbling* = apt to dribble or drip.

drudge. A willing lover—but applied rather to the penis than to the man. *Sonnet* 151: 'Proud of his pride, He is contented thy poor drudge to be, To stand in thy affairs, fall by thy side./No want of conscience hold it that I call Her "love" for whose dear love I rise and fall.'

dug, now applied only to animals, is by Shakespeare applied to a woman's nipple: *2 Henry VI*, III ii 393, 'The cradle babe Dying with mother's dug between its lips'.—R. & J., I iii 28 and 32–33: nipple and entire breast.

Etymologically, 'that with which one suckles'.

dull, stale, tired bed: *Lear*, I ii 13: a 'love-bed that has, through use, become uninteresting, the pleasure staled with custom and the body wearied with sexual intercourse.

dullness. Sexual torpidity and stupefaction. *A. & C.*, II i 27 (see **toy,** n.). The basic sense of *dull*, seems to be 'foolish, stupid'.

duteous to vices. Applied to that *cavaliere sirvente*, Oswald: 'A serviceable villain, As duteous to the vices of thy mistress As badness would desire' (*Lear*, IV vi 255–257).

eagerness. Sharp-set amorousness. 'Madding my eagerness with her restraint', *All's Well*, V iii 212.

Via Fr. *aigre*, ex L. *acer*, 'sharp', hence 'zealous, ardent'.

ear, v. 'He that ears my land spares my team', the Clown in *All's Well*, I iii 44, where *ear* = to **plough** (especially for corn), with implication of copulation.

Of common-Teutonic stock and cognate with L. *arare*, 'to plough'.

easy. Easy-virtued; readily accessible in the sexual way. '*Posthumus*. The stone's too bard to come by.—*Iachimo*. Not a whit, Your lady being so easy', *Cymbeline*, II iv 45–46.

Cf. **free** and **liberal.**

eat. To consume **flesh,** especially **mutton;** i.e., to have sexual intercourse. See quotations at **mutton** and **stomach.**—'*Apemantus*. O, they'—ladies—'eat lords; so they come by great bellies.—*Timon*. That's a lascivious apprehension', *Timon*, I i 208–209.

Cf. **meat, dish,** and the erotic **dumb glutton** (the vulva) for the semantics, which can also be apprehended in the **stomach** quotation.

edge, n. Sexual desire in a man, with especial reference to erection,—the semantics being: 'edge of sexual appetite'. *Hamlet*, III ii 265–269, 'H. I could interpret between you and your love, if I could see the puppets dallying.—*Ophelia*. You are keen, my lord, you are keen.—H. It would cost you a groaning to take off my edge.—O. Still better, and worse.'—See quotation at **motions.**—*The Tempest*, IV i 29.—'This bateless edge on his keen appetite', *Lucrece*, V. 9.

Of common-Teutonic stock (with sense of either 'edge' or 'point'): cognate with L. *acies*, 'point or sharp edge; hence, keenness'.

eel is erotic-suggestive of penis in 'Thunder shall not so awake the beds of eels as my giving out her beauty stir up the lewdly inclined', *Pericles*, IV ii 144–146; cf. the *double entente* of the erotically minded: *a snake in the grass* (a penis amid its circumambient hair): also cf. the entry at **conger.**

effect of love, the. The sexual fulfilment of love: copulation. 'I had him in mine arms With all th' effect of love', Mariana, referring to Angelo: *Measure*, V i 196–197. Cf. **effectual.**

effusion. Semen. *Measure for Measure*, III 30, 'The mere effusions of thy proper loins', where 'thy proper' = thine own.

Egyptian dish, his. See **dish.**

emballing. Old Lady to Anne Bullen (affectedly bashful), 'In faith, for little England You'ld venture an emballing' (*Henry VIII*, II iii, 46–47), where *emballing* is innuendo'd to = a *coïtus*. Cf. **brawl,** q.v.

embrace, v. To fold in one's arms, especially during sexual intercourse or sexual dalliance—see, e.g., the quotation at throbbing breast.— *Two Gentlemen*, I ii 129, 'Now kiss, embrace, contend, do what you will'.—See quotation at **strumpet,** adj.—*Much Ado*, IV i 48–50.—*Measure*, I iv 39.—And elsewhere.

Ex Old Fr. *embracer* (Mod. Fr. *embrasser*); lit., 'to enarm': L. *bracchium*, 'arm'.

embrace, n; **embracement.** A loving, an amorous, embrace, especially in reference to that which encircles a *coïtus.*, Volumnia to Virgilia, 'If my son were my husband, I should freelier rejoice in that absence wherein he won honour than in the embracements of his bed where he would show most love', *Coriolanus*, I iii 2–6.—'Clothed like a bride, For the embracements even of Jove himself', *Pericles*, I i 6–7.—See **hoop . . .** (for *embrace*).—*Venus*, v. 790 (-ment).

employ. To buy oneself, i.e. to be sexually intimate with (a woman); cf. the euphemistic *have something to do with*: *King John*, I i 98, 'Your tale must be, how he employ'd my mother'.

Via Fr. ex L. *implicare*, lit. 'to fold up', hence 'to iuclude'—to include for work.

empty vessel. '*Hostess*. One must bear . . .: you are the weaker vessel, as they say, the emptier vessel.—*Doll Tearsheet*. Can a weak empty vessel bear such a huge full hogshead?', 2 *Henry IV*, II iv 59–62: in reference to Falstaff; the implication that he may be genitally too big for Tearsheet.

Cf. **vessel,** q.v., and see **bear.**

enamonr'd. In love; infatuated: 'Methought I was enamour'd of an ass, *M.N. Dream*, IV i 78.—*Much Ado*, II i 156, 'He is enamour'd on Hero'.

Via Fr., ex L. *amor*, 'love'.

encounter, n. and v. A love-bout; to make love (with). 'I see our wars Will turn into a peaceful comic sport, When ladies crave to be encounter'd with', 1 *Henry VI*, II ii 44–46.—*L.L.L.*, v ii 32.—See **assail.**—See quotation at **press to death.**—'I will encounter darkness as a bride, And hug it in mine arms', *Measure*, III i 31–32.—*Cymbeline*, II v 19 (the n.).—See quotation at **lists of love.**

Lit., to come against; a coming-against, a meeting. (L. *contra*.).

encounterer. One (in the quotation, a woman) who encounters—hence, goes half-way to meet—love or lust. 'O, these encounterers, so glib of tongue, That gives a coasting welcome ere it comes, . . . set them down For sluttish spoils of opportunity And daughters of the game', *T. & C.*, IV v 58–63.

end has, for centuries, been used in bawdy innuendo to mean 'penis' or, less often, 'prepuce'. In *Measure*, I iii 2–6: 'Believe not that the dribbling dart of love Can pierce a complete bosom. Why I desire thee To give me secret harbour, hath a purpose More grave and wrinkled than the aims and ends of burning youth'. Compare a pun current in the late 1940's: 'He went away for a week-end and got a weak end'.

enforce. To violate (a woman: cf. **force** and **constrain**). 'She was enforced, stain'd and deflower'd', *Titus Andronicus*, v iii 38.— *M.N. Dream*, III i, 'Lamenting some enforced chastity'.—'Thy mistress enforced', *Cymbeline*, IV i 18.

To **force** (q.v.), with intensive prefix *en*.

enforcement. Enforced copulation. 'His enforcement of the city wives', *Richard III*, III vi 8.—*Lucrece*, v. 1622.

engender, 'to beget a child', occurs often in Shakespeare; e.g., *Timon*, IV iii 191.

Lit., 'to generate': cf. **generation.**

enjoy. 'It was Alençon that enjoy'd my love', Joan la Pucelle in 1 *Henry VI*, v iv 73.—'I speak no more than what my soul intends: And that is, to enjoy thee for thy love', 3 *Henry VI*, III ii 94–95.—'Now perforce we will enjoy That nice-preserved honesty of yours', *Titus Andronicus*, II iii 134–135.—'Out of heart you love her, being out of heart you cannot enjoy her', *L.L.L.*, III ii 44–46.—*R. & J.*, III ii 27–28, (Juliet) 'Though I am sold, Not yet enjoy'd'.—*Merry Wives*, II ii 254–256, Falstaff to Ford (purporting to be another), 'As I am a gentleman, you shall, if you will, enjoy Ford's wife'.—*As You Like It*, v ii 4–5.— *Othello*, I iii 326.—*Lear*, v iii 79, Goneril to Regan, 'Mean you to enjoy him?'—Cf. *Cymbeline*, II i 63.—And elsewhere, especially in *Venus* and *Lucrece*.

Etymologically = 'to give joy to' (now *joy*), it has long come to mean 'gain joy from'; via Old Fr., ex L. *gaudere*, 'to rejoice'; cf. **joy,** n. and v.

enraged. (Cf. **raging,** q.v.) 'Being so enraged, desire doth lend her force Courageously to pluck him from his horse', *Venus*, vv. 29–30.

Lit., 'made furious': French *enrager*: *en* + *rager*; L. *rabia*, 'raving, rage, fury'.

enseamed bed. A bed much creased (with violent love-making); *seam*, 'to furrow with wrinkles'. 'To live In the rank sweat of an enseamed bed, Stew'd in corruption, honeying and making love Over the nasty sty', *Hamlet*, III iv 92–95.

Perhaps better interpreted as a bed saturated with sweat— see *The O.E.D.* at *enseam*, v. 2—and soiled with sexual effusions.

entertaimnent. See **mutual entertainment.**

entice. To allure, to tempt, to wrong-doing or to sexual intercourse or to a combination of both. 'Bad child; worse father! to entice his own To evil should be done by none'. Induction (vv. 27–28) to Act I of *Pericles*.

Ex Old Fr. *enticier*, 'to set on fire' (L. *titio*, 'a firebrand'): C.O.D.: cf. **inflame.**

entreat. To beg amorously 'If for this might he entreat you to his bed, give him promise of satisfaction', *Measure*, III i 266–267.

Via Old Fr., ex L. *tractare*, 'to drag or draw'.

erection;, the, source of all erection. Mistress Quickly (an early Mrs. Malaprop), 'She does so take on with her men; they mistook her erection.—*Falstaff.* So do I mine, to build upon a foolish woman's promise', *Merry Wives*, III v 37–40.—(To a couple of whores) 'Plague all; That your activity may defeat and quell The source of all erection', *Timon*, IV iii 162–164.

A sexual distension and rigidity of the penis: 'the source' may, therefore, be either that organ itself or the testicles or the semen.

L. *erigere*, 'to put straight; to raise'.

eringo or **eryngo.** A root of sea-holly, supposed to be au aphrodisiac. *Merry Wives*, V v 18–22, 'Let the sky rain potatoes, let it thunder to the tune of *Green Sleeves*, hail kissing-comfits, and snow eryngoes; let there come a tempest of provocation, I will shelter me here. [*Embracing her.*]'.

Origin: a Latin shape of the diminutive of Gr. *errungos*, 'sea-holly', which may possibly be connected with:—

Eros. The Greek god (contrast Aphrodite, the goddess) of love: L. *Amor*, (and **Venus**). Referred to a score of times; e.g., punningly, 'Unarm, Eros; the long day's task is done, And we must sleep'; *A. & C.*, IV xiv 35–36: Antony, on hearing that Cleopatra is dead.

Gr. *éros*, '(physical) love; (sexual) desire'; cf. *éramai*, 'I long for, desire, love'. Perhaps ex, or cognate with, Aryan *aris*, 'filled with desire' (Wyld).

errors of the blood. ' "All my offences that abroad you see Are errors of the blood, none of the mind" ', says the woman-deceiving Adonis of *A Lover's Complaint* (vv. 183–184).

Errors = 'mistakes'; but there is also a reference to the etymological sense, 'wanderings'; cf. the phrase, *ranging blood*; and see **blood.**

eryngo. See **eringo.**

et cetera. Pudeud. 'O, that she were An open *et-caetera*, thou a poperin pear!', *R. & J.*, II i 37–38.

Lit., 'and the other things' (cf. **another thing**), this may be set beside the '——' ending of Sterne's *Sentimental Journey*: but see the entry at **medlar,** a medlar being slangily an *open arse*, (cf. physiologically, **loose**).

On a second reading, prompted by the reproaches of several friends and scholars, I conclude that the pun on *medlar*, slangily known as 'an *open-arse*', and *poperin pear*, shape-rcsembliug penis and scrotum, is so forcibly obvious that 'an open *et-caetera*', must here mean 'an open arse'. Yet my interpretation of Shakespeare's 'open *et-caetera*', as 'pudend' is correct, for the opening clearly refers to the female cleft, not to the human anus. With the human bottom regarded as involving and connoting the primary sexual area, compare the slangy use of *tail* for the human bottom in general and for the female pudend in particular. 'Open *et-caetera*', therefore suggests 'open cunt'—admissive organ—desirous girl. *The Shorter Oxford Dictionary* defines *medlar* as 'the fruit of the medlar tree, resembling a small brown-skinned apple, with a large cup-shaped eye between the persistent calyx lobes'. As a distinguished scholar has remarked, 'I thought the medlar had exactly the same symbolism as the cut pomegranate for the vagina, a tradition which Rossetti so openly employed in his painting *Proserpine*. . . . I think the association of medlar with the tradition of the cut pomegranate may be historically a real one.'

Note also, of course, that 'open *et-caetera*', fits the metre; 'open arse' does not. (I owe this reminder and several very valuable comments to Mr. Gershon Legman of New York City in a letter dated 14 November 1947.)

eunuch. (Cf. **capon.**) An emasculated male. 2 *Henry VI*, IV ii 161–163 (figuratively).—*Titus Andronicus*, VI iii 128.—*L.L.L.*, III i 196.— *Twelfth Night*, I ii 62.—*All's Well*, II iii 88–89, 'I would send them to the Turk, to make eunuchs of'.—*A. & C.*, I v 8–9, (Cleopatra) 'I take no pleasure in aught an eunuch has'.—And elsewhere.

From the Greek, *eunuch* is literally 'a bedchamber attendant': to be 'safe', he had to be castrated.

Europa. See **bull-Jove** and **hot-blooded.**

exchange flesh, to. (Generally of the woman) to coït. *The W. Tale*, IV iii 279–281, 'She was a woman, and was turn'd into a cold fish for she would not exchange flesh with one that loved her'.

For the semantics, cf. **fleshmonger** (and **whoremonger**) and the **trade, trader, tradesman** group of terms.

execute; execution. To perform, a performance of, the chief sexual act (cf. **performance**). For the n., see the T. & C., quotation at **act.**—'When my lust hath dined,—which . . . to vex her I will execute in the clothes that she so praised', *Cymbeline*, III v 26–28.

L. *exsequi*, to pursue to the end; to carry out, in a thorough way.

experiments. See **try experiments.**

eye. (For the semantics, cf. **O**; *eye* because of the shape, the garniture of hair, and the tendency of both organs to become suffused with moisture.) 'A whitely wanton with a velvet brow, With two pitchballs stuck in her face for eyes; Ay, and, by heaven, one that will do the deed, Though Argus were her eunuch and her guard', L.L.L., III i 193–196.

Cf. **naked seeing self,** q.v.

fading. 'The burden of a song': ostensibly, the commentators may be right; but I find it hard to believe that 'burdens of "dildoes" and "fadings"' (*The W. Tale*, IV iii 195: see full quotation at **dildo**) means 'burdens of dildoes and burdens (or refrains)': Shakespeare was not wont to be thus ineptly tautological, and the pairing of *fading* with *dildo* is suggestive, especially in conjunction with the next pairing of erotic terms. I propose that *fading* = *fading-away*, an orgasm–'death' (see **die**), normally accompanied by an amorous sighing and a steamy breath: *to fade* is cognate with L. *vapor*, 'steam, exhalation'. Or it may, as Webster implies, be connected with *fading*, 'an Irish dance' (cf. **dance**).

faint, adj. 1, Faint-hearted, timorous, in love-making. Following immediately on the quotation at **naked bed,** comes this: 'Who is so faint, that dares not be so bold To touch the fire, the weather being cold?', *Venus*, vv. 401–402.

2, As in 'He 'with his plenty prest, she faint with dearth' (faint with desire unsated), *Venus*, v. 545.

fair parts. In *A Lover's Complaint*, vv. 83–84, 'And when in his fair parts she'—Love—'did abide, She was new lodged, and newly deified', it is not merely possible, but (Shakespeare being ever sensual subtle) most probable, that the male generative organs are implied; probably all that is ostensibly intended is 'his handsome features and fine physique'.

fall, n. A woman's yielding to copulation, as in 'a fall off a tree' (*2 Henry VI*, II i).—See **wrestler.**

fall, v. (Of a woman) to fail from virtue, or from continence, to copulation or incontinence. See quotation at **take**

advantage.—'But I do think it is their husbands' fault, If wives do fail; say that they slack their duties, And pour out treasures into foreign laps . . .', *Othello*, IV iii 97–99.—*Henry VIII*, IV i 55–56 (concerning some countesses), 'Their coronets say so. These are stars indeed; And sometimes falling ones.'

Cf. **trip** and **stumble** and:—

fall backward. To fall, and then lie, on her back ('Then fell she on her back, fair queen', *The Passionate Pilgrim*, 4, v. 13): the time-honoured and most usual posture (*figura Veneris prima*) of a woman inviting or preparing for sexual intercourse. *R. & J.*, I iii, (to a baby girl) " 'Yea,' quoth he, "dost thou fall upon thy face? Thou wilt fall backward when thou hast more wit" '.— Cf. the quotation at **belly,** sense 2, and **downright way** and **perfect . . .**

fall in. 'Falling in after falling out may make them three' (*Troilus & Cressida*, III i 101) = falling into bed together as a proof of reconciliation has caused many a married couple to have an unplanned child.

fall to. Either it = the modem slang *fall for*, 'to take an amorous fancy to; to fall in love with' or it = to approach and accost sexually. 'She told the youngling how god Mars did try her, And as he fell to her, so fell she to him', *The Passionate Pilgrim*, 11, vv. 3–4.

false. Sexually unfaithful. Imogen, reading Posthumus's accusation: 'False to his bed! . . . I false! Thy conscience witness . . .', *Cymbeline*, III iv 41 . . . 47.—And elsewhere.

Probably cognate, derivatively, with Gr. *phelos*, 'deceitful'.

familiar, adj. Sexually familiar or on-coming: *T. & C.*, v ii 9 (see quotation at **sing**).—*Othello*, I iii 397–398, 'To abuse Othello's ear That he [Roderigo] is too familiar with his wife'.—*Lear*, v i 16.

Lit., 'on terms of family intimacy'.

fantasy. See **sinful fantasy,** and cf. **organs of fantasy.** Cf. also 'fancy' in *Lucrece*, v. 200.

father, v. To engender; also, acknowledge oneself the father of (see, eg., the first quotation of **bastard**).

favours, In reference to Fortune (the Roman goddess *Fortuna*), Hamlet, in II ii 234–235, says to the subservient courtiers Rosencrantz and Guildenstern, 'Then you live about her waist, or in the middle of her favours?'—See the second quotation at **allure:** here, *favours*, probably = breasts and thighs.

If a woman *bestows her favours on* or *grants the last favour to* her lover, she yields to his sexual importunity; what Hamlet implies, is therefore 'in that very area which is the goal of a lover's importunity': her sexual parts.

feasts of love. (A man says) 'Feasts of love I have been call'd unto', *A Lover's Complaint*, v. 181.—Cf. **revels,** q.v.

fee is used for 'fee of—reward consisting in—gratification of sexual lust' in *Titus Andronicus*, II iii 179–180, 'So should I rob my sweet sons of their fee: No, let them satisfy their lust on thee'.—*Venus*, v. 609 (see at **assay**).

feed, v. For the general idea, see the next two entries and cf. those at **eat** and **stomach.** 'Under her breast . . . lies a mole . . .: by my life, I kist it; and it gave me present hunger To feed again, though full', *Cymbeline*, II iv 134–138. (Cognate is 'When my lust hath dined', *Cymbeline*, III v 143.)—Venus to Adonis, 'Feed where thou wilt' (v. 232).

There is a combination of the idea of amorous roaming with that of feeling (cf. **taste**).

feed from home, to. To be false to one's wife. *The Comedy of Errors*, II i 100–101—see quotation at **break the pale.**

Cf. **feed,** q.v.

feeder. *A. & C.*, III xiii 109: see quotation at **leave a pillow unprest.**

Perhaps with an allusion to 'gross feeder'; certainly to be considered along with the two entries immediately preceding this, and with **eat.** Probably the sense is 'fornicator' or 'whoremonger'.

feel. '*Sampson*. Ay, the heads of the maids, or their maidenheads; take it in which sense thou wilt.—*Gregory*. They must take it in sense that feel it.—*Sampson*. Me they shall feel while I am able to stand: and 'tis known I am a pretty piece of flesh', R. & J., I i 24–28.

The same semantic idea—here again is Shakespeare the forerunner, perhaps the progenitor!—resides in the C.18 slang *old hat*, 'pudend' (because often felt), and the erotic stress on 'feeling', with the suggestive removal of the hyphen, in the C.20 fast girls' recast of the proverbial saying, a *fellow-feeling makes us wondrous kind*.

The word has an Aryan base that = 'to strike gently'.

fere. A companion; especially a woman and a bed-fellow. *Pericles*, Induction (v. 21) to Act I, 'This king unto him took a fere, Who died and left a female heir'.

O.E. *gefera*, a fellow-traveller (O.E. *faran*, to travel; to go).

fig me! '*Pistol*. When Pistol lies, do this; and fig me, like The bragging Spaniard', 2 *Henry IV*, v iii 117–118. A sexually allusive imprecation or adjuration—cf. *foutre*, on which it follows so closely.

Cf. the It. *fico*, used expletively by several Jacobean dramatists.

fill a bottle with a tun-dish. A tun-dish is a funnel: *bottle* = pudend; *tun-dish* = penis. Hence, the phrase = to have sexual intercourse. With reference to Claudio's arrest for lechery, '*Duke*. Why should he die?—*Lucio*. Why, for filling a bottle with a tun-dish', *Measure*, III ii 173–174.

fillip o' the head, to. To twit a person with cuckoldry, as in T. & C., IV v 45. The *head*, for there sprout the horns (see **horn**); cf. **brow** and **forehead**.

Fillip, (cf. *flip*) is probably echoic.

filthy. 'Dirty', smutty, impure, obscene. 'Ballads . . . sung to filthy tunes', 1 *Henry IV*, II ii 47–48.—2 *Henry IV*, II iv 126 (see first quotation at **know**).—'Ha fie, these filthy vices!',

Measure, II iv 43.—'*Fish Lady.* My lord, you take us even at the best.—*Apemantus.* Faith, for the worst is filthy; and would not hold taking, I doubt me', *Timon*, I ii 152–154.

Cf. **foul, greasy, muddy.**

finger, v.; **fingering.** To caress intimately (the vulgarism is 'to fingerfuck'); intimate caresses. 'You are a fair viol, and your sense the strings; Who, finger'd to make man his lawful music, Would draw heaven down . . . to hearken', *Pericles*, I i 81–83.—*Fingering*, occurs in the quotations at **penetrate** and **instrument.**

fire. Sexual ardour. 'Natural rebellion, done i' the blaze of youth; When oil and fire, too strong for reason's force, O'erbears it, and burns on', *All's Well*, V iii 8.—See quotation at **allure.**— *Tempest*, quotation at **dalliance.**—Several times in *Venus and Adonis*.

Cf. **ardour** and **heat.**

firk. To copulate; to copulate with. *Henry V*, IV iv 27–28, 'Pistol. Master Fer! I'll fer him, and firk him, and ferret him.'

Of dubious etymology, firk, probably, is partly from L. *facere*, and partly a euphemistic pronunciation of *fuck*. (Note that 'the firking thing!', often used in ignorance, is, in fact, 'the fucking thing!')

fish, n. A girl or a woman, viewed sexually; especially, a prostitute, as in R. & J., I i 29 (see quotation at **tool**).—Implied in **fishmonger,** q.v.

Cf. **cod's head** and **eel,** both of which are allusive to the male sexual organ, and **ling,** which—if the fish, and not the kind of heather, is intended—is as indubitably allusive to the female genitals. A fish is slimy.

fish, v., as used by Shakespeare, bears an erotic connotation: cf. the entries at **groping for trouts . . .** and **fishmonger.**

O.E. *fiscian*, 'to catch fish'; the n. is earlier, and it comes from a common-Teutonic root that is cognate with L. *piscis*.

fish nor flesh. reference to **fish** (n., as above) and **flesh** (as later).

'Why, she's neither fish nor flesh; a man knows not where to have her', 1 *Henry IV*, III iii 132–133.

fishmonger. A procurer; a pimp. *Hamlet*, II ii 73–76, '*Polonius*. Do you know me, my lord?—*Hamlet*. Excellent well; you are a fishmonger.—P. Not I, my lord.—H. Then I would you were so honest a man.'

A dealer in **fish;** cf. **fleshmonger.**

fit, n. and v. See **fitness.**

fit it, in L.L.L., IV i 129, like **fit,** v., in second quotation at **constable,** is probably allusive to copulation: see the passage (from 118 to near end of scene).

fitness; (to) fit. Suitability, aptness, aptitude for love-making; to coït with (a woman). 'Why should his mistress, who was made by him that made the tailor, not be fit [= fitted] too? the rather—saving reverence of the word—for 'tis said a woman's fitness comes by fits' (with pun on *by fits* = 'by fits and starts' and on *fit* = 'a fitting'), *Cyinbeline*, IV i 3–6, followed by 'Therein I must play the workman'.

flame, flames; flaming, adj. The physical ardour of conflagration of Eros-love or of lust; erotic, physically ardent. *Merry Wives*, V v 100 (see at **sinful fantasy**).—*Twelfth Night*, I v 262.—'To flaming youth let virtue be as wax', *Hamlet*, III iv 85.—'Girdle with embracing flames the waist Of Collatine's fair love, Lucrece the chaste', *Lucrece*, vv. 6–7.

Cf. **ardour** and **fire** and **heat.**

flax. Male pubic hair: see entry at **spin off.**

flesh. (Cf. **meat** and **mutton,** qq.v.). The flesh, hence the body, of a beloved woman or of a prostitute or plaything. 'Do nothing but eat, and make good cheer, And praise God for the merry year; When flesh is cheap and females dear, And lusty lads ream here and there', 2 *Henry IV*, V ii 18–21, where *roam* = to range, to be promiscuous.—In *All's Well*, I iii 27–29, '*Countess*. Tell me . . . why thou wilt marry. *Clown*. My peer body, madam, requires it: I am driven on by the flesh', *flesh* = 'the old Adam', man's carnal nature.—*Cymbeline*, I iv 135–137, 'If you buy ladies' flesh at a million a dram, you cannot preserve it from tainting'.—*The W. Tale*, II i 137. See also **pride** below

flesh one's will. (Of a man) to effect sexual ingression. 'He hath perverted a young gentlewoman here in Florence, of a most chaste renown; and this night be fleshes his will in the spoil of her honour', *All's Well*, IV iii 13–15, where 'will' probably = 'sexual desire': on the analogy of *flesh one's sword* (to thrust it into human flesh) and perhaps suggested by **sword,** q.v.

fleshmonger. One who trades in **flesh** (and especially in **mutton**); a wencher—on the analogy of the synonymous **whoremonger.** 'And was the duke a fleshmonger, a fool and a coward?', *Measure*, V i 330–331. (Cf. also **fishmonger.**)

flinch. to hold back in an amorous bout. Pandarus to Cressida, concerning Troilus, 'If my lord get a boy of you, you'll give him me. Be true to my lord: if he flinch, chide me for it', III ii 105–107.

The basic sense of *flinch* is 'to turn aside' (to the *flank*).

flirt-gill. A wanton, a light wench; a 'flirt-Gill' (flirtatious Gillian: cf. variant *Jill*, generic for 'girl' or 'young woman'). 'Nurse . . . I am none of his flirt-gills; I am none of his skainsmates', R. & J., II iii 155–156.

flower. The **rose** that is the maidenhead. '[I] threw my affections in his charmed power, Reserved the stalk, and gave him all my flower', *A Lover's Complaint*, vv. 147–148.

focative. See **fuck.**

foin, v.; **foining.** (Of a man) to copulate; copulation. *2 Henry IV*, II i 16 (see quotation at **stab:** with which compare the well-known (though undictionaried) proverb, 'A standing prick has no conscience'.—*Ibid.*, II iv 229–230, 'Doll Tearsheet [to *Falstaff*]. When wilt thou leave fighting o' days and foining o' nights . . .?'

Foin (ex Old Fr. *foisne, foine*, a fish spear), in fencing, is 'to thrust' (cf. **thrust, prick, stab** for the semantics).

folly. Sexual folly: wantonness, promiscuity; wildness. 'She turn'd to folly, and she was a whore', *Othello*, v ii 133.

A weakening of Fr. *folie*, 'madness', ex L. *follis*, 'bellows', and Low L. *follis*, 'an empty-headed person'.

fondling. Lovingly or lustfully caressing; or perhaps an amorous endearment in: (Venus, love-besieging Adonis) ' "Fondling," she saith, "since I have hemmed thee here Within the circuit of this ivory pale" ' (vv. 229–230).

From adj. *fond* + the frequent active suffix -*le* (cf. *handle*, ex *hand*). Ultimately of Scandinavian origin in a verb that has the basis sense: to act foolishly; hence, to dote.

foot, n. A copulation: copulation: obscurely at **yard** (first quotation).—See **coun.**

The allusion is to Fr. *foutre*, (of a man) to copulate with. See **foutre.**

foot, v. To copulate: Pistol, warning Ford against the amorous Falstaff's intentions towards Mistress Ford, 'Take heed; have open eye; for thieves do foot by night; Take heed, ere summer comes, or cuckoo-birds do sing', *Merry Wives*, ii i 121–122: foot, ostensibly, is 'to foot it' (to walk), but ulteriorly it represents the French *foutre* (cf. the preceding entry): *les voleurs d'amour foutent, la nuit, des femmes d'autrui.*

forbearance from sexual intercourse: see quotation at **pudency,** and cf. **abstinence.**

force, v. To rape (a woman). 'Forced in the ruthless, vast, and gloomy woods', Andronicus of Lavinia in *Titus Andronicus*, iv i 54; cf. quotation at **constrain.**—*Two Gentlemen,* v iv 58 and 59.—*Forcing,* adj.: see **violation.**—*Lucrece,* v. 182.

Lit., to apply force to; cf. **constrain.**

forefinger. 'As fit . . . as Tib's rush for Tom's forefinger, as a pancake for Shrove Tuesday' (*All's Well*, ii ii 21–24) = as suited, one to the other, as two things can possibly be. The bawdiness of 'Tib's rush for Tom's forefinger' emerges thus:

Tib, a pet-name for *Isabel*, is used generically for 'girl' or 'woman';

rush is short for *rush-ring*, a finger-ring made of rush; *forefinger* is euphemistic for 'penis'—which fact makes it clear that *rush* is here used for *ring* in the latter's sexual meaning, 'pudend';

Tib's rush for Tom's forefinger, therefore = copulation.

forehead, as the seat of a cuckold's horns (see **horn**): *Merry Wives*, IV ii 21–22; 'I have a pain upon my forehead here', *Othello* in III iii 284.

Cf. **brow.**

forfended place, the. Pudend. Regan, amorous, to double-crossing Edmund, 'But have you never found my brother's way To the forfended place?', *Lear*, V i 10–11.

Lit., the averted—the prohibited—place: cf. **secret parts** and **touch forbiddenly.**

forked plague. Cuckoldry. 'This forked plague is fated to us When we do quicken', *Othello*, III 276–277.

In reference partly to **horn,** q.v., and to the *fork*, that one finds in:—

forks, the. (Cf. 'a poor, bare, forkt animal as thou art', *Lear* III iv 110–111.) The fork or crutch of the body; cf. the slang phrase, *to get* (or *climb*) *on the old fork* (to coït), *King Lear*, IV vi 121–122.

Behold yond simpering dame, Whose face between her forks presages snow:

where 'forks' = buttocks and upper thighs, along with the gap between them (*les fourchettes*) and 'face' = the mons *Veneris*, and the pubic hair. She is growing old; the pubic hair whitens last on the human body.

Compare also 'He was . . . like a forkt radish' in *2 Henry IV*, III iii 320–321.

forkt one. One of the **horned herd:** a cuckold. Leontes to himself, 'Our head and ears a forkt one!', *The W. Tale*, I ii 186.

For the semantics, cf. **stag.**

fornication. Voluntary copulation between man (especially if unmarried) and unmarried woman. In *Merry Wives*, v v 159, Falstaff is charged with being 'given to fornications, and to taverns'.—See at **cardinally.**—'Claudie, Cendem'd upon the act of fornication', *Measure*, v i 70.—See the *Henry VIII*, quotation at **tool.**

Via Old Fr., ex Church Latin *fornicatio*, ex *fornicari*, 'to visit a *fornix* or brothel; to be a whoremonger'; *fornix* originally meant 'an arch' or 'a vault', many of the Roman brothels being in *vaults*, which, naturally enough, had *arched* roofs.

fornicatress. A girl, a woman, that fornicates. *Measure*, ii ii 15.

See preceding entry for the etymology.

fort. See quotation at **scale,** with which cf. 'this blemisht fort' (the female body) in *Lucrece*, v. 1175.

For the semantics, cf. **siege,** sense 1, q.v.

fortunate bed; fortune. (A bed as the scene of) happy love-making. 'Doth not the gentleman Deserve as full as fortunate a bed As ever Beatrice shall couch upon?', *Much Ado*, iii i 44–46.—'In your bed, find fairer fortune, if you ever wed', *All's Well*, ii iii 92–93.

Cf. *bonne fortune*, a love-bout, whether incidental or leading to a love-affair.

foul. Bawdy; obscene: see the quotation at **get the upshoot.**—For adv. (*foully*), see **desire,** v.—See **thump.**—Tarquin is 'full of foul hope' (*Lucrece*, v. 284).

Cf. **filthy** and **greasy.**

foul desire. Illicit lust. 'Why are yon sequester'd from all your train, ... And wander'd hither to an obscure plot, Accompanied but with a barbarous Moor, If foul desire had not conducted you?' *Titus Andronicus*, ii iii 75–79. Tamora, thus questioned, is, a few lines further on (109), called 'foul adulteress'.

Cf. **hot blood.**

foul-mouthed. Bawdy and scatological of tongue. Pistol is 'the foulmouth'dst rogue in England', *2 Henry IV*, ii iv 72.

foul thoughts. Lewd fancies and amorous plans. 'An index . . . to the history of lust and foul thoughts', *Othello*, II i 260–261.

Cf. **hot thoughts.**

fountain. Venus to Adonis (vv. 233–234), 'Graze on my lips; and if those hills be dry, Stray lower, where the pleasant fountains lie'. 'Lovely-breasted Ida': lovely-breasted Venus.

From *fountain* (L. *fons*, 'a spring, a river-source') = 'water-spring', to *fountain* = 'milk-spring or -source', is an easy semantic step.

foutre, n. As an imprecation: 'Pistol. A foutre for the world and worldlings base!', *2 Henry IV*, V iii 98; *ibid.*, v. 114, 'A foutre for thine office!'

Fr. *foutre*, 'to coït with (a woman)'. Pistol's 'a foutre for' has its exact equivalent in modem English vulgarism: *a fuck for!*

Foutre is from L. *futuere* (perhaps cognate with Gr. *phuteuein*).

frailty. Weakness in sexual matters. 'Though Page be a secure fool, and stands so firmly on his wife's frailty', *Merry Wives*, II i 222–223.—*Twelfth Night*, II ii 31.—*Hamlet*, I ii 145, 'Frailty, thy name is woman!'—*T. & C.*, IV iv 95–97.—*Othello*, IV iii 101–102, Emilia to Desdemona, 'Have not we affections, Desires for sport, and frailty, as men have?'—Elsewhere.

(The adj. *frail* occurs in *Cymbeline*, I vi 90.)

Via Old Fr., ex L. *fragilis*, 'easily broken or shattered'.

frame love, to. To devise and arrange a love-bout. 'She burnt with love, as straw with fire flameth; She burnt out love, as soon as straw out-burneth; She framed the love, and yet she foil'd the framing; She bade love last, and yet she fell a-turning', *The Passionate Pilgrim*, vv. 13–16.

Frame = to contrive, devise, make, elaborate.

free, adj. Of a woman that grants a man the freedom of her body; cf. **liberal,** which see for a quotation.—*2 Henry VI*, IV vii (near end).—See quotation at **unseminar'd.**

The origin, beyond O.E., is obscure: see *The O.E.D.*, Webster, Weekley, Wyld.

freeze. see **Priapus** and cf. **frosty.**

French velvet. See **piled . . .**

fresh. 'Your fresh whore', *Measure*, II ii 60: where there is probably a pun on two senses of *fresh*: new, hence not much shop-soiled; shameless (cf. German *frech* and the modern-slang use of *fresh* for 'impudent, cheeky').

Fresh, of common-Teutonic origin, is cognate with an Aryan word for 'to go' (cf. 'an oncoming girl') and with Gothic *fraiw*, 'seed; offspring'.

frosty. Sexually **cold.** 'He red for shame, but frosty in desire', *Venus*, v. 36.

I.e., frozen or as cold as, infected with, frost. Etymologically: *freeze* comes from an Aryan root for 'to burn': to touch an object that is extremely cold has much the same result as to touch one that is extremely hot.

fruit; fruits. 'The fruit within my womb', 1 *Henry VI*, v iv 63.—2 *Henry VI*, III ii 213.—3 *Henry VI*, III ii 58, 59, ('the fruits of love').—See quotation at **profit.**

fruitful, in quotation at **rain,** v., = fertilizing (male spermata fertilizing the ovaries).

fruition. Enjoyment: 1 *Henry VI*, v v 9, 'To . . . arrive Where I may have fruition of her love'.

fuck, occurring allusively in *focative*. 'Sir Hugh Evans. What is the focative case, William?—*William Page. O,—vocativo, O.—Evans.*, Remember, William; focative is *caret.—Mistress Quickly*. And that's a good root.—*Evans.* Oman, forbear', *Merry Wives*, IV i 42–47. That *focative* has been introduced for the sake of the punning innuendo is clear from the bawdy sequence—*O, caret* (punning *carrot*), and *root*; see **O, carrot, root.**

Fuck is probably one of the sadistic group of words for the man's part in copulation (cf. **clap, cope, hit, strike, thump,** and the modern slang term, **bang**), for it seems to derive from

Ger. *ficken*, 'to strike', as Klüge maintains. Probably confirmatory rather than contradictory is Sanskrit *ukshan* (a bull; lit., impregnator), which Bopp, in his *Comparative Grammar*, maintains to have originally been *fukshan*, (where *shan* = the agential *-er*): with cognates in Gr. *phutuein*, and Ger. *Ochse*.

full-acorn'd. See quotation at **mount**. Full-fed with invigorating food; hence, amorous. Cf. the modem phrase, *to feel one's oats*.

full of game. See **game, full of.**

fulsome. In heat; fired by, and submissive in, the act of breeding: *The M. of V.*, I iii 85, 'The fulsome ewes': see, too, the quotation at **rank** (vv. 79–80 of the same scene).

A specialization of the obsolete sense 'nauseating, disgusting' (ex the likewise obsolete senses 'copious' and, especially, 'excessive').

function. 'Even as her appetite shall play the god With his weak function', Iago in reference to Desdemona's sexual power over Othello: II iii 346–347: her appetite, like to Eros, god of physical love, shall exalt his passion and rouse him, merely a man, to godlike performance in love-making.

Function = activity, hence virility or potency.

fut. Foutre!: see quotation—most apposite—at **bastardizing.**

Ex **foutre,** n.

game, n.; mostly **the game.** Prostitution; promiscuous sexuality, or addiction to sexual intercourse. See quotation in next entry.

Cf. **disport** (and **sport**) and **toy,** n., and **play,** n.

game, daughters of the. Prostitutes; non-prostitute wantons. (See preceding entry.) 'O, these encounterers . . . That give a coasting welcome ere it comes, And wide unclasp the tables of their thoughts To every ticklish reader! set them down For . . . daughters of the game', *T. & C.*, IV v 58–63.

game, full of. Full of sexual **sport** and **toy**. *Othello*, II iii 20: cf. line 18, 'She is sport for Jove'. (See **game**.)

gamester. A prostitute, one who follows 'the **game**'. *All's Well*, v iii 184–185, 'She's impudent, my lord, And was a common gamester to the camp'.—'How long have you been at this profession . . . were you a gamester at five or at seven?', *Pericles*, IV v 72–75.

gate. The vulva. In conjunction with the quotation at **sluice,** take this:—'There's comfort in't, Whiles other men have gates, and those gates open'd, As mine, against their will', *The W. Tale*, I ii 196–198.

gay, in the senses 'sexually gay—wanton—promiscuous', is foreshadowed in Iago's ideal of a good woman: 'She that . . . Never lackt gold, and yet went never gay' (*Othello*, II i 149–151): *go gay* survives as a colloquialism.

geld. To emasculate. 2 *Henry VI*, IV ii (figuratively).—*Measure*, II i 231–235, '*Pompey*. Does your worship mean to geld and splay all the youth of the city?—*Escalus*. No, Pompey.—P. Truly, sir, in my poor opinion, they will to't, then'.—*Pericles*, IV v 125–126.—Quotation at **glib.**

From Old Norse; cf. *gelding*, 'a castrated horse', and **capon.**

gender. To procreate or to copulate: see quotation at **knot,** v.

generation. A begetting or engendering. Pandarus replies to Paris (see at **hot blood**), 'Is this the generation of love?', *T. & C.*, III i 130.—See second quotation at **bitch.**

Cf. **procreation.**

generation, work of. The act of breeding. (Of ewes and rams) 'When the work of generation was Between these woolly breeders in the act', *The M. of V.*, I iii 81–82.

See **generation** and **work,** n. and v.

genitive case is, in *Merry Wives*, IV i 49–54, taken to mean both 'generative case' and 'Jenny's case': see case. *Generative case*, is, naturally, that physical case which houses a generative organ: and *case* precludes the masculine one.

germen. (Rudiment—germ—of) a seed-vessel; the 'seed' itself— the fertilizing semen of a man. 'And thou, all-shaking thunder, . . . Crack nature's moulds, all germens spill at once, That make ingrateful man!', *Lear* III ii 6–9.

Medically, *germen* is an ovary (female reproductive element), *sperm* being the semen (male generative fluid): in the *Lear*, quotation, however, *mould* = 'matrix, womb', and *germen* 'the male seed'.

get. To beget. *Richard III* (see quotation at **unlawful**).—'He was gotten in drink', *Merry Wives*, I iii 20.—*T. & C.*, III ii 105.—See quotation at **increase.**—'When your sweet self was got', *All's Well*, IV ii 10.—*Measure*, III ii 119, 'Getting a hundred bastards',—Venus to Adonis, 'Thou wast begot; to get, it is thy duty' (v. 168).—And elsewhere.

Short for **beget,** which, in O.E., has basic sense 'to obtain': hence, to obtain (a child) from a woman's body.

get into corners. To segregate with a view to seduction or to mutual joyance. '*Lorenzo.* I shall grow jealous of you shortly, Launcelot, if you thus get my wife into corners', *The M. of V.*, III v 29–30.

Cf. **stair-work.**

get the sun of. See the quotation at **standard.** Ostensibly, to gain the advantage of the sun—i.e., of position; equivocally, to beget a son upon them (cf. **get with child**).

get the upshoot. L.L.L., IV i 134–136, '*Costard.* Indeed, 'a must shoot nearer, or he'll ne'er hit the clout.—*Boyet.* An if my hand be out, then belike your hand is in.—*Costard.* Then will she get the upshoot by cleaving the pin.—*Maria.* Come, come, you talk greasily; your lips grow foul.'

To receive a man's seminal emission.

get with child. 'At that time he got his wife with child', *All's Well*, v iii 299.—*Measure*, I ii 69–70.—*The W. Tale*, III iii 61–62, 'Getting wenches with child'.

Cf. **get** and the last quotation at **beget.**

getter; getting. Begetter; begetting. *All's Well*, III ii 41 (the latter: see **stand to**).—*A. & C.*, III xiii 107 (the latter).—'Peace is . . .

a getter of more bastard children than war's a destroyer of men', *Coriolanus*, v v 210–212.

getting-up. Either sexual penetration or impregnation: *The M. of V.*, III v 37–39, 'I shall answer that better to the common-wealth than you can the getting up of the negro's belly: the Moor's with child by you, Launcelot'.

gib-cat. An old tom-cat; with the implication of lost potency. '*Falstaff*. 'Sblood, I am as melancholy as a gib-cat or a lugg'd bear', *1 Henry IV*, I ii 76–77

An elaboration of *gib*, a tom-cat (especially if castrated) = Gib (hypocoristic for *Gilbert*), generic for any male cat.

giglot, adj. and n. Wanton. 'He answer'd thus, "Young Talbot was not born To be the pillage of a giglot wench', *1 Henry IV*, IV vii 40–41—*Measure*, v i 345.

Also *giglet*: connected with *gig* (M.E. *gigge*), 'a giddy girl; a wanton', the *-let* (or *-lot*), probably being the diminutive suffix. The radical sense of *gig* is 'anything that whirls or is whirled'.

give oneself. (Of girl or woman) to yield to a man's sexual desire. See last quotation at **desire**.—*Measure*, II iv 55 and 57 (*give up one's body*).

A euphemism of delicate-minded men (who *give* themselves at least equally) and of women that cloak their desires with the mantle of maidenly self-sacrifice.

glass of virginity. See **crack,** v.

glib, v.t. To castrate. 'I have three daughters . . . I'll geld 'em all; . . . And I had rather glib myself than they Should not produce fair issue', *The W. Tale*, II i 143–149 (where, by the way, *geld* is used in the rare application to women).

Webster adduces the Middle Dutch *lubben*, which is probably a cognate, and the now only dialectal *lib*, which, in this sense, has been common in M.E. and Mod. E. in sense 'geld'; *The O.E.D.* holds *glib* to be a corruption of *lib*.

globe. See **world.**

glove. See **Venus' glove.**

glow, v. To be warm with the ardour of love or the heat of lust. (Of Venus, passionately wooing Adonis) 'She red and hot as coals of glowing fire, He red for shame, but frosty in desire (vv. 35–36).

Of common-Teutonic origin, *glow* is cognate with the obsolete (and dialectal) *gleed*, 'an ember'.

glutton, adj. Amorous-greedy; having strong sexual appetite. See the quotation at **naked bed.** Cf. the *Venus* quotation at **surfeit,** v.

Ex the n., which, via Fr., comes from L. *glut(t)o*, 'a gormandizer', itself ex *glutire*, 'to gulp down', and cognate with *gula*, 'gullet, throat'; *glutire* may be echoic.

glutton-like. 'Now quick desire hath caught the yielding prey, And glutton-like she feeds, yet never filleth', of Venus as she hungrily kisses Adonis (vv. 547–548). Cf. preceding entry.

go. '*Charmian . . . O, let him marry a woman that cannot go, sweet Isis, I beseech thee!*', *A. & C.*, I ii 61–63. The sense is doubtful: but *go* must mean one of two things:—Either 'a woman that cannot **go to it**' (q.v.), i.e. cannot effectively copulate (unless she undergo the necessary operation); or 'one who cannot **come**' (q.v.). The latter is more likely: if *go*, bears this meaning, then *go* is probably elliptic for some such phrase as 'go all the way (with her sexual partner)'; modifying, or perhaps precising this fact, is the relation indicated at the end of the **come** entry (q.v.).

go-between (cf. **goer-between,** q.v.); **to go between.** A pandar; to play the pandar. 'I did go between them . . .; but more than that, he loved her,—for, indeed, he was mad for her', *All's Well*, v iii 255–257.

(One whose occupation it is) to go between—act as the intermediary of—a pair of lovers.

go in couples. See **stable** (below), 2nd paragraph.

go off. (See quotation at **Pistol**.) To discharge itself or oneself. '*Falstaff*. No more, Pistol; I would not have you go off here',

2 Henry IV, II iv 135, where the innuendo is that mentioned at **discharge,** q.v.

A pistol *goes off* when a bullet is discharged: cf. **bullets.**

go to bed. To have sexual intercourse: *All's Well*, v iii 260.—In *Pericles*, IV ii 101–103, masturbation is implied.—In *The W. Tale*, IV iii 105–106, it is used metaphorically of the marigold (bedding with the sun: pun on 'sun-down').

go to it. To copulate. See quotation at **lecher,** v. A few lines further on in *Lear* we find: 'Behold yon simpering dame . . . That minces virtue, and does shake the head To hear of pleasure's name,—The fitchew nor the soiled horse goes to't With a more riotous appetite' (IV vi 121–126).

See **it** and cf.—

go to work with. To embark upon a love-bout with (a woman). Allusively in *Measure*, v i 277–278, 'Escalus. I will go darkly to work with her.—Lucio. That's the way; for women are light at midnight.'

Cf. **go to it** and **work,** n. and v.

go with child. To be pregnant. *Richard III*, III v 85.

goatish. Lecherous. 'An admirable evasion of whoremaster man, to lay his goatish disposition to the charge of a star!': *Lear*, I ii 130–132.

See:—

goats; goats and monkeys! Goats and monkeys are Shakespeare's types of animal lechery. 'As prime as goats, as hot as monkeys', *Othello*, III iii 403; ibid., IV i 261, 'Othello. You are welcome, sir, to Cyprus.—Goats and monkeys! [*Exit.*]'

Cf. the entry at **monkey.**—*Goat* probably comes from an Aryan root meaning 'to leap' (cf. **leap**).

goer-between. A pandar. See second quotation at **pandar,** n., and cf. **go-between.**

goose. See **green goose** and **Winchester goose.**

gratify. 'She did gratify his amorous works With that recognizance and pledge of love Which I first gave her',

Othello, v ii 213–215: i.e., rewarded him with her sexual favours.

Via Fr., ex L. *gratificari,* 'to do a favour to': *gratus,* 'pleasant, pleasing' + *facere,* 'to make or do'.

grease. To render **greasy** or obscene; to defile. *Timon,* iv iii 195 (see quotation at **liquorish**).

Ex the n., which, via Old Fr., comes from the L. adj. *crassus,* 'fat'.

greasily; greasy. Obscene(ly). 'Come, come, you talk greasily; your lips grow foul', L.L.L., iv i 137.—*Merry Wives,* ii i 107, 'This greasy knight' (Falstaff).

great; great-bellied. Big with child. *Measure,* ii i 100 (the latter). Cf. **big.**

green, in Shakespeare and in many writers since, connotes 'vigour; virility; nubility', especially with a sexual undercurrent of implication. In L.L.L., I ii 83, Armando says, 'Green, indeed, is the colour of lovers'.

Green, of common-Teutonic stock, has the same base as that in *grass* and *grow*; growing grass is green; the Old High German *gruoan* = not only 'to grow' but also 'to grow green'. (Wyld.)

green goose. 'The spring is near when green geese are a-breeding', L.L.L., I i 97;, cf. 'This is the liver-vein, which makes flesh a deity, A green goose a goddess: pure, pure idolatry', L.L.L., iv iii 72–73: from the latter quotation, with its erotic sense of **flesh,** (q.v.), a *green goose* seems to be a fresh, young whore (for *goose,* 'prostitute', see **Winchester goose**). By Farmer & Henley, it is defined as 'a prostitute', *tout court.*

green sickness. *Chlorosis*–an anaemic sickness of young women (with consequent greenish complexion). The Elizabethan dramatists emblemized it as a sign of a girl's love-sickness, or of vague desire, for a man. R. & J., iii v 156, where Juliet is taxed with green sickness.

groaning. A woman's cry or groan of pain at losing her virginity. See the quotation at **edge.**

groom. Bridegroom. *The Taming*, III ii 150–151 and 210–211 ('a jolly surly groom').

groping for trouts in a peculiar river. Fishing in a private stream—copulating with a woman. 'Pompey. Yonder man is carried to prison.—*Mistress Overdone*. Well: what has he done?—*Pompey*. A woman.—*M. Overdone*. But what's his offence?—*P.* Groping for trouts in a peculiar river.—*M. Overdone*. What, is there a maid with child by him?': *Measure*, I ii 83–86.

Cf the low-slang *waterworks* (urinary organ) and **fish**.

gross. Lewd, obscene; (sexually) coarse. See quotation at **clasp**.

Gross: large; hence, very fat; hence, physically coarse; hence, indelicate.

grow to. See **smack**.

guinea-hen. A woman, a wanton; a whore, especially a courtezan. 'Ere I would say, I would drown myself for the love of a guinea-hen, I would change my humanity with a baboon', Iago to Roderigo (passion-sick for Desdemona): *Othello*, I iii 315–318.

The female to *peacock*: there is probably a sexual contrast to **cock**.

hackney, 'a horse for ordinary riding', is allusive for a woman in L.L.L., III i 32–33, 'The hobby-horse is but a colt, and you love perhaps a hackney'.

For the semantics, cf. **rider** and **hobby-horse** and **nag** (q.v.).

hair (cf. entries at **hare** and **hare-finder**) may be 'pubic hair' in the quotation at **heir** and in *Two Gentlemen*, III i 352–353, ' "She hath more hair than wit."—More hair than wit,—it may be: I'll prove it'; i.e., test it.—See **tale**, sense 1, where pubic hair is clearly meant.—In *Henry V*, III vii 61–62, a merkin (see Grose's dictionary) is alluded to.

half-blasted. See **blasted**.

half-worker. In 'Is there no way for man to be, but women Must be half-workers? We are all bastards' (*Cymbeline*, II v 1–2), the meaning is that women, thinks Posthumus, are not content with one man but must forever have a second sexual intimate.

With *worker*, cf. **work.**

hand in; hand out. 'An if my hand is out, then belike your hand is in' (L.L.L., IV i 135) is clearly—see the entire archery scene—a reference to a male hand caressively in or out of the placket-hole (see **placket.**)

handle, v.t. (Cf. **use.**) Concerning Falstaff, who has just died: '*Boy.* 'A said once, the devil would have him about women.— *Hostess.* 'A did in some sort, indeed, handle women; but then he was rheumatic, and talkt of the whore of Babylon', *Henry V*, II iii 37–41.—vbl. n., *handling*, 'caressing': *Henry V*, v ii 319.— *Measure*, v i 271–276 (punningly).

Lit., 'to use one's hands upon, to feel, to touch', it is a frequentative of *hand*; cf. **touch,** n. and v.

hang one's bugle in an invisible baldrick. '*Benedick.* That a woman conceived me, I thank her; that she brought me up, I likewise give her most humble thanks: but that I will have a recheat winded in my forehead, or hang my bugle in an invisible baldrick, all women shall pardon me', *Much Ado*, I i 223– 227. The relevant phrase = to set penis in pudend: for **horn,** 'penis', which has suggested **bugle,** see *The Taming of the Shrew*, IV i 25–27; cf. **pipe.** Hunting and music (though less than war) afford Shakespeare many sexual metaphors, puns, innuendoes.

happy nights. Nights happy with the physical expression of love. The Nurse to Juliet, 'Go, girl, seek happy nights to happy days', R. & J., I iii 108.

Cf. **fortunate bed.**

hard. (Of penis) in erection see the *Much Ado* quotation at **horn;** cf. *Henry V*, v ii, 303–308.

hardening of one's brows. A cuckolding. 'I find it,—And that to the infection of my brains And hardening of my brows',

Leontes, who fears that he is about to be cuckolded: *The W. Tale*, I ii 144–146.

See **brow:** Leontes means that 'horns' are growing upon his forehead: see also **horn.**

hare. A prostitute; a light wench. 'Mercutio. No hare, sir, unless it is a hare in a Lenten pie, that is something stale and hoar ere it be spent. [*He . . . sings.*] An old hare hoar, An old hare hoar, Is very good meat in Lent: But a hare that is hoar Is too much for a score, When it hoars ere it be spent', R. & J., II iii 135–142.

Probably punning **hair;** cf. the obsolete *cat*, 'a prostitute', and see **scut.** Hares and rabbits are notoriously repetitive in the act.

hare-finder. 'Cupid is a good hare-finder', *Much Ado*, I i 172: i.e. of light-wenches or, at the least, obliging wenches (see **hare**) and of the pubic hair (see **hair**).

harlot. A prostitute; a (very) loose woman. 'Tear the stain'd skin off my harlot-brow', *Com. of Errors*, II ii 135; IV iv 98 ('dissembling harlot') v i 205, 'While she with harlots feasted in my house'.—'Helen and Hero, hildings and harlots', R. & J., II iii 44.—(Following second quotation at **comfort**) 'Dwell I but in the suburbs Of your good pleasure? If it be no more, Portia is Brutus' harlot, not his wife', *Julius Caesar*, II i 285–287.—'The harlot's cheek, beautified with plastering art', *Hamlet*, III i 51; IV v 117.—*Coriolanus*, III ii 112.—*Timon*, I ii 67 and IV iii 79.—Leontes calls Polixenes 'the harlot king' (*The W. Tale*, II iii 4).

At first, masculine: 'a vagabond; a knave'. Via Fr., ex It. *arlotto*, 'a hedge-priest'.

harlotry. A harlot's trade; hence a pejorative adjective in 1 *Henry IV*, II iv 405, or a worthless woman (*ibid.*, III i 196); *Othello*, IV ii 235.

In the first reference, 'one of those harlotry players' means no more than one of these inferior—or even, perhaps, strolling—players; in the second, 'a peevish self-willed har-lotry' = 'a bitch'; in the third, 'He sups to-night with a harlotry' = '... with either a whore or, at the least, a very accommodating girl'.

harum. See **case.**

hatches. A nautical metaphor: see quotation at **boarding:** *hatches* cover cargo; hence, petticoats are presumably referred to, as covering women's cargo

have. To **possess** carnally. 'Was ever woman in this humour woo'd? Was ever woman in this humour won? I'll have her;—but I will not keep her long', *Richard III*, I ii 228–230.—R. & J., I iii 96.—See **fish nor flesh.**—*Cymbeline*, II iv 68.

Cf. **take.**

have a hot back. See **back . . .**

have (a woman's) **virginity.** To devirginate. 'Ask him upon oath, if he does think He had not my virginity', *All's Well*, V iii 182–183.

head. 'I will be cruel with the maids, and cut off their heads . . . Ay, the heads of the maids, or their maidenheads', *R. & J.*, I i 21–24; cf. *Measure*, IV ii 2–5, where *head*, in addition to meaning maidenhead, = the prepuce.

For *head* in reference to the horns of cuckoldry, see quotation at **horned.**

hearten and **dishearten,** 'to arouse (a man) sexually' and 'to abate his sexual urgency': see quotation at **provoke.**

heat, n. Amorous ardour; (of animals) rut. *Much Ado*, IV i 40–41, 'She knows the heat of a luxurious bed; Her blush is guiltiness, no modesty'.—See quotation at **affect.**—*Lucrece*, v. 706.—*Ibid.*, v. 1473, 'Thy heat of lust'.

heavier. 'Heavier by the weight of a man' and 'the heavier for a husband': *Much Ado*, III iv 25 and 32–33.

The same idea as that in **burden** and **buried . . .** and **load.**

heifer. A young woman engaged in harlotry or addicted to sexual looseness: see the quotation at **pagan.**—Cf. 'We must be neat;—not neat, but cleanly, captain: And yet the steer, the heifer, and the calf, Are all call'd neat', *The W. Tale*, I ii 123–125. Semantically cf **cow** and **bull**.

heir. 'Where France?—In her forehead; arm'd and reverted, making war against her heir' (*Com. of Errors*, III ii 19–121): *heir* puns *hair*, q.v.: her sexual parts fight against her intelligence.

hell, in *Sonnet* 144, 'I guess one angel in another's hell' = I suspect that my good male friend ('the better angel') is copulating with 'the worser spirit a woman colour'd ill'. Not impossibly, Shakespeare here alludes to the famous Boccaccio story of 'putting the devil in hell'.

hen. Wife; bed-partner. '*Katharina*. What is your crest? a coxcomb?—*Petruchio*. A combless cock, so Kate will be my hen.—*Katharina*. No cock of mine; you crow too like a craven', *The Taming*, II i 223–225.—*1 Henry IV*, III iii 54–55, 'Enter Hostess. [*Falstaff*]. How now, Dame Partlet the hen!'

herb-woman, in *Pericles*, IV v 86–87, is used allusively of a bawd.

herd, See **horned.**

hick and hack, to: *Merry Wives*, IV i 57–58: apparently = 'to womanize and to copulate'.

hillock. Venus, describing the 'park' that is her body, speaks of 'Sweet bottom-grass, and high delightful plain, Round rising hillocks, brakes obscure and rough' (*Venus*, vv. 236–237): not the breasts (for see quotation at **fountain**), but the posteriors: neither art nor myth is wholly silent on the theme of 'the callipygal Cytherean'. Shakespeare uses *hill* of the lips (*Venus*, v. 234).

hit, v.t. To copulate with (a woman): cf. *strike, thump,* and the modern low-slang term 'to bang' (a woman), and *fuck* itself. Allusively in quotation at **hit lower.** By implication in that at **hit it.** Costard's 'hit the clout' (*L.L.L.*, IV i 134) alludes to a pudend-cover.—*R. & J.*, I i 205–206.—See **swell.**—See **blackness.**

Hit, however, is as much a metaphor from archery as it is a

piece of sadism, whereas *cope, fuck, strike, thump* are clearly sadistic.

hit it. To attain the sexual target of the pudend. The *locus classicus* is the shooting-match in L.L.L., IV i, especially in vv. 118–130, where *hit it* is punned-on and mercilessly elaborated.—Cf. 'If love be blind, love cannot hit the mark' (effect inmission), R. & J., II ii 33.

See also **hit.**

hit lower. To attain sexually to the pudend (see **hit** and cf. **low-countries**). L.L.L., IV i 116–118, 'Maria . . . She strikes at the brow.—*Boyet*. But she herself is hit lower: have I hit her now?'

hit the mark. See **hit it.**

hoar. See **whore.**

hobby-horse. A wanton; a mistress. 'This is some minx's token . . . There,—give it your hobby horse', *Othello*, IV i 153–155; *The W. Tale*, I ii 275, 'My wife's a hobby-horse'. A hobby-horse is a rocking-horse: the sexual innuendo and pun are clear: *horse*, because it is ridden (see **horse** and **ride, rider,** and cf. **leap, mount, vault**); the 'rocking' element refers to female movement *in coitu*.

Cf. **hackney** and **nag.**

hold at a bay. To keep off a man from sexual intimacy. *The Taming*, V ii 56, ''Tis thought your deer does hold you at bay'.

I.e., to hold him off as a stag so faces and frightens the hounds that they bite not, but merely bark (*bay* is a deep bark or barking).

hold-door trade, the. Prostitution,—prostitutes lounging at brothel-doors to attract customers. 'Brethren and sisters of the hold-door trade', *T. & C.*, V x 51.

hole is still a vulgarism for 'pudend'. *Two Gentlemen*, II iii 17–19, 'This left shoe is my mother . . . it hath the worser sole. This shoe, with the hole in it, is my mother, and this my father; a vengeance on't!'—R. & J.: see **occupy.**

Cognate with *hollow* and *hell*, it is a shape-metaphor: of

circle and **ring.** During the war of 1914–18, one of Bairns-father's most famous cartoons became a catch-saying among those lower-class women who were willing to 'oblige' amorous soldiers: 'If you know of a better hole, (then) go—or you can go—to it!'

holland. The anal area. 'The rest of thy low-countries have made a shift to eat up thy holland', 2 *Henry IV*, II ii 22–24 (in ostensible reference to linen).

Cf. **low-countries** and **Netherlands,** qq.v., the pun being *Holland: Hole Land.*

holy puns 'holey' (see **hole**), both in **holy-thistle** and in the Clown's 'Faith, I have other holy reasons' (for marriage): see the passage at I iii 27–33 in *All's Well*; cf. quotation at **broach** and the entry at **wholly.**

holy-thistle. A kind of thistle, with a double innuendo in *Much Ado*, III iv 67–74, '*Margaret*. Get you some of this distill'd Carduus Benedictus, and lay it to your heart: it is the only thing for a qualm.—*Hero*. There thou prick'st her with a thistle.—*Beatrice*. Benedictus! Why Benedictus? you have some moral in this Benedictus.—*Margaret*. Moral! no, by my troth, I have no moral meaning: I meant, plain holy-thistle': where the innuendo may best be conveyed in the punning equivalent, 'holy prick' (see **hole** and **prick** n.).

honesty. Sexual virtue. 3 *Henry VI*, III ii 72–73, 'Why, then mine honesty shall be my dower; For by that loss I will not purchase them'.—See third quotation at **enjoy.**—*Hamlet*, III i 110.—See *A. & C.* quotation at **lie,** v.—And elsewhere.

So too **honest** (sexually virtuous), as in the *Merry Wives*, II i 227; *Hamlet*, III i 103; *Othello, passim.*

L. *honestus*, honourable.

honey, n. and v. The sweets of sexual pleasure; to indulge in sticky caresses. 'But when ye have the honey ye desire, Let not this wasp outlive, us both to sting', Tamora to her raping sons, *Titus Andronicus*, II iii 131–132.—The v. occurs in *Hamlet*, III iv

94 (see **enseamed bed**).—See second quotation at **delight**.—
Venus, v. 16, the adj. (see **secrets**).—*Lucrece*, v. 493, 'I know
what thorns the growing rose defends; I think the honey
guarded with a sting'; cf. v. 836.

Cf. **bliss**, q.v.

honour. 1, Female chastity: L.L.L., v ii 351, 'By my maiden
honour'.

2, In Shakespeare, *honour* or *honourably* is used at least twice to
convey a bawdy pun on the element *on* ('honour'): sexual (see
on) in *Much Ado*, iii iv 27 (taken in conjunction with the four
preceding lines); 'fundamental' in *Hamlet*, ii ii 398–401, the
quotation at *buz*.—Shakespeare, therefore, supplies the proto-
type of the catch-story, 'He married for honour: and he got
honour', as he is of so many other modern bawdinesses.

honour-flawed. (Of a woman) that has yielded her chastity-
honour. *The W. Tale*, ii i 142.

See **honour**, sense 1.

honourable; honourably. *Much Ado*, iii iv 27–29 (Essay, section 4). See **honour**, sense 2.

hook, n. In the quotation at **draw up,** *hook* may connote 'sexual
allurement' or even 'pudend'; in that at **diver,** *hook* probably
innuendoes 'penis'.

For the semantics of the latter sense, cf **cock;** of the former,
cf. **circle.**

hoop with embraces, to. To encircle, lovingly or amorously,
with one's arms. 'If ever henceforth thou . . . hoop his body
more with thy embraces', *The W. Tale*, iv iii 440–442.

Cf. **chain.**

horn. Penis (especially, *penis erectus*); but mostly the horns of
cuckoldry. 'Had I the power that some say Dian had, Thy
temples should be planted presently With horns, as was Actaeon's', *Titus Andronicus*, ii iii 61–63, and also in iv iii.—*Two
Gentlemen*, i i 79.—L.L.L., vi i (several times); v i 46–49 (and
after).—*M. N. Dream*, v i 230–234.—*The Taming*, iv i 25–27 (see

the entry at **three-inch fool:** the penis sense).—*Ibid.*, v ii 41.—2 *Henry IV*, I ii 48–50, 'He hath the horn of abundance, and the lightness of his wife shines through it'.—*Much Ado*, II i 25–26.—' "Scorn", "horn",—a hard rime', *ibid.*, v ii 38–39, with reference to priapism; *ibid.*, v iv 122–124 (ditto).—*Merry Wives*, several times (of cuckoldry).—*As You Like It*, IV ii 13–18 (*penis erectus*).—*T. & C.*, I i, in IV v 31 and 46, both senses occur.—*A. & C.*, I ii 4–5.—And elsewhere.

The horns arise from the legend of amorous Jove self-transformed to the likeness of a bull: *T. & C.*, v i 52–54.

horn-mad. Passionately angry at having been cuckolded. 'Why, mistress, sure my master is horn-mad.—*Adriana*. Horn-mad, thou villian!—*Dromio*. I mean not cuckold-mad', *Com. of Errors*, II i 57–58.—In Claudio's 'If this should ever happen, thou wouldst be horn-mad' (to Benedick scorning marriage), there may be the further implication, 'extremely amorous', with an allusion to the 'penis' sense of *horn*.—*Merry Wives*, I iv 49; cf. III v 148.

horn-maker. Causer of cuckoldry. 'Virtue is no horn-maker', *As You Like It*, IV i 61.

See **horn** and cf. **cuckold-maker.**

horned; horned herd. (Cf. 'They may jowl horns together, like any deer i' th' herd', *All's Well*, I iii 55–56.) Cuckolded; cuckolds in general. '*Iago*. Have you not hurt your head?—*Othello*. Dost thou mock me? . . . A horned man's a monster and a beast.—*Iago*. There's many a beast, then, in a populous city, And many a civil monster': IV i 60–65.—*A. & C.*, III xiii 126–128, 'O, that I were upon the hill of Basan, to outroar the horned herd!'

See **horn.**

horning, n. An effecting of cuckoldry. Cf, first quotation at **horn** with ''Tis thought you have a goodly gift in horning', Lavinia to the adulterous Tamora (*Titus Andronicus*, II iii 67).

horns. See **horn.**

horse, v. (Cf. **colt.**) To **mount** a woman—as though she were a horse. See quotation at **stew,** where *horsed* = provided with a woman-mount.—In transferred sense, Leontes, in reference to his wife Hermione and his friend Polixenes, speaks of their 'horsing foot on foot' (*The W. Tale,* I ii 287).

    Cf. also **hackney, hobby-horse,** and **nag.**

horsemanship. (Cf. **ride, rider,** q.v.) From the man's point of view: sexual intercourse: *Henry V,* III vii 56, the relevant passage being quoted in the Essay.

    For semantics, cf. also **leap, mount, vault.**

horum. See **case.**

hot. Amorous; sexually eager; ardent; appetent. In reply to Talbot's, 'Damsel, I'll have a bout with you again', Joan of Arc says, 'Are yet so hot, sir?' (1 *Henry VI,* III ii 59).—Quotation at **Spain.**—'My master is become a hot lover', *Two Gentlemen,* II v 46.—*R. & J.,* II iv 63, the Nurse to Juliet, 'Are you so hot?' (so amorous-eager to have news of Romeo).—'The blessed sun himself a hot fair wench in flame-colour'd taffeta', 1 *Henry the Fourth* I iii 10.—See **violation.**—'The hot passion of distempered blood', *T. & C.,* II ii 169.—'As hot as monkeys': see at **prime.**—*A. & C.,* III xiii 118–120, 'Besides what better hours, Unregister'd in vulgar fame, you have Luxuriously pickt out'.—See quotation at **mingle bloods.**—See that at **stair-work.**—The second at **stark-naked.**

    Passion heats the blood, inflames the cheeks; the opposite is **cold.**

hot back. See **back, have a hot.**

hot blood. Blood heated by amorous desire (cf. next entry). 'He eats nothing but doves, love; and that breeds hot love, and hot love begets hot thoughts, and hot thoughts beget hot deeds, and hot deeds is love', *T. & C.,* III i 126–129.

    See **hot** and cf. **blood.**

hot-blooded. Amorous; lecherous. *Merry Wives,* V v 2–4, '*Falstaff.*

Now, the hot-blooded gods assist me!—Remember, Jove, thou wast a bull for thy Europea; love set on thy horns.'

hot deeds. Amorous acts. See quotation at **hot blood.**

Cf. **deed . . .,** q.v.

hot dreams. Amorous dreams. Iachimo, referring to Posthumus and Imogen, 'He spake of her, as [though] Dian had hot dreams, And she alone were cold', *Cymbeline,* v v 180–181.

Cf. **offend in a dream.**

hot-house. A brothel. '. . . A bad woman; whose house, sir, was . . . pluck'd down in the suburbs; and now she professes a hot-house, which, I think, is a very ill house too', *Measure* II i 63–66.

For *hot,* cf. **stew** and the C. 18 *bagnio* (properly, Turkish baths).

hot thoughts. Thoughts or imaginings of physical love; amorous longings. See quotation at **hot blood.**

hotly. Amorously; lasciviously. See quotation at **lust,** v., and that at **burning eye.**

hour of love, an. A short period of love-making. The phrase has been trivialized in cheap novels and 'romantic' films. 'Come, Desdemona, I have but an hour Of love, of worldly matters and direction, To spend with thee', *Othello,* I iii 299–301; cf. 'Love and her soft hours' (*A.* & *C.,* I i 44).

house of profession; house of resort; house of sale. A brothel; the second phrase is generally applied to a better-class one. ' "I saw him enter such a house of sale",—Videlicet, a brothel', *Hamlet,* II i 60–61.—'Shall all our houses of resort in the suburbs be pull'd down?', *Measure,* I ii 98–99.—Ibid., IV iii 1–4, Pompey (the pimp), 'I am as well acquainted here as I was in our house of profession: one would think it were Mistress Overdone's own house, for here be many of her old customers'.

Cf. also **bawdy house** and **naughty house.**

hug, v. To embrace closely or amorously. See quotation at **strumpet,** adj.—See *Measure* quotation at **encounter.**—

'*Apemantus*, Thy flatterers ... Hug their diseased perfumes' (their whores, infected with venereal disease), *Timon*, IV iii 206–207.

Origin obscure; *hug* may be cognate with Icelandic *hugga*, 'to soothe or comfort' (Wyld).

hunger. Synonymous with **appetite** and **desire.** See quotation at **feed.**

hungerly. Hungrily: in the manner of one who is sating a sexual appetite. See quotation at **stomach.**

hungry. Avidly amorous: see quotation at **cloy.**

husband, v. To be a husband to, to be as a husband to, with especial reference to sexual intercourse. See **husband her bed.**—*Lear*, V iii 71, Goneril to Regan, in reference to Edmund, '. . . If he should husband you'.

Cf. **man,** q.v.

husband her bed. To be a potent husband in a woman's bed. 'You shall as easy Prove that I husbanded her bed in Florence', *All's Well*, V iii 125–126.

Cf.:—

husbandry. In 'Her plenteous womb Expresseth his full tilth and husbandry', *Measure*, I 42–43, and in the quotation at **unear'd,** we have the seeding-cultivation-harvesting metaphor so common in Shakespeare when he wishes to speak of semen-sowing and sexual **tillage.**

Hymen. The Greek and Roman god of marriage. *As You Like It*, V iv 145–148, ''Tis Hymen peoples every town; High wedlock, then, be honoured: Honour, high honour, and renown, To Hymen, god of every town'.—*Pericles*, Induction (vv. 9–11) to Act III, 'Hymen hath brought the bride to bed, Where, by the loss of maidenhead, A babe is moulded'.

Hymen comes from the Greek for 'membrane' (especially that which constitutes the maidenhead, still known medically as the *hymen*). Or perhaps—see my *They Came to Stay*—the 'membrane' sense derives from the Proper Name.

immaculate. Spotlessly pure, especially in regard to sex; undefiled, unspotted (*virgo immaculata*, as in 1 *Henry VI*: see first quotation at *chaste*).

Lit., 'unspotted': contrast, therefore, **spot**, q.v.

impudently; impudent. Sexual shamelessness or forwardness; forward or shameless. *All's Well*, II i 172–174, 'Tax of impudence,—A strumpet's boldness, a divulged shame,—Traduced by odious ballads'.—*Ibid.*, IV iii 325 (the adjective).

L. *impudens*, lacking shame (*pudere*, to feel shame).

in, be. See **out.**

incest. Sexual intercourse between father and daughter, or mother and son, or brother and sister; formerly also with deceased husband's brother or deceased wife's sister. See first quotation in next entry. Also in *Hamlet*: 'Let not the royal bed of Denmark be A couch for luxury and damned incest' (I v 82–83).—'Is't not a kind of incest, to take life From thine own sister's shame?', *Measure*, III i 135–136.—*Pericles*, 'Her to incest did provoke', Act I, Induction, v. 26; and elsewhere in the play.

Probably, L. *incestum*, 'an unchaste thing': a notion that seems to go back to a time when all other sexual intercourse was freely allowable.

incestuous; incestuous sheets. Hamlet, of his mother, 'O, most wicked speed, to post With such dexterity to incestuous sheets!': I ii 155–156.—*Ibid.*, III iii 90, 'Th' incestuous pleasure of his bed'.—*Ibid.*, V ii 334.—*Lear*, III ii 55.—And elsewhere.

See **incest.**

inclined. Inclined or disposed to love-making; as in *Macbeth*, IV iii 74–76, in reference to Malcolm's self-imputed lust.

Incline; via Old Fr. *encliner*, 'to cause to lean; to bend'. Cf. 'Incline our hearts to keep this law'.

incontinency; incontinent. Inability—unable—to resist sexual appetite. 'They made a pair of stairs to marriage, which they will climb incontinent, or else be incontinent before marriage', *As You Like It*, v ii 39–41.—'You must not put another scandal on him, That he is open to incontinency', *Hamlet*, ii i 29–30.—T. & C., v i 100 (the adj):—*Timon*, iv i 3, 'Matrons, turn incontinent!'—*Cymbeline*, ii iv 127, 'Her incontinency'.

Its etymological force—see also **continence**—appears best in its medical sense: 'inability to hold one's urine'; hence, 'inability to resist the semen-urge'.

increase, n. Increase of population, with direct or indirect allusion to sexual intercourse. *All's Well*, i i 127–129, 'Loss of virginity is rational increase; and there was never virgin got till virginity was first lost'—a theme elaborated, several times, in the Sonnets.—*Coriolanus*, iii iii 115.—*Venus* cleverly turns this argument on the beautiful Adonis, but she was wasting her time.

The basic sense of *increase* is 'growth' (L. *crescere*, to grow).

incurable bone-ache. See **Neapolitan bone-ache.**

infinite malady, the. (Cf. preceding entry and **malady of France.**) 'Of man and beast the infinite malady Crust you quite o'er!', *Timon*, iii vi 97–98. Not certainly = venereal disease; perhaps = leprosy, or some similar disease.

inflame; inflamed with Venus; inflaming. To kindle—kindled—kindling—with love. 'My tender youth was never yet attaint With any passion of inflaming love', 1 *Henry VI*, v v 81–82.—'His heart Inflamed with Venus', T. & C., v ii 165–166.—See second quotation at **act.**—*Pericles*, i i 20.—'Tarquinius being inflamed with Lucrece's beauty', *Lucrece*, Argument.—*A Lover's Complaint*, vv. 268–270.

Cf. **flame,** q.v.

insatiate. Sexually insatiable. *Richard III*, iii v 36, 'My mother went with child Of that insatiate Edward'; cf. iii vii 7, 'Th' insatiate greediness of his desires'.

The opposite is **satiate,** q.v.

inside lip, with. 'Kissing with inside lip', *The W. Tale*, i ii 285.

Either: with parted lips alternating thus: male, female, male, female (or vice-versa); or: a kiss that is either singly or reciprocally lingual. How like Shakespeare to deliberately leave his audience guessing!

instrument. (Cf. **organ** and **tool.**) Hortensio, amorous wooer in guise of music-teacher, says to Bianca, 'Madam, before you teach the instrument, To learn the order of my fingering, I must begin with rudiments of art', *The Taming*, III I 64–66: by innuendo, 'instrument' here = penis.

Cf. the entry at **finger.**

intemperance; intemperate. Loose living; unbridled. 1 *Henry IV*, III ii 156 (the former); *Much Ado*, IV i 59, 'Intemperate in your blood'.—*Macbeth*, IV iii 66, 'Boundless intemperance'.

The opposite is **temperance,** q.v. for etymology.

Ireland. Posteriors; or perhaps rather the urinary and defecatory organs of woman. 'In what part of her body stands Ireland?—Marry, sir, in the buttocks: I found it out by the bogs', *Com. of Errors*, III ii 114–116 (the passage on the geography of a woman's body). Grose, in his *Classical Dictionary of the Vulgar Tongue*, 1785, calls Ireland 'the Urinal of the Planets', because of its wet climate. In this Shakespearean passage, however, the clue is 'the bogs', for *Bogland* and *Boglanders* are very old names for Ireland and her people.

it. Sexual intercourse. ' "Had women been so strong as men, In faith, you had not had it then" ', *The Passionate Pilgrim: Sonnets to Music*, 4, vv. 23–24.

itch, n.; **itches.** A skin-disease or -irritation. In the quotation at **blain,** the itches are those which spring from some venereal disease.

itch, v. To have a sexual itch—(usually fugitive) amorous desire. See quotation at **scratch** and cf. the noun **itch.**

jade. See the quotation at **bear.**

A jade, here, is a worn-out stallion; hence, a **surfeit-**

exhausted man. (The usual sense is 'a battered, peevish, woman of little reputation'.) Kate's imputation is that Petruchio is insufficiently virile to be worthy to **ride** her.

Ex Old Norse *jalda*, 'a mare'.

jakes. (See also **Ajax**.) A privy. 'I will tread this unbolted villain into mortar, and daub the wall of a jakes with him', *Lear*, II ii 74–76: cf. 125–126 (again Kent in reference to Oswald), 'None of these rogues and cowards But Ajax is their fool' (*a jakes*).

Jacque's (or *Jack's*) *house*, the house being dropped: cf. 'I'll call at the baker's [shop]'; *Jack* in English, like *Jacques* in French, is generic for 'man', as in *every man Jack* and *every Jack shall have his Jill*.

jewel. Allusively for chastity incarnate in the maidenhead. '*Marina*, Whither wilt thou have me?—*Boult*. To take from you the jewel you hold so dear', *Pericles*, IV v 154–155.—'But, by my modesty,—The jewel in my dower,—I would not wish . . .', *The Tempest*, III i 53–54.—In *Lucrece*, v. 1191, *jewel* = that **chaste treasure** which is female married virtue.

Cf. *treasures* and *treasury*.—*Jewel*, via Old Fr., from L. *jocus*, 'jest, play'.

jordan. A chamber-pot. *1 Henry IV*, II i 19–21, 'Why, they will allow us ne'er a jordan, and then we leak in the chimney; and your chamber-lie breeds fleas like a loach'.—*2 Henry IV*, II iv 33, 'Empty the jordan'.

From the river *Jordan*. (See my *They Came to Stay*.)

Jove. See **bull Jove** and cf. **Europa**.

joy, n.; **joys of love.** Amorous pleasure; pleasure in sexual intimacy. See quotation at **a-weary** and the *Venus* quotation at **clip** and the last quotation at **kiss**.

Cf. **bliss** and **delight**.

Ex Old Fr. *joie*, it ultimately represents L. *gaudia*, plural of *gaudium*, joy or a rejoicing [cf. a college *gaudy*]'.

joy, v. To enjoy sexually (see **enjoy**); i.e., to possess sexually, to copulate with. 'Let her joy her raven-colour'd love', *Titus Andronicus*, II iii 83.

In French, *jouir de*: contrast *faire quelqu'un(e) jouir*, to cause a man or a woman to experience an orgasm.

juggle, v.i.; **juggling,** adj. To copulate, there being a word-play on 'jugglers' balls' and 'testicles'; pertaining to copulation. 'She and the Dauphin have been juggling', 1 *Henry VI*, v iv 68.—'A juggling trick', *T. & C.*, v ii 25. (See **secretly open**).

Via Old Fr. *jogler* ex L. *joculare*, 'to jest', ex *jocus*, 'a joke, a jest': and so cf. **play** and **sport**.

juggler. (Cf. the preceding.) Fornicator. Doll Tearsheet to Pistol, who has just spoken bawdily to her: 'Away . . . you basket-hilt stale juggler, you!' 2 *Henry IV*, IV iv 129–130.

jump. (Cf. **leap** and **vault**.) To coït athletically and vigorously with (a woman). 'Such delicate burdens of "dildos" and "fad-ings", "jump her and thump her"', *The W. Tale*, IV iii 194–196.

'Medieval L. *jumpare*, of obscure origin' (Webster).

Kate. See **Keep-Down.**

keen. Sexually ardent or excited. Perhaps in *Hamlet*, III ii 267 (see quotation at **edge**).

Cf. 'a keen knife-edge' and 'sexually sharp-set'. *Keen* is of common-Teutonic stock; it may, in its Aryan origin, = 'know-ing; alertly shrewd'.

Keep-Down, Mistress Kate. A woman known to Mistress Over-done and therefore probably a whore or at least a wanton: *Measure*, III ii 202.

Kate, perhaps punning *cat*, 'a prostitute', has, like *Doll* and *Moll*, been for centuries a common name for whores; *Keep-Down* may well imply that she kept men down (on the bed: cf. **down-bed**).

keep fair quarter with one's bed. To remain faithful to one's wife, as in *Com. of Errors*, II i 108; cf. the quotation at **break the pale** and:—

keep league and truce. To remain faithful in marriage. 'Keep, then, fair league and true with thy true bed; I live unstain'd, thou undishonoured', *Com of Errors*, II ii 144–145.

keep out, v.t. To keep a man away from the pudend. '*Helena.* Man is enemy to virginity; how may we barricade it against him?—*Parolles.* Keep him out'; *All's Well*, I i 112–114.

Synonym: **hold at a bay.**

kicky-wicky. Parolles to Bertram, who has just wedded Helena but refuses to *bed* her: 'To th' wars, my boy, to th' wars! He wears his honour in a box unseen, That hugs his kicky-wicky here at home, Spending his manly marrow in her arms, Which should sustain the bound and high curvet Of Mars's fiery steed', *All's Well*, II iii 281–286.

Perhaps Fr. *quelquechose* (cf. **thing** and **thing, another),** which normally yields *kickshaw(s)*. Note the endearing suffix -*y* and the love-expressive rhyming in the word *kicky-wicky*.

kind, be after. To seek, sexually, one's mate; mostly applied to animals. 'If the cat will after kind, So be sure will Rosalind', *As You Like It*, III ii 104–105.

Kind is in the obsolete sense 'nature', which may come from the also obsolete sense 'offspring'; not irrelevant, therefore, is the obsolete French literarism, *la nature*, the pudend, the female *genitalia*. Cf. **do the deed of kind,** q.v. at **do it.**

kind, do the deed of. See **do it.**

kindle. To engender; to conceive. 'The cony, that you see dwell where she is kindled', *As You Like It*, III ii 343.—See the *Venus* quotation at **warm.**

kiss, n. and v. 'A sovereign kiss', *Two Gentlemen*, I ii 116; II ii 9, 'Seal the bargain with a holy kiss' (Julia to her wooer, Proteus).—Juliet 'breath'd such life with kisses in my lips, That I revived, and was an emperor', *R. & J.*, V i 8–9.—'A second time I kill my husband dead When second husband kisses me in bed' (coïts with me; it is a euphemism—cf. Fr. *baiser*): *Hamlet* III ii 203–204.—Similarly, in defence of cuckoldry, the Clown in *All's Well* (I iii 50) says, 'He that kisses my wife is my friend'.—*Coriolanus*, v iii 44–48.—*Venus* to Adonis, 'I'll smother thee with kisses' (v. 18).—'Were kisses all the joys in bed, One woman would another wed', *The Passionate Pilgrim: Sonnets to Music*, 4, vv. 47–48.

Of common-Teutonic origin, *kiss* is echoic.

kiss with inside lip. See **inside lip.**

kissing, vbl. n. '[Thy lips] were made For kissing, lady', *Richard III*, I ii 172–173.

knog his urinals. 'Welsh' for *knock his urinals.*: 'Sir Hugh Evans. I will knog his urinals about his knave's costard when I have goot opportunities for the 'ork', *Merry Wives*, III i 13–15. Knock his *urinals* or the glass vessels in which doctors kept, for observation, specimens of their patients' urine. Evans means that he will smash an undignified part of Caius's laboratory equipment over his skull' (Mr E. Phillips Barker, letter of 4 May 1948).

knot; virgin knot. Maidenhead: 'Untied I still my Virgin knot will keep. Diana, aid my purpose!', *Pericles*, IV ii 150–151.—'If thou dost break her virgin-knot . . .', *The Tempest*, IV i 15.

Cf. the entries at **Hymen** and **maidenhead.**

knot, v.i. To come together in sexual congress. *Othello*, IV ii 61–62, 'A cistern for foul toads To knot and gender in!'

From the close inter-knitting of the two bodies: *knit* is, in fact, a cognate.

know. To have carnal knowledge of; to be sexually intimate with (usually a woman), to the point and inclusion of coïtion. Doll Tearsheet to bawdy Pistol, 'Away, you mouldy rogue, away! I am meat for your master.—*Pistol*. I know you, Mistress Dorothy.—*Doll*. Away, you cut-purse rascal! you filthy bung, away!', *2 Henry IV*, II iv 123–127.—*Much Ado*, IV i 48–49.—*Merry Wives*, I i 236.—*Measure*, v i 186–187, 'I've known my husband: yet my husband knows not That ever he knew me'; cf. 200–202.—' Before I know myself, seek not to know me', Adonis to Venus (v. 525). The word is a Hebraism.

know as a wife. To **know** as one knows one's wife in the marriage-bed. 'Tuesday night last gone, in's garden-house, He knew me as a wife', *Measure*, v i 227–228.

know carnally. To **know,** to have sexual intercourse with. See second quotation at **cardinally.**—Shakespeare also uses the phrase **to know** (a person's) **body.**

laced mutton. (See also **mutton.**) A loose woman; a prostitute. 'I, a lost mutton, gave your letter to her, a laced mutton', *Two Gentlemen*, I i 96–97, where, however, Julia is a woman of good repute.

ladies' flesh. See **flesh** (quotation from *Cymbeline*).

lady-bird. When in *Romeo and Juliet* (I iii 4–5) the Nurse, being told by Lady Capulet to summon her daughter Juliet, calls: 'What, lamb! What, lady-bird', and immediately adds, 'God forbid!'—she realizes that, although she has used *lady-bird* as an endearment, equivalent to 'sweetheart', the term slangily means 'a wanton'.—This kind of anachronism is extremely interesting but hardly the point here.

lag end. 'They may, *cum privilegio*, wear away The lag end of their lewdness, and be laugh'd at', *Henry VIII*, I iii 33–34. They may exhaust the remainder of their lewdness: but there is, one may suspect, an indelicate pun intended: *lag end* may = *latter end* (the posteriors) or it may be vaguely allusive to the male generative organ.

Then, *lag* comes ex the v., which = 'to linger *behind*'.

lance. A penis. See quotation at **sunburnt.**

Cf. **pike, sword,** and, more vaguely, **weapon.** Even today, *to break a lance with* (a woman) = to copulate with her and thereby experience an orgasm.

lap. 'In thy sight to die, what were it else But lie a pleasant slumber in thy lap', *2 Henry VI*, III ii 389–390.—See quotation at **perfect in lying down.**—'*Hamlet.* Lady, shall I lie in your lap?—*Ophelia.* No, my lord.—H. I mean, my head upon your lap?—*O.* Ay, my lord': III ii 116–119.—See quotation at **fall,** v.—See that at **lust-wearied.**—And elsewhere.

Lap in the ordinary sense, but with an implied localization in the pudend.

Ex the now obsolete sense, 'flap of a garment': cf., therefore, **codpiece** and **placket.**

lascivious. Gloster to Winchester in *I Henry VI*, at III i 20–21, 'Lascivious, wanton, more than well beseems A man of thy profession and degree', where the chief sexual sense, 'lustful', appears very clearly; of words or music, it means 'inciting to lust'.—'Lascivious Edward', *3 Henry VI*, V v 34.—'The lascivious pleasing of a lute', *Richard III*, I i 13.—See quotation at **adulterer.**—See second quotation at **loose.**—See quotation at **eat.**—And elsewhere.

The L. *lascivus* = sportive. Ultimately ex, or cognate with, a Sanskrit base meaning 'to desire'.

latter end. See **ass.**

lawlessly. Immodestly; without sexual restraint. 'He bears an honourable mind, And will not use a woman lawlessly', *Two Gentlemen*, V iii 13–14.

lay down. To dispose, suitably persuade and position, a woman for the sexual act. (Of English courtiers that have lived in France) 'The sly whoresons Have got a speeding trick to lay down ladies; A French song and a fiddle has no fellow', *Henry VIII*, I iii 38–40.

lay it. (Of a woman) to cause an erection to disappear. 'To raise a spirit in his mistress' circle . . ., letting it there stand Till she had laid it and conjured it down' (by causing the male orgasm): *R. & J.*, II i 24–26. The subtle-sexual Shakespeare probably innuendo'd the 'conjure' of magic and implied an auditory allusion to L. *cunnus.*

lay it to one's heart. To admit the male organ and induce an emission: see *Much Ado*, III iv 67–69, where first 'it' = the penis; 2nd 'it' = emission.

lay knife aboard. (Cf. **board a land carrack** and **stab** and **set up one's rest.**) '*Nurse* . . . O, there is a nobleman in town, one Paris, that would fain lay knife aboard; but she, good soul, had as lief see a toad, a very toad, as see him', R. & J., II iii 205–207: to board sexually. Cf. 'Then laid his leg over my thigh, and sigh'd, and kist' (*Othello*, III iii 424–425).

Cf. the modern saying *Once aboard the lugger and the girl is mine*, drawn from a song.

lay one's arms before the legs. To clasp amorously, there being a pun on *arms* in 'I here am come by chance, And lay my arms before the legs of this sweet lass of France', L.L.L., V ii 549–550.

lead apes in hell. To die an old maid. 'I must dance barefoot on her wedding-day, And, for your love to her, lead apes in hell', *The Taming*, II i 33–34.—*Much Ado*, II i 40.

With cruel irony on the semantic idea present in **monkey** . . ., q.v.

leak, n. See **boat hath a leak.**

leak, v. To urinate: see quotation at **jordan.**

To *have a leak* (cf. *shed a tear*) is the modern equivalent.

Ex Old Norse *lika*, 'to drip, to leak', cognate with O.E. *leccan*, 'to water; to lave', itself connected with O.E. *lacu*, 'a stream'.

leaky. 'I'll warrant him for drowning; though the ship were no stronger than a nutshell, and as leaky as an unstanch'd wench': *The Tempest*, I i 45–47: leaking as much as a girl that, during menstruation, wears no sanitary pad (or towel or clout), *stanch* being 'to check the flow of (particularly, blood)'; or, perhaps, rather, it = as much as a girl whose menstrual flow has not ceased.

lean. Worn thin by sexual excess. 'How like a prodigal doth she'—a ship—'return, With over-weather'd ribs, and ragged sails, Lean, rent and beggar'd by the strumpet wind!', *The M. of V.* II v 73–75.

Lean may originally have been = 'inclined to droop or *lean*'.

leap, v. (Cf. **jump** and **vault;** also **climb** and **mount.**) Allied though not strictly relevant is 'If I could win a lady at leapfrog, . . . I should quickly leap into a wife' (*Henry V*, v ii 137–141).—See second quotation at **bull Jove.**

leap into one's seat. 'I do suspect that the lusty Moor hath leapt into my seat', *Othello*, II i 298–299: has usurped Iago's place in Emilia's bed.

leaping-house. A brothel: see quotation at **dial** and cf. **leap** and **vault.**

leave a pillow unprest. To neglect one's husbandly sex-attentions to a woman. Antony to Cleopatra, 'Have I my pillow left unprest in Rome, Forborne the getting of a lawful race, And by a gem of women, to be abused By one that looks on feeders?': III xii 106–109.

lecher, n. An habitual fornicator; a womanizer. 'I will now take the lecher; he is at my house; he cannot scape me', *Merry Wives*, III v 140–141.—See quotation at **whorish.**—'Now a little fire in a wild field were like an old lecher's heart,—a small spark, all the rest on's body cold', *Lear*, III iv 114–116; cf. IV vi 15.— 'And so did kill the lechers in their deed', *Lucrece*, vv. 1636–1637.—In *The Passionate Pilgrim*, &, v. 17, it is a woman: 'Was this a lover, or a lecher whether?'

The n. is probably, in English, earlier than the verb: the n. comes ex Old Fr. *lecheor*, 'a lecher', from *lechier*, 'to live in debauchery and glutton' (C.O.D.), lit. 'to lick'—ultimately of common-Teutonic origin.

lecher, v. To copulate. 'The wren goes to't, and the small gilded fly Does lecher in my sight', *Lear*, IV vi 115–116.

See etymological note to the n.

lecherous. Addicted to lechery. ''A was . . . lecherous as a monkey', 2 *Henry IV*, III ii 324–325—*Hamlet*, II ii 590–591, in the outburst against Claudius, 'Bloody, bawdy villain! Remorseless, treacherous, lecherous, kindless villain!'—See quotation at **sparrows.**

lechery. Habitual or frequent fornication outside wedlock. 'A man can no more separate age and covetousness than 'a can part young limbs and lechery: but the gout galls the one, and the pox pinches the other', 2 *Henry IV*, i ii 235–238.—*Twelfth Night*, i v 125.—*T. & C.*, ii iii 76, 'War and lechery confound all!'; *ibid.*, v. i 100 and ii 57.—And elsewhere.

leman. A mistress; a man's illicit amorous female companion. 'A cup of wine that's brisk and fine, And drink unto the leman mine', 2 *Henry IV*, v iii 45–46.—*Merry Wives*, iv ii 150–151.

M.E. *leofmon*, lit. 'man-dear'—i.e., dear to a man.

leprosy. In the quotation at **blain,** *leprosy* may = venereal diseases of all kinds; especially since *lepra Graecorum*, now psoriasis, was not, strictly, leprosy at all, but a hideous, scaly skin-disease.

let in and **let out.** 'Be it concluded, No barricado for a belly; know't; It will let in and out the enemy With bag and baggage', *The W. Tale*, i ii 203–206. To admit the sexual aggress of the male genitals (bag = scrotum; baggage, here, probably = penis [? and testicles]) and the inmission, and then release the attacker-captive.

Cf. the metaphor at **siege.**

levity. (Cf. **lightness.**) Sexual wantonness. 'Her reputation was disvalued In levity', *Measure*, v i 219–220.—Applied to Antony in *A. & C.*, iii vii 13.

A too-light sense of virtue and reputation; a too-light hand on the reins of sexual restraint.

lewd. Of persons: unchaste or lascivious. Of words or actions: unchaste or indecent. 'Thy lewd, pestiferous, and dissentious pranks', 1 *Henry VI*, iii I 16.—'He is not lolling on a lewd day-bed', *Richard III*, iii vii 72, where *day-bed* (either a bed used in the day-time, when a man should be manfully busy, or a couch) increases the notion of lasciviousness.—See second quotation at **turn to.**—Lucio is described as 'this lewd fellow', *Measure*, v i 508.—'. . . Where, like a virtuous monument, she lies, To be admired of lewd unhallowed eyes', *Lucrece*, vv. 391–392.

In O.E., it = 'ignorant; lay (as opposed to clerical, ecclesiastical)'; the transition to 'vile' and thence to 'unchaste' is easy. Shakespeare may be said to have firmly established and popularized the 'unchaste' sense, for even in the Authorized Version of the Bible we find the old sense used, as in 'Lewd fellows of the baser sort' (see my *A New Testament Word-Book*).

lewdly given; lewdly inclined. Addicted or inclined to fornication and loose living. 1 *Henry IV*, II iv 437 (the former); *Pericles*, IV ii 146 (the latter).

lewdness. Unchastity. 'Virtue, as it never will be moved, Though lewdness court it in a shape of heaven', *Hamlet*, I v 53–54.— See **lag-end.**

liberal. (Cf. **free.**) Of a woman, liberal with her body to a man; of a man, licentious, or broad of speech. 'It's sign she hath been liberal and free', 1 *Henry VI*, v iv 82.—*Two Gentlemen*, III i 342 (see **another thing**).—Concerning flowers, 'Long purples That liberal shepherds give a grosser name, But our cold maids do dead men's fingers call them', *Hamlet*, IV vii 169–171: what name? Some name, presumably, allusive to **prick**—cf. **carrot.** Perhaps the *snapdragon*, 'a bag-like flower that can be made to gape' (C.O.D.).

Dr Onions, in his *Shakespeare Glossary*, says that 'long purples' = the early purple orchis. The O.E.D. shows that certain kinds of orchis are named *ballocks grass, ballocks wort, sweet ballocks; lover's wanton; priest's pintle*, i.e. penis. See especially Vernon Rendall's *Wild Flowers in Literature*, 1934, the article on 'Long Purples', where that fine scholar—for some years editor of *Notes and Queries*—made it clear that 'Wild Arum has been suggested, but this is to ignore the names formerly current for the Early Spring Orchis, which from Elizabethan times down to the

19th century was called "Fools' Stones". "Dead Men's Fingers" was a name applied to the Purple Orchis from the shape of its roots. *Orchis maculata* possesses these palmate roots, but not *Orchis mascula*; but to expect Shakespeare or ordinary folk to make these distinctions is to ask too much. All were regarded as aphrodisiacs.' As Mr. F. Murray H. Mayall has remarked, 'There is little doubt that Shakespeare confused *Orchis maculata* ("Dead Men's Fingers") with *Orchis mascula* ("Priest's Pintle") and made them into one plant in the *Hamlet* passage'. Note Salvador de Madariaga's *On Hamlet*, 1948, and its reference to Shakespeare's probable source: Henry Lyle's *Niewe Herball*—'translated out of French'—1578.

L. *liberalis* (ex *liber*, 'free'); *Liber* was also the 'name of an ancient Italic god of plenty and fruitfulness' (Wyld).

libertine. A man habitually dissolute with laxly hedonistic ideas and no conscience towards women. *Much Ado*, II i 133.—*As You Like It*, II vii 75–76, 'Thou thyself hast been a libertine, As sensual as the brutish sting itself'.—'A puft and reckless libertine', *Hamlet*, I iii 49.—'Tie up the libertine in a field of feasts . . .; Epicurean cooks Sharpen with cloyless sauce his appetite . . .!', *A. & C.*, II i 23–25.

For the semantics, cf. the preceding and the following entry; also **free.**

liberty. Excessive freedom from restraint or temperance in sexual matters, gaming, drinking. See quotation at **drabbing;** cf. *Othello*, III iv 39.

licentious. Addicted to illicit sexual indulgence. 'How dearly'—says Adriana—'would it touch thee to the quick, Shouldst thou but hear I were licentious', *Com. of Errors*, II ii 129–130.—*Henry V*, II iii 22 ('licentious wickedness').—'Fill'd the time With all licentious measure', *Timon*, V iv 3–4.

Ex. *licence*, 'freedom from, or a flouting of, moral restraint, especially in sexual matters'; L. *licentia*, 'liberty to do just as one likes'.

lie, n. See **chamber-lie.**

lie, v.; **lying,** vbl. n. To lie down, to recline (especially in bed): in reference to sexual intercourse. See the ensuing *lie* phrases. Of virginity, Parolles says, "Tis a commodity will lose the gloss with lying; the longer kept, the less worth' (*All's Well*, I i 154–155), where ostensibly *lying* = lying unused.—*A. & C.*, V ii 251–253, 'A very honest woman, but something given to lie; as a woman should not, but in the way of honesty'.—*Henry VIII*, IV i 70–71, 'She is the goodliest woman That ever lay by man'.—Venus to Adonis, 'Lo, I lie between that sun and thee' (v. 194).—*Sonnets*, 138, V v. 13–14, with a pun on lie-telling, 'Therefore I lie with her and she with me, And in our faults by lies we flattered be': cf. 'I'll lie with love, and love with me' (*The Passionate Pilgrim*, v. 13).

lie between a maid's legs. Immediately after the lines quoted at **country matters,** comes this passage: 'That's a fair thought to lie between maid's legs.—*Ophelia.* What is, my lord?—H. Nothing.—O. You are merry, my lord.'

lie down. See **perfect . . .**

lie long. In 'Had I so good occasion to lie long As you, Prince Paris, nothing but heavenly business Should rob me of my bed-mate' (*T. & C.*, IV i 46), there is probably a sexual pun on 'lie-long' (*? penis erectus*).

lie on. To coït with (a woman). '*Iago.* Lie— *Othello.* With her?— *Iago.* With her, on her; what you will.—*Othello.* Lie with her! lie on her!': IV i 34–35.

lie on one's back. In reference to the female posture during sexual intercourse. (Concerning Mab, Queen of the Fairies) 'This is the hag, when maids lie on their backs, That presses them, and learns them first to bear, Making them women of good carriage', *R. & J.*, I iv 91–93.—See **defend one's belly.**

Cf. **lie,** v., and **fall backward.**

lie under. Mistress Page, referring to the amorous Falstaff, 'I had rather be a giantess, and lie under Mount Pelion', *Merry Wives*, II i 78–79. Cf. the implications of *succubus*.

lie with. To have sexual intercourse with; chiefly of a man in reference to a woman. King Edward to Lady Grey, 'To tell thee plain, I aim to lie with thee', *3 Henry VI*, III ii 69.—*Richard III*, I ii 108–113, elaborates the theme of 'lying in a lady's bed-chamber . . . with her'; V iii 337.—*R. & J.*, IV v 36.—*The M. of V.*, V i 259–262.— *Merry Wives*, II ii 283.—*Measure*, III ii 283–284.—See **lie on.**—*Pericles*, IV ii 22.—And elsewhere (see, e.g., *Sonnets* quotation at **lie,** v.).

Perhaps the oldest euphemism for 'to copulate' in the English language; cf. the also long-prevalent *sleep with*.

light, adj. 'Light wench', *Com of Errors*, IV iii 51.—*L.L.L.*, I ii 118 and IV iii 382 and V ii 15.—*R. & J.*, II i 141.—*Much Ado*, II iv 41–43 and III iv 75–76.—'Women are light at midnight', *Measure*, V i 278.

The sense, then, is 'sexually immoral' or 'given to—engaged in—prostitution'. But why *light*? Probably because a light woman is easy to persuade, to *move*, to participation in sexuality.

lightness. Female wantonness or immodesty or unchastity. 2. *Henry IV*, I ii 49 (see quotation at **horn**).—'Can it be That modesty'—woman's modesty—'may more betray'—i.e., seduce—'our sense Than woman's lightness?', *Measure*, II ii 168–170 (Angelo, overcome by suppliant Isabella's charm and modesty).

See light and **levity.**

like, v.; **liking,** n. To be amorously fond of; amorous fondness. 'If you like elsewhere, do it by stealth', *Com. of Errors*, III ii 7.—*R. & J.*, I iii 98–99, 'Lady Capulet. Speak briefly, can you like of Paris' love?—Juliet. I'll look to like, if looking liking move'.—*All's Well* (see at **board**).

The basic sense of *to like* (of common-Teutonic origin) is 'to be equal, to be like or similar to', thence (as Wyld remarks) 'to be harmonious, suitable, agreeable'.

line. To coït with (a woman), as in *As You Like It*, III ii 106–107, 'Winter garments must be lined, So must slender Rosalind'. To *line* is to cover (originally, with linen) on the inside; hence, to fill as if with lining; hence, to cram, to stuff. (See *The O.E.D.*) Cf. the slang 'to *stuff*'.

ling, old. Woman as pudend; what, in modern vulgarism, is known generically as 'cunt'. '*Clown*. I have no mind to Isbel, since I was at court: our old ling and our Isbels o' th' country'—cf. **country matters,** q.v.—'are nothing like your old ling and your Isbels o' th' court', *All's Well*, III ii 14–16.

Ling is perhaps the kind of heather so named: the reference, then, would be to the pubic hair (cf. **hair**). If, however, *ling* is here the coarse fish allied to the cod, then the semantics are comparable with those of **fish.**

lip, n. 'This is no world To play with mammets and to tilt with lips', 1 *Henry IV*, II iii 92–93.—*Timon*, III vi 63–64, (inviting guests to sit at the dinner table) 'Each man to his stool, with that spur as he would to the lip of his mistress'.

Of common-Germanic stock and cognate with L. *labium*, it is probably echoic: cf. **pap.**

lip, v. To kiss intimately; properly, lips to lips (and cf. 'with inside lip': see **inside lip**). 'O, 'tis the spite of hell, the fiend's arch-mock, To lip a wanton in a secure couch, And to suppose her chaste!', *Othello*, IV i 71–73.—*A. & C.*, II v 30.—And elsewhere.

liquorish. Amorous to the point of lechery. 'Dry up thy marrows, vines, and plough-torn leas; Whereof ingrateful man, with liquorish draughts And morsels unctuous, greases his pure mind', *Timon*, IV iii 193–195, where the primary sense of *liquorish* is 'of strong liquor'. Strictly, it is a misuse (as *The C.O.D.* points out) of *lickerish* or *lickerous*, 'lecherous' (see **lecher,** n.).

lists of love. 'Now she is in the very lists of love, Her champion mounted for the hot encounter', *Venus*, vv. 595–596.

A jousting simile: cf. **set up one's rest.** *Lists* = a jousting-tourney ground.

litter'd under Mercury. Spawned (or, rather, given birth to) under the star representing the god of thieves: *The W. Tale*, IV ii 25.

little finger. (Cf. **potato-finger.**) Penis. '*Lady Percy.* In faith, I'll break your little finger, Harry, An if thou wilt not tell me all things true.—*Hotspur.* Away, away, you trifler!—Love?—I love thee not', 1 *Henry IV*, II iii 89–91.

Still current, among women, as a euphemism, and originates in *The Bible*; to be precise, at 1 *Kings*, 12, 11, 'My little finger is thicker than my father's loins'; this is where women found the euphemism—only one of the numerous sexual euphemisms *The Bible* contains.

load, n. 1, The **burden** (cf. also **weight**) of a man's body. '*Old Lady.* What think you of a duchess? have you limbs To bear that load of title?—*Anne Bullen.* No, in truth.—*O.L.* Then you are weakly made: pluck off a little; I would not be a young count in your way, For more than blushing comes to: if your back Cannot vouchsafe this burden, 'tis too weak Ever to get a boy', *Henry VIII*, II iii 38–44.

2, (emitted) semen: see last quotation in the **bankrout beggar** entry.

lock, 'pudend': **see pick the lock.**

loins, in transferred sense 'a man's or a woman's generative organs'. 3 *Henry VI*, III ii 126, 'That from his loins no hopeful branch may spring'.—Of a woman: see quotation at **whorish.**—*Coriolanus*, III iii 112–116, 'I do love My country's good with a respect more tender, More holy, and profound, than . . . treasure of my loins'.

Via Fr., ex L. *lumbus*; 'ultimate meaning perhaps "hollow, depression"' (Wyld).

long purples (*Hamlet*, IV vii 169–171). See **liberal,** above.

loose, adj. Of women (men are generally said to be *loose-living*);

hence, of acts: wanton; unchaste. 'Her bonds of chastity are but loose' perhaps explains the semantics, but the metaphor may be physiological (reference: pudend). 'What, is Lavinia, then, become so loose, Or Bassianus so degenerate, That for her love such quarrels may be broacht Without controlment, justice, or revenge?', *Titus Andronicus*, II i 65–68.—'I would prevent The loose encounters of lascivious men', *Two Gentlemen*, II vii 40–41.—See second quotation at **salt.**

Ex Old Norse *lauss*, '**free,** unimpeded; hence, dissolute'.

loose-wived. Having a wanton wife. 'As it is a heart-breaking to see a handsome man loose-wived, so it is a deadly sorrow to behold a foul knave uncuckolded', *A. & C.*, I ii 70–72.

loss. Loss of semen. See quotation at **stand to,** and cf. **bereave** and **bankrupt** and **load** (sense 2), q.v.

Apparently ex 'to *lose*', of which the O.E. original, *forleosan* = both 'to lose' and 'to destroy'.

love. For a general reference to Shakespeare's attitude towards and opinions on love, see the Essay, section 5. Quotations could be adduced for every shade of that elastic word *love*, from incipient liking to all-pervasive adoration, devotion, desire; from bestial appetite, through hearty lusts and vagrant letches, to nigh-ethereal, starry loves of the most spiritual sort. The lowest, Shakespeare, endowed with an awe-inspiring degree of sympathy and perception, could understand; honest lust, fugitive libidos, and ordinary love (half sensuality, half sublimation) he knew in his own life; superior love, true love, was what he himself was also capable of—and what he aspired to. Full supporting quotations and an adequate elaboration of the theme would be out of place in this book, even in the Essay; they shall come at another time and in another place, for the subject has never been more than skimmed, which is an astounding omission on the part of British and American critics and scholars: for of all English-speaking writers, indeed of all poets, dramatists, novelists whatsoever, Shakespeare has dealt the most profoundly and the most shrewdly, the most spiritually (he out-Dante's Dante), the most lyrically (bettering even Meredith's *Love in the Valley*), the most sympathetically, the most humorously, the most materialistically and cynically, and, above all, the most comprehensively and comprehendingly, with that passion and that affection, that *alter-egoing* and that sublimation, that selfishness and selflessness, which are: love.

Love comes from O.E. *lufu* ('love; affection; friendliness'), which is cognate with O.E. *leof*, archaic *lief*, 'dear'; cognate also with L. *libet*, 'it pleases', and *libido*, 'desire'; traceable to Sanskrit *lubhyati*, 'he desires strongly'. (Wyld).

love, rite of. 'I must not yield to any rites of love', Joan of Arc in I ii 13 of 1 *Henry VI*.—*Richard III*, v iii 102.—See quotation at **prerogative and rite of love**.—*Sonnets*, 23, v. 6, 'The perfect ceremony of love's rite'.

love-performing night. Night, when love finds its easiest and hence its most frequent physical expression. 'Spread thy close curtain, love-performing night', R. & J., III ii 5.

Cf. **love** and **performance**.

lover. One who loves (generally, the man); one who is engaged in an intimate love-affair. *Two Gentlemen*, I i 106, where it refers to the respectable Julia.—*L.L.L.*, II i 126 and often afterwards.—*M.N. Dream*, v i 7–8.—*Measure*, I iv 39, 'Your brother and his lover have embraced'.—*Pericles*, IV ii 122 (of brothel favourites).—*Venus*, v. 573.

lover, v. To act the sexual lover with (a woman). 'Who, young and simple, would not be so lover'd?': *A Lover's Complaint*, v. 320.

low. Both in next entry and in 'O, sir, I did not look so low' (*Comedy*, III ii 136), low = 'positionally low' and 'obscene(ly)'. With the latter, cf. *to have a low mind* and ' "A rather questionable type of entertainment entitled *Sweet and Low*". "The man who thought of that title had genius", Maxwell interjected', E. C. Vivian, *Ladies in the Case*, 1933.

low countries. (Cf. **Netherlands** and **country matters.**) See the quotation at **holland.** Low, because low on the trunk of the body and because of the eliminatory orifices serving the lowly functions of the body; and cf. preceding entry.

Lucrece as the type of female married chastity: *The Rape of Lucrece* and *The Taming*, II i 289.

lust, n. A powerful—generally with the connotation 'animal-like'—desire for sexual intimacy (especially copulation); lascivious desire, whether in general or in particular. 'Polluted with your lusts'. *1 Henry VI*, v iv 43.—*Richard III*, III v 80.—See second quotation at **strike.**—'O, keep me from their worse than killing lust', *Titus Andronicus*, II iii 175.—'Ruffian lust' (see **contaminate**).—See at **mettle.**—See **sinful fantasy.**—*Hamlet*, I v 45 and 55.—Elsewhere, especially in *Venus and Lucrece*.

Etymologically no more than 'desire; pleasure'. Cf. *the lusts of the flesh*: all bodily appetites.

lust, v. To desire amorously. 'Thou rascal beadle, . . . Why dost thou lash that whore? . . . Thou hotly lusts to use her in that kind For which thou whipst her', *Lear*, IV vi 161–164.

lust-dieted. 'Heavens, . . . Let the superfluous and lust-dieted man, That slaves your obedience, that will not see, Because he doth not feel, feel your power quickly', *Lear*, IV i 68–71. One expects it to mean 'dieted, or stinted, in one's lust', but here it may mean 'fed on lust'.

lust-stained. Othello, in reference to his impending suffocation of Desdemona, 'Thy bed lust-stain'd shall with lust's blood be spotted', v i 36.

lust-wearied. 'Let us rear The higher our opinion, that our stirring Can from the lap of Egypt's widow pluck The ne'er-lust-wearied Antony', *A. & C.*, II i 35–38.

lustful. Full of or moved with excessive, especially of illicit, sexual desire. 'Lustful paramours', *Henry VI*, III ii 53.—*Titus*

Andronicus, IV i 80.—(Of Venus, wooing Adonis) 'And kissing speaks, with lustful language broken, "If thou wilt chide, thy lips shall never open"' (vv. 51–52).

See **lust, n.**

lusty. Full of health and strength, with a connotation of youth (or prime manhood) and of aptitude for love. 'Lusty young men', *R. & J.*, I ii 26.—*Ibid.*, II iii 153.—'I' faith, he'll have a lusty widow now, That shall be woo'd and wedded in a day', *The Taming*, IV ii 50–51.—*Othello*, II i 298.—See **stealth.**

luxurious. Sensual, amorous. 'She knows the heat of a luxurious bed', *Much Ado*, IV i 40.—See quotation at **whoremasterly.**—*Macbeth*, IV iii 58.—For adv., luxuriously: *A. & C.*, III xiii 120.

Ex:—

luxury. Luxurious living, especially in reference to sexual excesses (cf. L. *luxuria*). 'Urge his hateful luxury, And bestial appetite in change of lust', *Richard III*, III v 79–80.—'Dauphin. Shall a few sprays of us, The emptying of our father's luxury, Our scions . . .', *Henry V*, III v 5–7.—See quotation at **sinful fantasy.**—See quotation at **incest.**—*T. & C.*, v ii 56–57, 'The devil luxury, with his fat rump and potato-finger'.—*Measure*, V i 499.—*A Lover's Complaint*, vv. 314–315, 'When he most burnt in heart-wisht luxury, He preacht pure maid, and praised cold chastity'.

L. *luxuria*, 'riotous living' (cf. **riot**, n. and v.): ex *luxus*, 'excess, debauchery'.

lying. See **lie**, v.

mackerel. A pimp. Perhaps there is a vague allusion in 'You may buy land now as cheap as stinking mackerel.—*Prince Henry*. Why, then, is it like, if there come a hot June, . . . we shall buy maidenheads, as they buy hob-nails, by the hundreds.—*Falstaff*. By the mass, lad, thou say'st true; it is like we shall have good trading that way', *1 Henry IV*, II iv 370–375.

Old Fr. **makerel** (Mod. Fr. **maquereau,** both 'fish' and 'pimp'). Perhaps semantically relevant are **cod, eel, fish, ling.**

mad. Infatuated; madly in love. 'Cupid is a knavish lad, Thus to make poor females mad', M.N. *Dream*, III ii 440–441.—Troilus, 'I tell thee, I am mad In Cressid's love', I i 51–52.—*All's Well*, v iii 257, 'He was mad for her'.—*Venus*, v. 249, 'Being mad before, how doth she now for wits?': Venus, at this stage, is enraged with lust.

mad, v. See at **eagerness.**

maid; maiden. 'I, a maid, die maiden-widowed', Juliet in reference to her being a virgin and to her unconsummated marriage: R. & J., III ii 135.—'Let in the maid, that out a maid Never departed more', *Hamlet*, IV v 54–55.—*All's Well*, II iii 67–68.

Maid is short for *maiden*, of common-Teutonic stock; probably with an Aryan original, meaning 'unmarried'.

maiden, adj. Of a maiden; physically pure: l *Henry VI*, v iv 52.

maiden loss. Loss of maidenhead; devirgination. '*Angelo.* A deflower'd maid! . . . But that her tender shame Will not proclaim against her maiden loss, How might she tongue me!', *Measure*, IV iv 22–26.

Contrast **loss,** q.v.

maidenhead. The hymen or 'virginal membrane, stretched across external orifice of vagina' (C.O.D.); since it disappears only at a woman's first experience of sexual intercourse, it has always been held as equivalent to, symbolic of, and hence synonymous with virginity. 'There shall not a maid be married, but she shall pay to me her maidenhead ere they have it', 2 *Henry VI*. IV vii. (With allusion to the not wholly mythical *droit de seigneur*.)—'Now by my maidenhead,—at twelve year old' (*sc.*, I lost it), R. & J., I iii 3; *ibid.*, III ii 137.—*The Taming*, III ii 22, 'Carouse full measure to her maidenhead'.—See **mackerel.**— 'A pottle-pot's maidenhead', 2 *Henry IV*, II ii 77.—See first quotation at **secret parts.**—Frequently elsewhere.

Hence, get or **take a maidenhead,** to deflower a girl.

maidenhood and **maidhood.** 'Two stainless maidenhoods' (Juliet's and Romeo's virginities). R. & J., III ii 13.—*Maidhood: Twelfth Night,* III i 153 and *Othello,* I i 174.

Maid(en) + *-hood,* a suffix indicative of quality or condition.

make. See **mar.**

make a monster of. To cuckold. 'At your den, sirrah, with your lioness, I'ld set an ox-head to your lion's hide, And make a monster of you', *King John,* II i 292–295.—'Or, if thou wilt needs marry, marry a fool; for wise men know well enough what monsters you make of them', *Hamlet,* III i 139–141.—Cf. 'In all Cupid's pageant there is presented no monster', *T. & C.,* III ii 73–74. (—*Othello,* IV i 63: see **horned.**)

For the semantics: see the originating terms, **bull Jove** and **horn.**

make a son out of one's blood. Helena to Fourth Lord (*All's Well,* II iii 97–98), 'You are too young, too happy, and too good, To make yourself a son out of my blood'.

Cf. **get the sun of.**

make defeat of virginity. To persuade a virgin, before marriage, to yield her virginity, as in 'If you ... Have vanquisht the resistance of her youth, And made defeat of her virginity', *Much Ado,* IV i 45–47.

make holes in a woman's petticoat. (Cf. 2 *Henry IV,* II ii 81–82.) Falstaff to a tailor whom he is impressing for military service, 'Wilt thou make as many holes in an enemy's battle as thou hast done in a woman's petticoat?', 2 *Henry IV,* III ii 159–161. This phrase is perhaps not sexual at all—but I shouldn't care to wager on it.

make love. 'Honeying and making love', *Hamlet,* III iv 94. To indulge in sexual caresses and intercourse—Fr. *faire l'amour.*

make one's heaven in a lady's lap. 'I'll make my heaven in a lady's lap, And deck my body in gay ornaments, And witch sweet ladies with my words and looks', 3 *Henry VI,* III ii

148–150. Either 'to womanize' or 'to devote myself to love-making'.

make one's play. For an erotic pun, see quotation (*Henry VIII*) at **thing**, sense 2.

make the beast with two backs. To engage in sexual intercourse, the phrase being applied equally to both of the partners in the act and to the conventional and prevalent *figura Veneris*. 'Your daughter and the Moor are now making the beast with two backs', *Othello*, I i 107–109.

(Cf. **beastly.**) A man and a woman *in coitu* obviously resemble a two-headed animal with two backs, four arms, and four legs.

Graham Greene, *Brighton Rock*, 1938, ' "I'm not one for dancing." He eyed the slow movements of the two-backed beasts: pleasure, he thought, they call it pleasure',—this is a deliberate reminiscence.

make the diseases. To form—or to infect with—venereal diseases. 'You help to make the diseases, Doll; we catch of you, Doll', *2 Henry IV*, II iv 44–45.

make water. To urinate. 'Where didst thou see me heave up my leg, and make water against a lady's farthingale?', *Two Gentlemen*, IV iv 39–41: There is also an allusion to sexual emission.—*Twelfth Night*, I iii 126, 'I would not so much as make water but in a sink-a-pace' (a dance).—See **urine.**

making. Effectual copulation regarded as an act of creation—in short, procreation. 'There was good sport at his making, and the whoreson must be acknowledged', *Lear*, I i 23–24.

malady of France. Syphilis. *Henry V*, V i 84–85, (Pistol) 'News have I, that my Nell is dead i' th' spital of malady of France'.

Cf. **infinite malady.** Syphilis seems to have come to England from France; to France from Italy; to Italian ports (cf. **Neapolitan bone-ache**) from the Levant; and perhaps the disease-breeding filth of the Levant received its accretion from the pullulating populousness of the farther East.

male varlet. A pathic; a passive homosexual. '*Thersites*. Thou art thought to be Achilles' male varlet!—*Patroclus*. Male varlet, you rogue! what's that?—*Thersites*. Why, his masculine whore', *T. & C.*, v i 14–16.

Varlet: from Old Fr., where it = a groom; a youth.

mammets. Female breasts. '*Hotspur*. I care not for thee, Kate: this is no world To play with mammets and to tilt with lips', 1 *Henry IV*, ii iii 92–93.

L. *mamma*, a breast (especially of a woman): an echoic word, symbolizing the baby's gurgle of satisfaction when given its mother's breast.—Cf. **pap.**

man, v. To be sexually man to a woman; to possess (a woman). Juliet, apostrophizing Night: 'Hood my unmann'd blood, bating in my cheeks, With thy black mantle', *R. & J.*, iii ii 14–15.

Perhaps traceable to an Aryan radical, meaning 'human being': only modern civilization has weakened the idea that the human being *par excellence* is man, not woman.

manage, n. and v. For the noun, see the quotation at **pace.** Lit., 'training of a horse, mainly with reference to its schooled movements, in the short gallop'; the erotic force of the metaphor is clear (cf. the low-colloquial *short time*).—An instance of the verb occurs in the *Venus* quotation at **mount.**

Fr. *manege*, It. *maneggio* (*maneggiare*, to handle; L. *manus*, the hand): cf., therefore, **handle** and **touch** (n. and v.).

mandrake. '*Falstaff*. Thou whoreson mandrake', 2 *Henry IV*, i ii 15.—Ibid., iii ii 324–325, ''A was the very genius of famine; yet lecherous as a monkey, and the whores call'd him mandrake: 'a came ever in the rearward of the fashion'; there is some obscure sexual allusion in the last sentence: perhaps he was insatiable and monstrously perverted in his sexual practices.—Cf. *mandragora* in *Othello*, iii iii 330.

M.E. *mandragge*; ex *mandragora*, which, via Late L., comes from Gr. *mandragoras* (of unknown origin). The form *mandrake* 'shows association with *man* and *drake* in sense of "dragon, monster"'

(Wyld). 'European herbaceous plant, narcotic and emetic, with a root'—? cf. **root**—'formerly supposed to resemble the human form; said to shriek when pulled out of the ground' (*id.*).

This plant was famed as an aphrodisiac.

mansion of love. The human body as the vehicle of love's physical activities,—contrast **temple,** the body as the home of the spirit. Juliet (R. & J., III ii 26–28), 'O, I have bought the mansion of a love, But not possesst it; and, though I am sold, Nor yet enjoy'd'. Cf. *Lucrece*, v. 1164, 'Her mansion batter'd by the enemy'.

mar. Synonymous with **take down** and **take off,** qq.v. It is the opposite of *make*: for an example of both **make** and **mar,** see the quotation at **provoke.**

Literally, 'to impair fatally or effectually' (the exact sense in the **provoke** quotation).

mare. A girl, or a woman, regarded as the bearer of amorous man (cf. **rider, mount, leap**): M.N. *Dream*, III ii 461–463, 'Jack shall have Jill; Naught shall go ill; The man shall have his mare again'.

mark, n. A target in archery—hence that sexual mark or target at which a man sexually aims: the pudend. That this is so appears from the shooting-match in L.L.L., IV i (especially vv. 118–139); and above all in the words, 'Let the mark have a prick in't'.—R. & J., I i 203–207; II I 33.—*Pericles*, II iii 113–114.

The word still occurs allusively in the sense 'the male's centre of sexual attraction'. A correspondent recalls that, in the 1930's, he saw a vulgar postcard in which a young man appeared—naturally the picture was very discreet—to have his hand under a girl's skirt. The caption was, 'Feeling up to the mark at Southend?'

market-price. A prostitute's fee. 'I had that which any inferior might At market-price have bought', *All's Well*, v iii 217–218.

Cf. **mart.**

marriage joys; marriage pleasures; marriage rite. 'The sweet silent hours of marriage joys', *Richard III*, IV iv 231.—'In marriage-pleasures play-fellow', v. 34 of Induction to Act I of *Pericles*.—*Ibid.*, IV, Prologue, 16–17, 'One daughter, and a wench full grown, Even ripe for marriage-rite'.

Marriage is perhaps cognate, ultimately, with the Sanskrit word for 'man or youth; lover': which tends to constitute an etymological indication that, originally, marriage was not a legal but a sexual relationship (*C'est mon homme*).

marrow. Mettle, spunk, semen: see quotation at **kicky-wicky.**—'Lust and liberty, Creep in the minds and marrows of our youth, That 'gainst the stream of virtue they may strive . . .!', *Timon*, IV i 25–27.

Properly, the soft fatty substance resident in bone-cavities; hence, the best—the most essential part—of anything.

mart, v.i. To bargain, as though in the market-place, for a woman's body. 'A saucy stranger, in his court, to mart As in a Romish stew, and to expand His beastly mind to us', *Cymbeline*, I vi 150–152.

(Cf. **cheapen.**) *Mart, market*: from L. *mercari*, 'to do business, to trade; to buy'.

masculine whore. A pathic—or passive homosexual. See the quotation at **male varlet.**

See **whore.**

match. A bout of love. 'Come, civil night, . . . And learn me how to lose a winning match, Play'd for a pair of stainless maiden-hoods', *R. & J.*, III ii 10–13 (Juliet *loquitur*).—*Measure*, v i 209.

O.E. (*ge)maecca*, 'one of a pair; a mate' (M.E. *make*); hence, one who is a match for another; hence, a contest (originally between persons actually or supposedly a fair match).

meacock. Spiritless; without vigour. *The Taming*, II i 305–306, 'How tame, when men and women are alone, A meacock wretch can make the curstest shrew'.

Of dubious etymology, *meacock* may well be *mi-coq*, a

demicock (or rooster)', hence sexually weak or unenterprising ('Faint heart never won fair lady').

measure, in the quotation at **trip,** contains an erotic pun: for the exact allusion, cf. the entry at **short.**

meat. (Cf. **mutton** and **flesh,** qq.v.) The flesh of a whore or of a wanton; hence, a whore or a wanton. R. & J., II iii 139 (see at **hare**).—2 Henry IV, II iv 123–124, 'Doll Tearsheet [to Pistol]. Away, you mouldy rogue, away! I am meat'—food, a dish—'for your master'.—'By Juno, that is a queen of marriage, All viands that I eat do seem unsavoury, Wishing him my meat.—Sure, he's a gallant gentleman', (Thaisa loquitur in Pericles, II iii 30–32).

Originally, meat = any food; cf., therefore, **eat,** q.v.

meddle with. To be intimate with (a woman): allusive in Twelfth Night, III iv 252 and 283.—'How, sir! do you make with my master?—Coriolanus. Ay; 'tis an honester service than to meddle with thy mistress', Coriolanus, IV v 43–45.

Via. Old Fr. medler, from the Low L. equivalent of miscere, 'to mix': cf. **compound** and the euphemistic modern **mingle,** v.i., 'to coït'.

medlar; rotten medlar; medlar tree. In Shakespeare, 'medlar' means either pudend or podex or the pudend-podex area (the lower posteriors and the crutch). 'Now will he sit under a medlar-tree, And wish his mistress were that kind of fruit. As maids call medlars when they laugh alone' (and see continuation at **poperin pear**): R. & J., II i 34–36.—'They would else have married me to the rotten medlar', says Lucio of a 'wench' that he 'got with child', where rotten medlar apparently = a professed whore.

See **et cetera** above. In Timon, IV iii 306–312, the word—as Professor Oswald Doughty has noticed—'seems curiously ambiguous, and suggestive of . . . homosexual, but it might perhaps as well, or better, mean a woman'; but then, all Shakespeare's mature work is characterized by a deliberate ambiguity and a deliberate ambivalence.

Old Fr. *medler* (ex L. ex Gr.). There is probably a pun on **meddle.**

medlar-tree. See preceding entry.

mell with. To mingle sexually with (a member of the opposite sex). 'Men are made to mell with, boys are but to kiss', *All's Well*, IV iii 229.

Old Fr. *meller* or *mêsler* (Mod. Fr. *mêler*): *miscere*, 'to mix'.

melt. 'Thou wouldst have plunged thyself In general riot; melted down thy youth In different beds of lust', *Timon*, IV iii 255–257: dissolved thy **marrow,** thy youthly ardour, virility, strength.

Cf. the euphemistic *melt* (of either sex), to experience an orgasm.

merry (cf. **gay**)**,** on several occasions in Shakespeare (e.g., at **lie between a maid's legs**)**,** = bawdily witty or humorous.

mettle, 'natural ardour', as early as Shakespeare had the derivative sense, 'abundance (and vigour) of semen'; cf. the variant *spunk. Mettlesome* and *spunky*, besides meaning 'courageous', 'high-spirited', mean 'sexually vigorous or ardent'. (*Mettle* is a variant of *metal*; etymologically, *spunk* is 'tinder, or a spark'.)

Henry V, III v 27–31, '*Dauphin*. By faith and honour, Our madams mock at us, and plainly say Our mettle is bred out, and they will give Their bodies to the lust of English youth To new-store France with bastard warriors'.

middle. See the quotation at **favours.**

milk-paps. Female breasts (or, less probably, nipples): see **pap.** 'Let not the virgin's cheek Make soft thy trenchant sword; for those milk-paps, That through the window-bars bore at men's eyes, Are not within the leaf of pity writ, But set down horrible traitors', *Timon*, IV iii 114–118.

mingle bloods. To participate in sexual intercourse. 'Too hot, too hot! To mingle friendship far is mingling bloods', *The W. Tale*, I ii 108–109.

Cf. **compound** and **mell with.**

mingle eyes, to. To carry on an ocular flirtation, an exchange of flirtatious glances. Antony to Cleopatra, 'To flatter Caesar, would you mingle eyes With one that ties his points?': III xiii 156–157.

Cf. the preceding entry.

minion. 1, A man's—especially a king's or a prince's—male favourite; not necessarily a homosexual. 'Go, rate thy minions, proud insulting boy!', *3 Henry VI*, II ii 84 (Queen Margaret to Prince Edward).

2, Applied to the lovely, chaste Lavinia in *Titus Andronicus*, II iii 125; and in *Othello*, V i 33, to the chaste and lovely Desdemona.

Ex Fr. *mignon*, 'small, delicate; sweet, charming': ex Old High Ger. *minne*, 'love'.

minx. A sexually forward or on-coming girl or young woman; a flirt. 'Damn her, lewd minx! O, damn her!', *Othello*, III iii 466.—*Ibid.*, IV i 153, 'Some minx's token'.

Etymology doubtful, but cf. Low Ger. *minsk*, 'a man (Mod. Ger. *Mensch*); also, however, an impudent woman'. (Wyld.)

mire, v. To befoul; to urinate, or to defecate, upon. 'Paint till a horse may mire upon your face: A pox of wrinkles!', *Timon*, IV iii 147–148.

Cf. the figurative use of the n. for 'dirt, defilement'.

mirth (cf. **merry**), in *A. & C.*, I iv 18 (see **tumble,** sense 2), probably = a bout of love-making.

Cf. **one moment's . . .**

mistress. A man's illicit woman; the woman one loves. 'My mistress is my mistress' (i.e., only my mistress), *Titus Andronicus*, IV ii 107.—'Now you are metamorphosed with a mistress' (good sense), *Two Gentlemen*, II i 129; II i 86–87, 'His mistress doth hold his eyes lockt in her crystal looks' (likewise).—So too *L.L.L.*, I i, 'Study where to meet some mistress fine, When mistresses from common sense are hid'.—See at **be out.**— 'Thy wedded Mistress', *Coriolanus*, IV v 115.

The mistress of one's heart, she who rules one's heart. Old

Fr. *maistresse*, f. of *maistre*, 'master', ex L. *magister*: the base is the *mag* of L. *magnus*, 'big, great', ex equivalent Sanskrit *mahamt*.

Mitigation, Madam. A brothel-proprietress or -keeper. '*Lucio.* Behold, behold, where Madam Mitigation comes!—*First Gentleman.* I have purchased as many diseases under her roof as come to—', *Measure for Measure*, I ii 44–46.

   She provides the means of mitigating sexual desire: L. *mitigare*, 'to render *mitis* or gentle': cf. *to gentle a horse*.

moist. '*Othello.* This hand is moist, my lady . . . This argues fruitfulness and liberal heart:—Hot, hot, and moist: this hand of yours requires A sequester from liberty', III iv 35–39.

   A hot, moist palm may indicate amorous desire.

momentary trick, the. Copulation. *Measure*, III i 110–112, Claudio to Isabella in reference to Angelo's offer to free the former if the latter will 'sleep' with him, 'If it were damnable, he being so wise, Why should he for the momentary trick Be perdurably fined?' Cf. the elaboration on this theme in *Lucrece*, vv. 211–218, and Chesterfield's amorous epigram on 'a man's short time' with a whore.

   Momentary because, in a man unschooled in the art of restraint, the orgasm so quickly follows the ingression: cf. **one moment's fading mirth** and the French epigram, 'Plaisir d'amour ne dure qu'un instant: chagrin d'amour dure toute une vie'.

monkey, lecherous as a. (Cf. **goats and monkeys!**) See quotation at **lecherous.** Shakespeare makes goats and especially monkeys the types of lechery-addicts; monkeys, at least, deserve the imputation, and Shakespeare returns to it in *Othello*, III iii 403 (see quotation at **prime**), where the phrase he uses is **hot as monkeys.**

monster. See **make a monster of** and the first quotation at **horned.**

morsel. See quotation at **dish.**

mort o' the deer, the. 'To be paddling palms and pinching fingers . . .; and making practised smiles . . .; and then to sigh, as 'twere The mort o' the deer; O, that is entertainment My bosom likes not, nor my brows!', *The W. Tale*, I ii 115–119. 'The mort, or death, of the deer (or dear one)': the sexual 'dying' (see **die**) that is caused by the orgasm.

motions; raging motions. The hot impulses and the actual physiological stirrings and bodily movements of physical desire. 'A man whose blood Is very snow-broth; one who never feels The wanton stings and motions of the sense, But doth rebate and blunt his natural edge With profits of the mind, study and fast', *Measure*, I iv 57–61.

Via Fr. ex L. *movere*, 'to move', ex Sanskrit.

mount, v. (Cf. **climb, jump, leap, vault.**) To assume the man's 'superior' posture in a *coïtus*. 'Perchance he . . ., like a full-acorn'd boar, a German one, Cried "O!" and mounted; found no opposition but what he lookt for should oppose', *Cymbeline*, II v 15–18.—Of Adonis in connection with *Venus*, 'He will not manage her, although he mount her' (v. 598).

Ex. Fr. *monter*, 'to go up hill' (L. *mons*, hill, mountain): the basic sense of the Sanskrit original is 'to project'.

mountain. Venus, referring to the *park* that is her body, says to Adonis (vv. 232), 'Feed where thou wilt, on mountain or in dale'. *Mountain* is probably generic for all the pleasant eminences: breasts and buttocks, certainly; and thighs, probably; and the *mons Veneris*, perhaps.

Cf. **hillock.**

mouse. A term of sexual endearment; a beloved woman. 'Let the bloat king tempt you again to bed; Pinch wanton on your cheek; call you his mouse', *Hamlet*, III iv 193–194.

The term occurs frequently in C. 17 plays and pamphlets. Of common-Teutonic origin, *mouse* goes back to an Aryan base that means 'to steal'.

mouse-hunt. A whoremonger; a womanizer, '*Lady Capulet.* Ay, you have been a mouse-hunt in your time, But I will watch you from such watching now.—*Capulet.* A jealous-hood, a jealous-hood!', *R. & J.*, IV iv 11–13.

I.e., a **mouse**-hunter.

mouth, v. To kiss amorously. See quotation at **mutton** and perhaps cf. **inside lip.**

Immediately from the n., which comes from a base that has the meaning, 'to chew'.

muddy. Smutty, dirty, indelicate, bawdy. See the quotation at **calm;** *ibid.,* II iv 54, '*Doll Tearsheet* [to *Falstaff*]. Hang yourself, you muddy conger, hang yourself!'

For semantics, cf. **filthy, foul, nasty** and **obscene.** Mud is of Low Ger. origin and cognate with *mother,* 'scum produced by fermentation in alcoholic liquors, or the sticky sediment that forms in fermenting vinegar'.

mutton. (Cf. **flesh, meat;** and **eat.**) Woman regarded as food for the satisfaction of man's sexual appetite. 'The duke . . . would eat mutton on Fridays. He's now past it; yet . . . he would mouth with a beggar, though she smelt brown bread and garlick', *Measure,* III ii 183–186.

Old Fr. *moton,* 'a sheep', ex Low L. *multo* (probably of Celtic origin).

mutual entertainment. Mutual caressing and, with it, sexual intercourse (cf. **cherish** and **comfort** for the semantics). 'The stealth of our most mutual entertainment With character too gross is writ on Juliet', *Measure,* I ii 151–152.—Cf. the quotation at **raw.**

Via Fr., ex L. *mutuus,* 'borrowed, lent; exchanged': *mutare,* 'to change'.

mutually committed. Committed willingly and freely by both parties to the act of sexual intercourse. '*Duke.* So, then, it seems your most offenceful act Was mutually committed?—*Juliet.* Mutually': *Measure for Measure,* II iii 26–27.

Cf. **commit** and **mutual entertainment.**

n, innuendoed or concealed or—specially in *and* (pronounced 'n')—representing *in*; connected with the ways in which words or sounds are—for instance, with suggestive pauses—delivered on stage.

Mr Aylmer Rose, in a long and valuable letter dated 2 October 1955, writes thus, concerning *Twelfth Night*, II v 87–89: ' "Her very C's, her U's, and [pronounced 'n', i.e. N] her T's; and thus makes she her great P's" [where, he implies, there is a significant pause before P's]. If my suggestion about the innuendoed N is correct, it draws attention to the necessity of considering the sound of words and the way in which they are delivered on the stage. Examples:—'*Antony and Cleopatra*, I ii 59.—Not in my husband's . . . nose. *Troilus and Cressida*, III i 125.—In love, i' faith, to the very tip . . . of the nose. *Henry the Fifth*, II i 34–35.—A dozen or fourteen gentlewomen that live honestly by the prick . . . of their needles. The last words are altered as if by an afterthought, when what has gone before has had time to deliver its shock and produce its roar of laughter. So, too, words often conceal other and more dangerous words—your examples "constable" and "focative"—even most seemingly innocent words like "and". It yields the required N in *Twelfth Night*, and is perhaps equivalent to "end" (an erotic word) and it may even suggest "in" (see your note on Pillicock for vowel change). In *As You Like It* "and" in "Love's prick and Rosalind" could easily be made by the speaker to convey "in" (justified by III ii 208—"put a man in, etc.")'

nag. A pejorative for 'a small riding horse'. 'Yon ribaudred nag of Egypt' (i.e. Cleopatra), *A. & C.*, III x 10: Antony is the **rider:** see **ride**; cf. **mount** and especially **hackney** and **hobby-horse.**

Etymology: cf. Middle Dutch *negge*; anterior history obscure.

naked. '*Iago*. To be naked with her friend in bed, An hour or more, not meaning any harm?—*Othello*. Naked in bed, and not mean harm! It is hypocrisy against the devil': IV i 3–6.

Cognate with L. *nudus*, it is of Aryan origin.

naked bed, (Cf. *Othello* quotation at **naked.**) 'Who sees his true love in her naked bed, Teaching the sheets a whiter hue than white, But, when his glutton eye so full hath fed, His other agents aim at light delight?', *Venus*, vv. 397–400: naked in her bed.

naked seeing self. The pudend: for the semantics, cf. **eye** and **O**, qq.v. 'Can you blame her, then, being a maid yet rosed-over with the virgin crimson of modesty, if she deny the appearance of' [Cupid, who is] 'a naked blind boy in her naked seeing self?', *Henry V*, v ii 303–307.

nasty. Sexually dirty or otherwise sexually objectionable. See quotation at **enseamed bed.**

Cf. **filthy, foul, greasy, muddy,** and also **beastly.** Etymologically, *nasty* appears to = dirty.

naughtily. Indelicately. Cressida to Troilus, 'You smile and mock me, as if I meant naughtily', IV ii 37. Cf.:—

naughty. Obscene; inclined to love-making. Pandarus to Cressida, 'Would he not—a naughty man—let it sleep?': T. & C., IV ii 25 and 32–33.

Naughty originally meant 'worthless' (a thing of *naught*).

naughty-house. (Cf. **bawdy-house** and **bad woman.**) A brothel. 'This house, if it be not a bawd's house, . . . is a naughty house', *Measure*, II i 75–76.

See **naughty** and cf. the C.19–20 euphemism, *house of ill fame.*

Neapolitan bone-ache. Syphilis; cf. **malady of France,** q.v. 'Vengeance on the whole camp! or, rather, the Neapolitan bone-ache! for that, methinks, is the curse dependant upon those that war for a placket', T. & C., II iii 19–21; in v i 21, it is called *incurable bone-ache.*

neat. Cattle, in the sense 'horned herd' (see at **horned**). 'Come, captain, we must be neat', says jealous Leontes in *The W. Tale*, 1 ii 122–123.

As *cattle* and *chattel* are doublets, coming from a L. word meaning 'property', so *neat* probably comes from a common-Teutonic base that means 'to use'.

neck. A woman's bosom. See the quotation at **paddle**. Here, *neck* is used instead of *bosom* for the sake of the metre—not as a euphemism.

needle. (Cf. **prick** and **thorn**, qq.v.) In 'Hostess. We cannot lodge and board a dozen, . . . gentlewomen that live honestly by the prick of their needles, but it will be thought we keep a bawdy-house', *Henry V*, II i 33–36, the term bears its literal sense, then there is a reference to the **eye** of the needle, and there is an allusion to **prick**, n. and v.

ne'er lust-wearied. See **lust-wearied**.

nest of spicery. The pudend and the circumambient hair. 'Eliza-beth. But thou didst kill my children.—*Richard*. But in your daughter's womb I'll bury them: Where, in that nest of spicery, they shall breed Selves of themselves, to your recomforture', *Richard III*, IV iv 424–426.

Semantics: a lark's nest. As for *spicery*: well, that olfactory and gustatory allusion hardly requires explanation; but cf. **honey** and **sweetness**.

Netherlands, the. (Cf. **holland** and **low countries**.) The pudend and adjacent area. 'I could find out countries in her . . . Where stood . . . the Netherlands?—O, sir, I did not look so low'. *Com. of Errors*, III ii 112–135; cf. *R. & J.*, II i 19, '[Rosalind's] quivering thigh, and the demesnes that there adjacent lie'.

In relation to the nether *trunk* of the human body, for, after all, 'the nether limbs' are the legs.

nipple. The terminal projection on a human breast; especially either teat of a woman's bosom. 'When it did taste the wormwood on the nipple Of my dug, and felt it bitter . . .', *R. & J.*, I iii 32–33.—*Macbeth*, I vii 57.

Origin obscure: but may it not be 'that little thing which the baby *nips* as it sucks the breast'?

nose. Penis. 'Iras. Am I not an inch of fortune better than she?—Charmian. Well, if you were but an inch of fortune better than I, where would you choose it?—Iras. Not in my husband's nose', A. & C., I ii 56–59.

This entry must be compared with the next: here, nose = proboscis = trunk = dangling projection.

nose-painting. Lechery; (excessive) copulation. 'Macduff. What three things does drink especially provoke?—Porter. . . . Nose-painting, sleep and urine', Macbeth, III iii 27–28. The remainder of the Porter's speech makes it clear that lechery, not the nose-reddening that results from over-drinking, is primarily meant, though there may be a pun. (Cf. Othello's 'O, I see that nose of yours, but not that dog I shall throw it to' (IV i 142–143), to Cassio whom he believes to be Desdemona's paramour.)

See **parson's nose** and consider its potentialities: there is, I surmise, a very greasy allusion.

nunnery, in 'Go thy ways to a nunnery' (Hamlet, III i 131) and 'Get thee to a nunnery (138–139), both spoken by Hamlet to Ophelia, bears the fairly common Elizabethan slang sense 'brothel'.

nuptial, n, and adj. Bridal. 'This union stood upon . . . her nuptial vow', Titus Andronicus, II iii 125.—R. & J., I v 37.—M.N. Dream: see quotation at **desire.**—'Nuptial rites', The M. of V., II viii 6.—'In heart As merry as when our nuptial day was done. And tapers burnt to bedward!', Coriolanus, I iv, 30–32.

L. nuptiae, 'a wedding', ex nubere, 'to become a wife'.

nymph. A girl or young woman, especially if pretty and oncoming. 'To strut before a wanton ambling nymph', Richard III, I i 17.—Titus Andronicus, II i 22 (see at **siren**).—Favourably in 'Thou gentle nymph, cherish thy forlorn swain!', Two Gentlemen, V iv 12.

Derivative from the Classical sense, 'one of the many maiden deities supposed to haunt, and considered as the

spirits of woods, hills, springs, rivers, the sea, &c.' (Wyld). Via
L., ex Gr. numphë. Cognate with nubile, 'marriageable'.

O. For the semantics, cf. the entries at **circle** and **eye.** 'Rosaline. O
that your face were not so full of O's!—Princess. A pox of that
jest!', L.L.L., v ii 45–46.—R. & J., iii iii 88–89, 'Nurse. For
Juliet's sake, . . . rise and stand, Why should you fall into so
deep an O?', where 'O' ostensibly refers to a cry of
lamentation.—See the revealing quotation at **fuck.**—Probably
implied in the first quotation at **mount.**

obscenely. 'Most incony [i.e., dainty] vulgar wit! When it
comes so smoothly off, so obscenely, as it were, so fit', L.L.L.,
iv i 142–143, at the end of that thicket of sexual innuendoes
and puns which is the latter part of the archery scene.

   obscene comes from L. obsc(a)enus, 'filthy; disgusting': L. ob +
easement s + caenum, 'mud, filth' (cf. cunire, 'to defecate', and
inquinare, 'to defile'). Therefore cf. **filthy, foul, greasy, muddy,
nasty.**

occupation. The n. corresponding to **occupy.** There is a vaguely
allusive passage in Measure, iv ii 33–39, where Pompey, servant
to a bawd, and Abhorson, part-time executioner and part-
time pimp, make much play with the word, especially in the
former's 'Painting [? cf. **nose-painting**] . . . is a mystery; and
your whores, sir, being members of my occupation, using
painting, do prove my occupation a mystery'.—Perhaps, too,
there is a prophetic relevancy in 'Othello's occupation's gone'
(iii iii 337).

occupy. To copulate with (a woman), with an allusion to the
two senses, 'take and retain possession of' (as in warfare) and
'to keep (a person) busy'. 'Mercutio. Thou desirest me to stop in
my tale against the hair.—Benvolio. Thou wouldst else have
made the tale large.—Mercutio. O, thou art deceived; I would
have made it short: for I was come to the whole depth of my
tale; and meant, indeed to occupy the argument no longer', R.

& J., II iii 97–103; where 'whole' puns on **hole**.—2 *Henry IV*, II iv 146–149, 'A captain! God's light, these villains will make the word as odious as the word "occupy"; which was an excellent good word before it was ill sorted'.

œilliades. Amorous glances. '. . . Page's wife, who even now gave me good eyes too, examined my parts with most judicious œilliades', *Merry Wives*, I iii 56–58; 'Strange œilliades and most speaking looks', *Lear*, IV iv 25.

French *œillades*: L. *oculus*, 'an eye'.

offend in a dream. To have an amorous dream (cf. **hot dreams**). 'He hath but as offended in a dream! All sects, all ages smack of this vice; and he To die for't!', *Measure*, II ii 5–7.

Did the hen or the egg come first? Does the dream cause the physical condition, or the physical condition the dream? No irrefutable answer has been given: perhaps sometimes it is the one, sometimes the other: but probably it is the physiological condition which determines the dream, for the dream, though usually of an amorous episode, is occasionally of one's overpowering desire to urinate.

old ling. See **ling**.

on. See quotation at **thing,** where 'on' = lying, in sexual intercourse, on.—*Much Ado*, III iv 23–27, 'Hero. My heart is exceeding heavy.—*Margaret*. 'Twill be heavier soon by the weight of a man.—*Hero*. Fie upon thee! art thou not ashamed?—*Margaret*. Of what, lady? of speaking honourably?' (Honourably.)

For another bawdy **on** pun, see the second quotation at **buz;** and cf. *Hamlet*, II ii 415.

on the way. Pregnant. 'She is two months on her way', *L.L.L.*, V ii 666–667.

one moment's fading mirth. *Two Gentlemen*, I i 30 (passage on love) may refer to that sexual act which is no sooner begun than, with so many males, it ends in the orgasm.

Cf. **momentary trick,** q.v.

orchard. The female pelvic region, with especially reference to the pudend and the womb. See quotation at **plant** and cf. **rose, husbandry, tillage, plough.**

organ. See the next two entries.

Ex. L. *organum*, 'implement, **instrument**', ex Gr. *organon*, 'instrument, **tool**', cognate with *ergon*, 'work'.

organs of fantasy, in *Merry Wives*, v v 52, probably = imaginative faculties; but there may be also an erotic implication (see **sinful fantasy**).

organs of increase. Ovaries. *Lear*, I iv 284–287, 'Into her womb convey sterility! Dry up in her the organs of increase; And from her derogate body never spring A babe to honour her!'

out and **in, be.** (Cf. '**let in** and **let out**', q.v.) L.L.L., IV i 133–135, especially 'An if my hand be out, then belike your hand is in', in reference to the target or **mark,** the innuendo being *digitae in vulvam inmissae* (or *impositae*)—or, at best, *vir sub indusio mulieris praetentans*, or not doing so.

out-paramour, to. (Cf. **paramour.**) To have more paramours than. 'In woman [I] out-paramour'd the Turk', *Lear*, III iv 92.

Overdone, Mistress. A bawd in *Measure for Measure*: many whores, when they are *overdone* (worn out), become bawds or procuresses.

ox. A cuckold (see **horn**): L.L.L., v ii 3–6.—Cf. **monster** and see **neat.**

pace, v.t. To train a woman, regarded as **hackney** or **nag,** to walk 'correctly' along 'the primrose paths of dalliance'. Bawd, to Lysimachus, concerning Marina, 'My lord, she's not paced yet: you must take some pains to work her to your manage' (the manage of horsemanship), *Pericles*, IV v 62–63.

paddle, v. To caress with the palm of the hand. A *paddle* is a 'small spade-like implement with long handle' (C.O.D.): the hand, especially the palm, is the digging part, and the arm is the handle. *Hamlet*, III iv 196, Paddling in your neck with his damn'd fingers'.—'Didst thou not see her paddle with the palm of his hand?', *Othello*, II i 256–257.—'To be paddling palms and pinching fingers . . . ', *The W. Tale*, I ii 115.

pagan. A prostitute. '*Page*. . . . Mistress Quickly and Mistress Doll Tearsheet.—*Prince Henry*. What pagan may that be?—*Page*. A proper gentlewoman, sir, and a kinswoman of my master's.— *P.H* Even such kin as the parish heifers are to the town bull', 2 *Henry IV*, II ii 150–156.

Pagan: from the cult of physical beauty in Pagan Greece and Rome and from the beauty of the Greek *hetairai*.

pandar, n.; **Pandarus.** See second quotation at **contaminate.**—'I would play Lord Pandarus of Phrygia, sir, to bring a Cressida to this Troilus', *Twelfth Night*, III i 53–54.—'If ever you prove false one to another, since I have taken such pains to bring you together, let all pitiful goers-between be call'd to the world's end after my name; call them all Pandars; let all inconstant men be Troiluses, all false women Cressids, and all brokers-between Pandars!', *T. & C.*, III ii 195–200.—*All's Well*, II i 97–98.—*Lear*, II ii 22 (*pandar*)—Pandar: a character in *Pericles*.—*Cymbeline*, III iv 31, 'Thou art the pandar to her dishonour'.—*The W. Tale*, II i 45.

The Homeric Pandaros was not a pandar; his pandering is a medieval fabrication.

pandar, v. To play the pandar to; to subserve the lust of. 'When . . . reason pandars will', *Hamlet*, III iv 89.

See the preceding entry.

Pandarus. See **pandar,** n.

pant, n. A panting; especially the quick breathing that accompanies and ensues upon the orgasm. In reference to Othello, 'That he may . . . Make love's quick pants in Desdemona's arms', II i 78–79. —*A. & C.*, IV viii 17.

pap. Nipple. L.L.L., IV iii 24 (of a man).

Echoic: of same semantics as **mammets,** q.v.

paramour. A clandestine or illicit lover (especially of a married person). 'Lustful paramours', 1 *Henry VI*, III ii 53; cf. v iii

82.—R. & J., v iii 103–106, 'Shall I believe That unsubstantial Death is amorous; And that the lean abhorred monster keeps Thee here in dark to be his paramour?'—M.N. *Dream*, IV ii, where it is Malapropized.

In M.E., it means 'wooer, or person wooed': one who acts *par amour*, 'by (or out of) love': which corresponds to L. *per amorem: amor*, 'love' (further etymology is obscure).

parcel-bawd. A part-time pimp, a partial procurer. 'He, sir! a tapster, sir; parcel-bawd; one that serves a bad woman', *Measure*, II i 62–63.

Cf. the alliterative sense-reduplicative *part and parcel*; see **bawd.**

park as 'the female body regarded as a domain where a lover may freely roam', is elaborated in **Venus,** vv. 229–240. Quoted in the Essay, section 1, near end.

parling looks. See **speaking looks.**

parson's nose. There is a pun on the literal meaning of these two words and on the transferred sense ('rump of a fowl') in: 'And sometimes comes she'—Queen Mab—'with a tithe-pig's tail Tickling a parson's nose as 'a lies asleep, Then dreams he of another benefice', R. & J., I iv 78–80.

passion and **passions.** Sexual love; physical desire. (Of the young lovers) 'But passion lends them power, Time means, to meet, Tempering extremities with extreme sweet', R. & J., II, Prologue.—*Ibid.*, II i 146, 'My true love's passion'.—*Much Ado*, II iii 109–111, 'There was never counterfeit of passion came so near the life of passion as she discovers it'.—'Nor wit nor reason can my passion hide', *Twelfth Night*, III i 155.—T. & C., III ii 35.—'Love's strong passion', *All's Well*, I iii 134, and elsewhere in the play.—See quotation at **salve.**—(Venus's) 'swelling passion' (*Venus*, v. 218).—And in *Lucrece, A Lover's Complaint*, etc.

L. *passio* = from *pati*, 'to suffer': 'strong feeling in general' becomes specialized, particularized: cf. the entry at **passion** in my *A New Testament Word-Book*.

pastimes. (Cf. **sport** and **disport; play** and **game.**) Sexual play—intercourse and caresses. 'We may, each wreathed in the other's arms, Our pastimes done, possess a golden slumber', *Titus Andronicus*, II iii 26–27.

pear. See **poperin pear.**

peculiar river. See **groping . . .**

pen. (Cf. **pin.**) Penis; there being a pun on clerk-Nerissa's quill-pen. 'I'll mar the young clerk's pen', *The M. of V.*, v i 237, says Gratiano to his wife, Nerissa, when she threatens to sleep with that clerk.

penance. See quotation at **confessor,** where, obviously, it = sexual compliance. (It is not inept to compare Boccaccio's story of 'putting the devil into hell'). There may even be a pun on **pen.**

penetrate. To influence a person sexually, to act as an aphrodisiac upon; *subagitare feminam*. 'I am advised to give her music o' mornings; they say it will penetrate.—[*Enter Musicians.*] Come on; tune: if you can penetrate her with your fingering, so; we'll try with tongue too', *Cymbeline*, II iii 12–16. (See **finger** and **try with tongue.**)

Penetrate comes directly ex a L. verb that is cognate with, or derived from, *penitus*, 'inwardly'.

perfect in lying down. Apt in love-making. 'Hotspur. Come, Kate, thou art perfect in lying down: come, quick, that I may lay my head in thy lap', 1 *Henry IV*, III i 226–228.

Cf. **fall backward;** also **down-bed** and **downright way.**

performance. (Cf. **execution** and **action.**) Effective virility; sexual potency. (Concerning Falstaff) 'Is it not strange that desire should so many years outlive performance?', 2 *Henry IV*, II iv 260–261.—*T. & C.*, III ii 84–86, 'They say, all lovers swear more performance than they are able, and yet reserve an ability that they never perform'.—See quotation at **provoke:** *Macbeth*, II iii 30.

Cf. the use of 'commission' in *Venus*, v. 568.

pervert. Of a heartless, eloquent Don Juan: 'O, all that borrow'd motion seeming ow'd [i.e., genuine], Would yet again betray the fore-betray'd, And new pervert a reconciled maid', *A Lover's Complaint*, vv 327–329.

Pervert, like **betray** = 'to lead astray' (from the path of female chastity).

Phrynia, in *Timon of Athens*, is Shakespeare's adaptation of Gr. *Phryne*: a type-name for a prostitute.

pick the lock. To **force** a woman's chastity. 'On her left breast A mole cinque-spotted, like the crimson drops I' the bottom of a cowslip: here's a voucher, Stronger than ever law could make: this secret Will force him think I have pickt the lock, and ta'en The treasure of her honour', *Cymbeline*, ii ii 37–42.— Cf. the proverbial *love laughs at locksmiths* (cf. vv. 575–576 of *Venus and Adonis*).

piece. A girl (or a woman) regarded sexually—a sense that has, since ca. 1870, been slang. 'He, like a puling cuckold, would drink up The lees and dregs of a flat tamed piece', *T. & C.*, iv i 62–63.—Boult, a pandar's servant, who has found Marina and taken her to a brothel-keeper: 'I have gone through for this piece . . . : if you like her, so; if not, I have lost my earnest', *Pericles*, iv ii 43–45.

Probably elliptic for *piece of flesh*. Cf. *Twelfth Night*, i v 262, 'As witty a piece of Eve's flesh as any in Illyria'; and *a nice piece of horseflesh* (a good horse); and the slang *nice piece of goods*, 'a pretty or attractive girl'.

pike. Penis. Falstaff to Doll Tearsheet, 'To serve bravely is to come halting off, you know: to come off the breach with his pike bent bravely, and to surgery bravely', *2 Henry IV*, ii iv 49–52.— See at **vice**.

Cf. **lance** and **poll-axe** and **sword**.

piled for a French velvet. Infected with venereal disease (cf. **malady of France:** syphilis); *velvet* is an obscure allusion to the clitoris (see **tip the velvet** in *A Dict. of Slang*). 'I had as lief be a list of an English kersey, as be piled, as thou art piled, for a French velvet. Do I speak feelingly now?', *Measure*, I ii 33–35.

Pillicock; Pillicock Hill. Lear's ' 'Twas this flesh begot Those pelican daughters' prompts Edgar (outcast, and posing as idiot Poor Tom) to chant, 'Pillicock sat on Pillicock Hill' (III iv 74–75).

The usual *langue-verte* explanation is that *Pillicock* (*penis* [cf. *pin*] + *cock*) = penis, and that *Pillicock-hill* = pudend; but more probably *Pillicock* = male generative organs (*pill*, 'testicle'; i, euphony-convenient; *cock*, 'penis') and *Pillicock-hill* = the mount of Venus + the *pudendum muliebre* itself. It is a common error, even among the less 'innocent' of Shakespeare's commentators, to over-simplify his subtle sexuality.

pinch, n. A pinching caress in love-making. (Cleopatra) 'Think on me, That am with Phoebus' amorous pinches black', *A. & C.*, I v 26–27.—'The stroke of death is as a lover's pinch, Which hurts, and is desir'd', says Cleopatra, whose dictum exacts respect (v ii 295–296).

The n. derives from the v., which is of doubtful etymology: cf. Fr. *pincer*. Perhaps echoic, from the sound emitted by the material, or the person, that has been painfully nipped.

pinch, v. 1, Of the distress caused by syphilis: see quotation at **lechery:** cf. *ibid.*, I ii 250, (Falstaff) 'A pox of this gout', or, a gout of this pox!'

2, In ordinary sense, but with a sexual connotation. 'You might have pincht [with a pun on *pinch*, 'to steal'] a placket,— it was senseless [Another pun: 'idiotic; insensible']; 'twas nothing to geld a codpiece of a purse', *The W. Tale*, IV iii 614–616.

pine. To waste away for love: see quotation at **achieve.** Via Fr., ex L. *poena*, 'penalty; pain'.

pipe, n. Penis. Vaguely relevant in *Much Ado*, II iii 14–15.—Insinuatingly in *R. & J.*, IV v 96.

Perhaps from both the water-pipe (cf. **cock**) and the musical pipe (cf. **bugle** and **horn**).

piss, n. Only in 'Monster, I do smell all-horse-piss; at which my nose is in great indignation', *The Tempest*, IV i 199–200.

Cf. **stale,** n. sense 2.

Ex the v. Both *piss* (to urinate) and *cack* (to defecate) are undoubtedly echoic.

Note also the famous nursery spell-out of both *cunt* and *piss* in *Twelfth Night*, II v 87–90: 'By my life, this is my lady's hand' [handwriting: these be her very C's, her U's, and her T's; and thus makes she her great P's. It is, in contempt of person, her hand.' Note that Shakespeare has not, after all, omitted the n; it occurs in 'and no T's', as several discerning scholars have noted; *cunt* is spelt out clearly enough, despite Professor Dover Wilson's assertion that C-U-T is a typographical error for C-U-E, with a presumable pun on 'P's and Q's', a phrase apparently unknown at the time. One can hardly doubt that in 'her great P's', P's = piss. It should be recorded that Mr. David Garnett was, so far as I know, the first scholar to deal adequately with this spell-out; this he did in *The New Statesman*, 1933, n.s., 6: 812. See also '**n,** inneundoed' above.

piss one's tallow. Literally, to lose weight by freely sweating; hence, in *Merry Wives*, V v 15–16 (see quotation at **rut-time**), to be so sexually excited as to experience a seminal emission.

Originally, hunting slang; its appositeness to Falstaff is clear—did he not 'lard the lean earth' with his sweat?

pissing-conduit. 'I charge and command, that, of the city's cost, the pissing-conduit run nothing but claret wine this first year of our reign'; *2 Henry VI*, IV, vi 2–5. The *Pissing-Conduit* was the mob's 'name for a small conduit near the Royal Exchange' (*The O.E.D.*).

pissing while, a. A minute or two. 'He had not been there . . . a pissing while, but all the chamber'—roomful—'smelt him', *Two Gentlemen*, IV iv 19–21.

Long enough to be able to urinate. See **piss.**

Pistol. In *2 Henry IV*, II iv there are several sexual puns on Pistol's name, in reference to *pistol* = penis (cf. **weapon**); e.g., 'Falstaff. Here, Pistol, I charge you with a cup of sack: do you discharge upon mine hostess.—*Pistol.* I will discharge upon her, Sir John, with two bullets.—*Falstaff.* She is pistol-proof, sir; you shall hardly offend her.—*Hostess.* Come, I'll drink no proofs nor no bullets' (II iv. 111–117). See **go off.**—See **cock.**

pistol-proof. Immune to impregnation: see preceding entry.

pizzle. 'You bull's pizzle, you stock-fish', 1 *Henry IV*, II iv 249.

An animal's, especially a bull's, penis: from *piss*, the implication is probably of 'penal' largeness.

In 2 *Henry IV*, II iv 160, the Hostess calls Pistol 'Peesel'—an obvious pun on *Pistol* and *pizzle*.

placket. An opening in—or the opening of—a petticoat; a petticoat-pocket, or a dress-opening that gives access to it. It is placed in contiguity with the pudend—hence the sexual connotations of *placket*, as in L.L.L., III i 181, where Cupid is hailed as 'dread prince of plackets, king of codpieces'.—T. & C., II iii 21 (see quotation at **Neapolitan bone-ache**).—*Lear*, III iv 97–99, 'Keep thy foot out of brothels, thy hand out of plackets, thy pen from lenders' books, and defy the foul fiend'.—'Is there no manners left among maids? will they wear their plackets where they should bear their faces?', *The W. Tale*, IV iii 253–255; must they speak from out their placket-holes, i.e. bawdily?

Semantically parallel to **lap,** q.v.; etymologically parallel—maybe!—with *placard*, 'a stomacher'.

plain. Venus, expatiating to Adonis on the topographical attractions of the **park** she places at his disposal in her proffered body, speaks of 'Sweet bottom-grass, and high delightful plain, Round rising hillocks' (vv. 236–237): *plain* is certainly her belly and perhaps also her back.

plant, n. A child, a baby, regarded as the result of **seed**-sowing. *A Lover's Complaint*, vv. 169–172, 'For further I could say, "This man's untrue", And knew the patterns of his foul beguiling;

Heard where his plants in others' orchards grew, Saw how deceits were gilded by his smiling'.

play, n. Amorous sport (cf. **game**). See *Henry VIII* quotation at **thing,** sense 2.

The O.E. noun, *plega*, means not only 'game, sport', but also quick movement' (Wyld).

play, v.i. To disport oneself sexually. Iago, ironically satirizing women, 'You are . . . Players in your housewifery, and house-wives in your beds.—*Desdemona.* O, fie upon thee, slanderer!—*Iago.* Nay, it is true, or else I am a Turk: You rise to play, and go to bed to work', *Othello*, II i 110–116.—'As well a woman with an eunuch play'd As with a woman', says Cleopatra, who was certainly no Lesbian, in *A. & C.*, II v 5–6.—'A bank for love to lie and play on', *The W. Tale*, IV iii 123.—Venus, amorously to Adonis, 'Be bold to play, our sport is not in sight' (v. 124).

Cf. **sport,** v., and **toy,** v.; also **game** and **riggish.**

play fair, to. To be faithful to one's partner in marriage. 'Heaven shield my mother play'd my father fair?', *Measure*, III i 137.

Cf. **keep fair quarter with one's bed.**

play-fellow. A sharer in sexual pleasures. ' . . . To seek her as a bed-fellow, In marriage-pleasures play-fellow', Induction (vv. 33–34) to Act I of *Pericles*.

For the semantics, cf. **play, sport, toy** and **game.**

play on one's back. (Of a woman) to copulate. 'Lulls him whilst she playeth on her back', *Titus Andronicus*, IV i 100.

Cf. to **fall backward** and **make the beast with two backs.**

play the maid's part. To refuse verbally and accept (or submit) in act; especially in reference to an amorous wooing or pro-posal. 'Play the maid's part,—still answer nay, and take it' (see **take it**), *Richard III*, II vii 51. Cf. 'Maids, in modesty, say "No" to that Which they would have the profferer construe "Ay"!', *Two Gentlemen*, I ii 54–55.

play the strumpet. To act like a strumpet; to be unfaithful to a man: *Cymbeline*, III iv 21–22.

play upon, in *Pericles*, I i 84, continues the musico-sexual metaphor of the first quotation at **finger:** cf. slangy *strum*.

please oneself upon. (Of a man) to indulge one's amorous desires upon the body of (a woman). 'Perhaps they will but please themselves upon her, Not carry her abroad. If she remains, Whom they have ravisht must by me be slain', *Pericles*, VI i 101–103.

Cf. **enjoy,** the euphemistic *take one's pleasure with a woman*, and:—

pleasure and **pleasures.** Sexual pleasure; pleasures of sexual intimacy. *R. & J.*, II iii 160–164, 'Peter [*addressing the Nurse*]. I saw no man use you at his pleasure; if I had, my weapon should quickly have been out, I warrant you: I dare draw as soon as another man, if I see occasion in a good quarrel'.—*As You Like It*, V iv 194.—'Th' incestuous pleasure of his bed', *Hamlet*, III iii 90.—*T. & C.*, II ii 147 and 171–173.—*All's Well*, II iv 45.— *Othello*, I iii 373.—And elsewhere.

A specialization (arising partly from the distinction between *pleasure* and *happiness*) of the general sense.

plough, v.t. To coït with; to impregnate (a woman). Agrippa, concerning Cleopatra, 'Royal wench! She made great Caesar lay his sword to bed: He plough'd her, and she cropt', *A. & C.*, II ii 240–242.—'An if she were a thornier piece of ground than she is, she shall be plough'd', *Pericles*, IV v 145–146.

Cf. Lucretius's 'plough (*arare*) the fields of woman (*muliebria arva*)', another Latin author's *alienum fundum arare* (to till another man's farm), and other such agricultural metaphors as **tillage, tilth, unear'd, husbandry,** and, above all, **ear.**

pluck; pluck a sweet. (Cf. the entry at **velvet leaves,** which read before the present entry). 'But, alack, my hand is sworn Ne'er to pluck thee from thy thorn;—Vow, alack, for youth unmeet, Youth so apt to pluck a sweet', *L.L.L.*, IV iii 109–112. Hence, to *pluck a sweet* is to despoil the beloved of her **rose,** here conventionally narrowed to 'maidenhead'.—*The Taming*, II i 211.

Cf. **sweet.** Pluck (of common-Teutonic stock) = to nip off, break off; to gather.

plum; plum-tree. Pudend; the legs (limbs of body: limbs of tree) leading to it. In the punning passage in 2 *Henry VI*, II i, 'What, art thou lame? . . . 'A falls off a tree. A plum tree . . . Wouldst climb a tree? . . . Mass, thou lovest plums well, that wouldst venture so.— Alas, good master, my wife desired some damsons, And made me climb, with danger to my life', *damsons*, however, would seem to allude to testicles, and *plum-tree* apparently = the pudend, the whole female pubic basin, and the thighs (In Cotgrave's French dictionary, *hoche-prunier* is defined as 'a Plum-tree shaker; a man's yard'), whereas *plums* seems to be collect-ively used for 'pudend as a fruit grateful to man's appetite'.

Compare with the German use of the cognate *Pflaume* for the vulva. An erudite correspondent adds, 'especially for the hair-less organs of a little girl, *because of the shape* (note the groove down the side of some kinds of plum). A German announcing the birth of a daughter will say that they "have received a plum" (cf. our "cushion with tassel").'

ply. To woo, pay court (to a woman). 'He plies her hard; and much rain wears the marble', 3 *Henry VI*, III ii 50.

Literally: to work hard at: hence, to assail (with eloquence).

pocky. Pitted—or infected—with the **pox** (syphilis): *Hamlet*, V i 175.

poll-axe. Penis: see quotation at **close-stool.** For the semantics, cf. **lance, pike, sword** and **weapon:** weapons of sexual attack. In '*poll-axe*', there may also be a pun on the homophonous *pole*, which has, for centuries, been used for *penis erectus*; in modern low slang, *to get up the pole* = (of a woman) to coït.

point, in the first quotation at **sword,** = head (or gland) of penis; with vague allusion to the entire phallus.

pollute. To defile sexually. 'Polluted with your lusts', 1 *Henry VI*, v iv 43.—*Lucrece*, v. 1726.

For origin, see:—

pollution. Sexual defilement. 'Before his sister should her body stoop To such abhorred pollution', *Measure*, II iv 182–183.

Pollute = to destroy the purity of (cf. **defile** and **stain**); literally, to drench (a person) dirtily (L. *per*, often pejorative, becomes *pol* before *luere*—a form of *lavare*).

pond. Allusively for 'pudend' in *Cymbeline*, I iv 87–88 (see quotation at **strange fowl**).—See quotation at **sluice**.

Cf. slang *waterworks* in same sense, and *river* in **groping for trouts** . . .

poop. To infect with venereal disease. 'Ay, she quickly poopt him; she made him roast-meat for worms', *Pericles*, IV ii 23–24.

With reference to the stern.

poperin pear. (Following the first quotation at **medlar,** q.v.) 'O, Romeo, that she were, O that she were An open *et-caetera*, thou a poperin pear!', *R. & J.*, II i 37–38. *Poperin* (generally *poperine*) *pear* by its shape makes it clear that 'penis + scrotum' is meant; cf. the pun on **Pistol** (likewise allusive to 'penis + scrotum'). Shakespeare, often delighting in a treble innuendo, may be— indeed, probably he is—punning on *pop her in*, especially as the old folk-song *pop goes the weasel!* refers to the emission-explosion of a *penis erectus*, a weasel being allied to a ferret, which burrows.

Poperin = *popperin* = *poppering* = *Poperinghe* (the township in West Flanders).

possess. To have a man, a woman, by way of sexual intercourse. See quotation at **mansion of love.**

Cf. **have,** q.v.: in both, the idea is to take and then to hold.

posteriors. Buttocks; the behind. '*A*. The posteriors of this day, which the rude multitude call the afternoon.—*Holofernes*. The posterior of the day . . . is liable, congruent and measurable for the afternoon: the word is well cull'd . . . , I do assure you, sir', *L.L.L.*, V i 83–88: there is, perhaps, an allusion to afternoon dalliance.

The vague 'hinder parts' (of the body) have become particularized to the jutting buttocks.

posture. Referring to the prospective Roman triumph Cleopatra says, 'I shall see Some squeaking Cleopatra boy my greatness I' the posture of a whore' (*A. & C.*, v ii 218–220): *posture* is, ostensibly, a theatrical term; ulteriorly, however, there is an erotic allusion to a sexual posture—a *figura Veneris*.

A posture is a deliberate position (L. *ponere*, 'to place') of the body.

potato-finger. In '*Thersites*. How the devil luxury, with his fat rump and potato-finger, tickles these together! Fry, lechery, fry!' (*T. & C.*, v ii 56–58), 'these' refers to flirtatious Cressida and amorous Diomedes, 'luxury' is licentiousness or lasciviousness, and 'potato-finger' seems to be the penis (cf **little finger**)—from the basic sense of the compound noun 'a long, thick finger'.

potent regiment. Maecenas to Octavia, in reference to Cleopatra: 'Th' adultrous Antony . . . turns you off; And gives his potent regiment to a trull' (III vi 93–95). The phrase undoubtedly = penis and testicles: cf. 'her **privates** we' and the sexual meaning of *potent*. Yet another of Shakespeare's warfare-metaphors in the sphere of love-making!

powder'd bawd. Face-powdered to hide the ravages of age and her former profession (prostitution) and subjected to the treatment of the **powdering-tub**. 'Your fresh whore and your powder'd bawd', *Measure*, III ii 60.

powdering-tub. 'From the powdering-tub of infamy Fetch forth the lazar kite of Cressid's kind, Doll Tearsheet she by name', *Henry V*, II i 78–80.

(Cf. the preceding entry.) A powdering-tub was a heated tub used in the cure of syphilis; the patient sweated in it.

pox. Syphilis; in exclamations, it may be compared with *a plague take it!*, as in 'A pox of that jest!', *L.L.L.*, v ii 238 (see quotation at **lechery**).—See that at **prick**, v.—'*Pandar.* Now the pox upon her green-sickness for me!—*Bawd.* Faith, there's no way to be rid on't but by the way to the pox', *Pericles*, IV iv 14–16.— *Cymbeline*, II i 17–18, 'A pox on't! I had rather not be as noble as I am'.—*The Tempest*, I i 39.

Pox = pocks: a pock is 'a small sore or eruptive spot', at first in small-pox and then also in other diseases. The word *pock* is of common-Teutonic origin.

pranks. Tricks, caresses, sexual congress in the **game** of love-making; cf. **disport, sport, play, toy, trick.** 'There's none so foul, and foolish thereunto, But does foul pranks which fair and wise ones do', *Othello*, II i 142–143; cf. III iii 203.

prat, in *Merry Wives*, IV ii 168–169, '*Mistress Page.* Come, Mother Prat . . . *Ford.* I'll prat her.—[*Beating him*] Out of door, you witch', seems to = 'strike on the buttocks'. (In cant and low slang, **prat(t)** = buttocks.)

pregnant. Either merely 'having conceived (a child)' or 'well on the way to giving birth to a child'. Shakespeare uses the adjective some fourteen times; nearly always with an undertone of sexual metaphor.

Cf. **big, great, quick.**

L. *prae*, 'before' + (g)*nasci*, 'to be born': *praegnans*, 'gravid' (although there is no verb *praegnare*, 'to be with child').

prerogative and rite of love. 'The great prerogative and rite of love, Which, as your due, time claims, he does acknowledge; But puts it off by a compell'd restraint', *All's Well*, II iv 39–41. The privilege of consummating one's marriage by the solemn custom (or practice) of sexual intercourse.

Cf. **love, rite of.**

press, v.t. To press down in the sexual act: see quotation at **lie on one's back:** the passage implies, almost describes, a female erotic dream.

To caress: 'Her breast—Worthy the pressing', *Cymbeline*, II iv 134–135.

press to death. 'Which bed, because it shall not speak of your pretty encounters, press it to death', *T. & C.*, III ii 205–206.

prevail. To prevail with a woman—persuade her to sexual intimacy: *1 Henry VI*, v iv 78.

Priapus. The Roman god of male potency and virility; hence, a penis-like statue or symbol.

In *Pericles*, IV v 3–4, the Bawd says of Marina, 'Fie, fie upon her! she's able to freeze the god Priapus, and undo a whole generation'. *Freeze* = deprive of sexual ardour.

In medical language, a *priaprism* is a persistent turgidity of the penis; in literary English, it is often used as a synonym of *erection*. The god *Priapus* is a direct adoption of the Greek *Priapos*.

prick, n. (Cf. **needle** and **thorn.**) In the 'greasy' latter part of the archery scene in L.L.L. (IV i), reference is made to the **mark** (or target), thus:—'*Maria.* A mark marvellous well shot, for they both did hit it.—*Boyet.* A mark! O mark but that mark! A mark, says my lady! Let the mark have a prick in't, to mete at, if it may be'; cf., a few verses further on, 'She's too hard for you at pricks, sir: challenge her to bowl'.—*R. & J.*, II iii 113–116, '*Mercutio.* Give ye good den [= good evening], fair gentlewoman.—*Nurse.* Is it good den?—*Mercutio.* 'Tis no less, I tell you; for the bawdy hand of the dial'—cf. **O**, q.v.—'is now upon the prick of noon' (see the quotation at **dial**).—See **bawd's house** (*Henry V* quotation).—See at **rose.**

Prick basically = any sharp, piercing object—e.g., the prickle of a thorn, or a goad.

prick, v. (Cf. **foin** and **stab.**) Of love,—'It pricks like thorn . . . Prick love for pricking, and you beat love down' (lay it on the bed,—or perhaps, satiate it), *R. & J.*, I iv 25–27.—*Much Ado*, III iv 67–70. 'Get you some of this Carduus Benedictus, and lay it to your heart . . . *Hero.* There thou prick'st her with a thistle'.—'When you have our roses, You barely leave our thorns to prick ourselves, And mock us with our barrenness', *All's Well*, IV ii 18–20.— See:—

prick out. 'To furnish with a **prick** or penis', is the under-sense of *Sonnets*, 20, vv. 13–14. (Cf. the preceding entry.)

pricking. Copulation regarded as penetration as if by a prick or thorn. See preceding entry; and cf. **prick,** n.

pride. In *Sonnet* 151, the lines 'Flesh stays no farther reason; But, rising at thy name, doth point out thee As his triumphant prize. Proud of this pride, He is contented thy poor drudge to be, To stand in thy affairs, fall by thy side' clearly shows that, as 'flesh' here denotes 'penis', so 'pride' denotes 'insurgent penis'; compare the modern euphemism, *morning pride*; compare also *in pride* at *pride in*, below.

pride, in. (Of animals) in heat. See quotation at **prime.**

This phrase is obsolete: **in heat** and **in rut** survive. There seems, here, to be a cast-back to the centuries-obsolete sense 'prowess': *proud* and *prowess* are cognates.

prime. Lecherous. 'It is impossible you should see this, Were they as prime as goats, as hot as monkeys, As salt as wolves in pride, and fools as gross As ignorance made drunk', *Othello*, III iii 402–405.

Prime, 'important; excellent', may imply excellence—extreme aptness—in breeding.

principal, in *All's Well*, I i 148–150, refers to the pudend + the womb. *Parolles*, concerning virginity, 'Out with't! within ten year it will make itself ten, which is a goodly increase, and the principal itself not much the worse for wear', *principal* punning 'the principal **thing**' and the commercial principal and interest.

print off. (Of the woman) to conceive, gestate and produce a child in the likeness of (her partner): 'Your mother was most true to wedlock, prince, For she did print your royal father off, Conceiving you': *The W. Tale*, V i 123–125. Cf. *Sonnets*, II vv. 13–14.

Cf. **stamp,** which is applied to the male partner in the act—as *print* itself might, with propriety, have been applied.

privates. Immediately following Hamlet's question—quoted at **favours**—is Guildenstern's reply, 'Faith, her privates we', which Hamlet caps with 'In the secret parts of Fortune? O, most true, she is a strumpet.'

Ostensibly, Guildenstern means that Rosencrantz and he are merely private soldiers in Fortune's service; but the innuendo is directed at the physiological sense, 'testicles': these two courtiers are the lowly intimates of Fortune.

procreant, adj. and n. Procreative—a procreator of children. *Othello*, IV ii 28 (the n.).—*Macbeth*, I vi 7–8, 'This bird hath made his pendent bed and procreant cradle'. Cf.:—

procreation. The engendering, conception, and reproduction of a child. *Timon*, IV iii 4.

Pro connotes prolongation or continuation; *creation* is ex L. *creare*, 'to cause to grow; hence, to make'.

procure. To obtain girls for a brothel; to be a procuress. Lucio to pimping Pompey, 'How doth my dear morsel, thy mistress? Procures she still, ha?', *Measure*, III ii 55–56.

Lit., 'obtain by care or effort' (C.O.D.); 'to see to [L. *curare*] for (oneself)'.

profession. See **house of profession** and cf. *Pericles*, IV v 72 (quotation at **gamester**).

profit. The physical enjoyment of the love that one has achieved. 'The purchase made, the fruits are to ensue; That profit's yet to come 'twixt me and you', *Othello*, II iii 10–11.

From a L. verb, meaning 'to advance the cause of'.

prompture of the blood. Sexual desire, whether fugitive (a letch) or enduring. 'Though he hath fall'n by prompture of the blood', *Measure*, II iv 178.

Prompture = prompting; via the verb, ex the adj., which comes from L. *promere*, 'to bring forward to view'. See **blood.**

propagate. To beget or engender. 'I sought ... a glorious beauty, From whence an issue I might propagate', *Pericles*, I ii 72–73.

L. *propagare* = 'to multiply plants by fastening down (*pangere*, to fasten) slips for growth'; hence, 'to multiply by successive generation' (Wyld).

propt under. As Shakespeare uses it, it contains a pun on the senses 'sustained' and 'upheld, from beneath, by a prop—a **stake** or a *pole* (see at **poll-axe**)'; cf. the pun on *understand* and *understandings* (legs).

[**prostitute,** n. A woman selling her body for sexual intercourse: a **harlot, strumpet, whore,** or, if 'superior', **a courtezan;** but never—at least, if properly used—is it applied, as these Shakespearean synonyms are, to a **wanton,** 'a promiscuous woman'.

Shakespeare does not use this noun.

L. *prostituta*, 'a woman put up for sale'; ex the L. verb that gives us:—]

prostitute, v. 'Prove that I cannot, take me home again, And prostitute me to the basest groom That doth frequent your house', *Pericles*, IV v 189–191.

Ex L. *prostituere*, 'to put up for sale'.

provocation and **provoker.** A tempting or a stimulating to sexual desire and sexual activity; one who—that which—does this. *Merry Wives:* see at **eringo.**—*Othello*, II iii 21–23, 'Cassio. Indeed, she's a most fresh and delicate creature.—*Iago*. What an eye she has! methinks it sounds a parley to provocation'.—Cf. 'And when she speaks, is it not an alarum to love?' (line 25).

For etymology, see:—

provoke. To excite sexually. In *Macbeth*, II iii 29–38, the Porter says of drink: 'Lechery, sir, it provokes, and unprovokes; it provokes the desire, but takes away the performance: therefore, much drink may be said to be an equivocator with lechery: it makes him, and it mars him; it sets him on, and it takes him off; it persuades him, and disheartens him; makes him stand to, and not stand to; in conclusion, equivocates him in a sleep, and, giving him the lie, leaves him'.

Ex. L. *Provocare*, 'to call forth; to challenge' (as to a combat).

public commoner. See **commoner.**

pucelle. Medieval French (Old Fr. *pucele*: Late L. *pullicella*, 'a maid': Classical L. *puella*, 'a girl') for 'a virgin'. Joan la Pucelle in 1 *Henry VI*: cf. the quotation at **puzzel.**

pudency. Modesty; a sense of shame (L. *pudere*, 'to feel shame'). *Posthumus*, concerning Imogen, 'Me of my lawful pleasure she restrain'd, And Pray'd me oft forbearance; did it with A pudency so rosy, the sweet view on't, Might well have warmed old Saturn; that I thought her As chaste as unsunn'd snow', *Cymbeline*, II v 9–13.

Cf. **bashful.**

punk. A prostitute; a very loose woman. Pistol, concerning Mistress Quickly, 'This punk is one of Cupid's carriers' (of love-letters), *Merry Wives*, II ii 134.—'Your French crown for your taffeta punk', *All's Well*, II ii 22.—'She may be a punk; for many of them are neither maid, widow, nor wife', *Measure*, v i 179–180.

Etymology obscure: The O.E.D. and *Webster*. It may be a piece of erudite slang: L. *punctum*, 'a small **hole**' (cf. **crack**), especially one caused by **pricking:** *punctum*: punc-tum: punk.

purse, in the quotation at **pinch,** v., sense 2, = the scrotum. (Cf. the entry at **let in.**)

put a man in one's belly. To take a man; to admit, sexually, a male ingression. *As you Like It*, III ii 205–208, '*Rosalind*. I prithee, take the cork out of thy mouth, that I may drink thy tidings.— *Celia*. So you may put a man in your belly.'

put down. To force, or lay a woman down in sexual intercourse: *The Taming*, v. ii 35–36, 'My Kate does put her down.— *Hortensio*. That's my office'.—*Much Ado*, II i 272–276.

put in. See quotation at **vice.**

put to. To subject a woman to sexual intercourse. 'If their daughter be capable, I will put it to them' (i.e., organ to organ): *L.L.L.*, IV ii 34–35.—Cf. quotation at **stuff,** n.

put-to, v.i. (Of a woman) to engage in the sexual act: she puts her body to the man's. '[She] deserves a name As rank as any flax-wench that puts-to Before her troth-plight', *The W. Tale*, I ii 255–257.

put to sea, in quotation at **boarding,** is 'to have sexual intercourse'.

puzzel. A whore. 'Puccelle or puzzel, dolphin or dogfish, Your hearts I'll stamp out with my horse's heels' (1 *Henry VI*, I iv 107), with especial reference to Joan of Arc, *la Pucelle* (or Virgin) *de France*.

Perhaps a deliberate perversion of *pucelle*.

quail. A prostitute; a wanton girl or woman. (Cf. the modern slang, *bird*.) 'An honest fellow enough, and one that loves quails', *T. & C.*, v i 50–51.

Ex Late L. *quacule*, via the Old Fr. *quaille* (Mod. Fr. *caille*, which likewise has the secondary sense 'whore'); the L. word was probably echoic. (Wyld.)

quench. Shakespeare uses it several times in connection with love-abatement; e.g., 'I do not seek to quench your love's hot fire, But qualify the fire's extreme rage', *The Two Gentlemen*, II vii 21–22.

Lit., 'to extinguish or to damp down (a fire); to slake (thirst)', *quench* represents O.E. *cwencan*, 'to extinguish', which had a cognate *cwincan* (? rather a thinning of both the sound and the sense), 'to be extinguished; to die'.

quick. With child. 'The poor wench is cast away; she's quick; the child brags in her belly already', *L.L.L.*, v ii 670–672.

Cf. **big, great, pregnant.**

M.E. *quik*, 'alive; lively'; O.E. *cwick*, 'alive': the use of *quick* for 'gravid' may, therefore, be described as both pregnant and proleptic..

quivering. See **thigh.**

R. See **Roger.**

raging (appetites, eye, motions, etc.). Filled with or expressive of lust. 'Where his raging eye or savage heart, Without control, listed to make a prey', *Richard III*, III v 82–83.—Cf. quotation at **sensuality** and 'They are in the very wrath of love' (*As You Like It*, v ii 41).— 'Raging appetites', *T. & C.*, II ii 181.— *Othello*, I iii 333 (see at **cardinally**).

Cf. the French saying, *Ce n'est plus l'amour—c'est la rage.* Ex L. *rabia*, a form of *rabies*, 'madness'—*rabere*, 'to rave'.

rain, postulated at **fruitful,** q.v. on p. 118. In Feste's closing song (*Twelfth Night*, at end), the refrain 'For the rain it raineth every day' may bear a sexual connotation; and there are several other passages where this particular deliberate ambiguity seems to occur—e.g., in *M.S.N.*, I; 128; 130, 'How now, my love! Why is your cheek so pale?/How chance the roses there do fade so fast?/— Hermia. Belike for want of rain.'

raise; raise up. To cause a priapism or erection: for *raise*, see **circle;** *raise up* occurs, *ibid.*, II i 29, 'I conjure only to raise up him' (ostensibly, to make him appear).

Old Norse *reisa*, M.E. *reisen*, vowel-influenced by O.E. *raeran*, M.E. *reren*, 'to rear' being the causative of 'to *rise*' (Wyld).

ram, n. Allusively as 'the Ram' in *Titus Andronicus*, IV iii.—'His hand, that yet remains upon her breast,—Rude ram, to batter such an ivory wall', *Lucrece*, vv. 463–464.

Cf. **bull** and:—

ram, v. In 'Ram thou thy fruitful tidings in mine ears, That long time have been barren' (*A. & C.*, II v 24–25), Cleopatra, amorous-hungry because of Antony's absence in Italy, uses an animal-copulation metaphor: cf. **tup.**

ramp, n., with which cf. **tomboy.** A wild-living whore; a low, vicious wanton. 'Should he make me Live, like Diana's priest, betwixt cold sheets, Whiles he is vaulting variable ramps, In your despite, upon your purse? Revenge it', Iachimo, maligning Posthumus to Imogen: *Cymbeline*, I iv 131–134.

Ex Fr. *ramper*, 'to assume a threatening upright posture', as in *rampant*. There seems to be a reminiscence of the M.E. *rampen*, 'to rage, to be furiously angry'.

range, v.i. 'If once I find thee ranging, Hortensio will be quit with thee by changing', *The Taming*, III i: i.e., straying afield—away from me—in your love and affections.

Lit., to run, lie, be, in a (Fr. *rang*) line, rank—hence, to be found in, to inhabit—hence (?), to move about, to wander.

rank, adj. In heat; sexually exacerbated or sexually dirty; obscene. 'The ewes, being rank, In the end of autumn turn'd to the rams', *The M. of V.*, I iii 79–80.—'The rank sweat of an enseamed bed', *Hamlet*, III iv 93.—'Lust and rank thoughts, hers, hers', *Cymbeline*, II v 24.—*The W. Tale*, I ii 256 (see quotation at **put-to**).—'To blush at speeches rank', *A Lover's Complaint*, v. 307.

Originally, (of grass) 'coarse', *rank*, of common-Teutonic origin, has had its sense influenced by Fr. *rance*, 'musty or stale'.

ransack. To rape or ravish. Paris, referring to Helen, 'What treason were it to the ransackt queen . . . !', *T. & C.*, II ii 150.—*Lucrece*, violated by Tarquin, says (vv. 836–838), 'My honey lost, and I, a drone-like bee, Have no perfection of my summer left, But robb'd and ransackt by injurious theft' (cf. v. 1170, 'Her house is sackt').

Of Old Norse origin, its basic sense is 'to search a house, as for plunder': Old Norse *rann*, 'a house', and *saka*, 'to seek'; the latter element is independent of *sack*, 'to pillage': Fr. *sac*, a bag. (Wyld.)

rape, n. Forcible violation of a woman. 'Many unfrequented plots there are Fitted by kind for rape and villainy', *Titus Andronicus*, II i 115–116; cf. **Tereus,** second quotation, and elsewhere in *Titus Andronicus* (see note at **ravisher**).—*King John*, II i 97–98, '[Thou hast] done a rape Upon the maiden virtue of the crown'.—Paris, concerning Helen, 'I would have the soil of her fair rape Wiped off', *T. & C.*, II ii 148.

Probably ex the v. 'to rape', which comes from L. *rapere*, 'to seize'; or perhaps ex, or cognate with, Old Norse *hrapa*, 'to hasten'.

rapine. Rape—see comment at **ravisher.**

Ex L. *rapina*, plunder: *rapere*, 'to carry off'.

raven, v. To copulate with (a woman) roughly or even brutally. 'The cloyed will,—That satiate yet unsatisfied desire ... , ravening first the lamb, Longs after for the garbage', *Cymbeline*, I vi 46–49.

Ex Old Fr. *raviner*, the v. corresponding to Fr. *rapine*: ex L. *rapere*. Therefore cf. **rape** and **rapine.**

ravish. To violate; to abduct and then violate. 'Ravish our daughters?', *Richard III*, V iii 338.—*Titus Andronicus*, II iv 2, and elsewhere.—M.N. *Dream*, II i 78.—'The ravisht Helen, Menelaus' wife, With wanton Paris sleeps', *T. & C.*, Prologue, 9–10.—*Coriolanus*, IV vi 82.—See quotation at **please.**—*Cymbeline*, III v 139.—*Lucrece*, Argument.

Ex Fr. *ravir*, which comes ex L. *rapere*, 'to seize'; it is, therefore, cognate with **rape** and **raven.**

ravisher. Violator of a woman—or of women. 'Good Rapine, stab him; he's a ravisher', *Titus Andronicus*, V ii 103, where there is a deliberate linking-up of 'Rapine' with **rape:** cf. v. 134, 'Nay, nay, let Rape and Murder stay with me'.—'As war ... may be said to be a ravisher', *Coriolanus*, IV v 213–214.—*Lucrece*, v. 770.

ravishing, adj. Pertaining to the violation of a woman. See quotation at **Tarquin.**

Ex **ravish,** q.v.

ravishment. 'He will steal, sir, an egg out of a cloister: for rapes and ravishments he parallels Nessus', *All's Well*, IV iii 250–251.—'In bloody death and ravishment delighting', *Lucrece*, v. 430.

Either *ravish* + -ment, or straight from Fr. *ravissement.*

raw. Inexpert, unpractised, tyro-clumsy; in especial reference to sexual intercourse. Pandar, concerning Marina (sold to a bawd), 'Wife, take her in; instruct her what she has to do, that she may not be raw in her entertainment', *Pericles*, IV ii 53–55.

Synonymous with **unripe, raw** is of common-Teutonic stock and cognate with L. *crudus*, 'raw, uncooked'.

rearward. See the second quotation at **mandrake.** There is possibly a vague charge of monosexuality.

rebel, v.; **rebellion.** (Of the passion, the appetite, of love) to stir, in one, against oneself; an amorous mutiny of the blood. 'Best safety lies in fear: Youth to itself rebels, though none else near', *Hamlet*, I iii 43–44.—For *rebellion*, see the fourth quotation at **codpiece.**

L. *rebellare*, 'to renew war; to revolt, after being conquered'; *rebellis*, 'rebellious'.

refrain. To withhold oneself from sexual intercourse; to forgo it. *Hamlet*, III iv 166 (see quotation at **abstemious**).

From Fr. *refrêner*, 'to hold in (a horse) with—L. *fraenum*—a bit or bridle'; contrast *unbridled passions*.

relief. In reference to the spacious **park** of her body, a park wherein she has already invited Adonis to 'Feed where thou wilt', Venus, sweetly reasoning (if not wholly reasonable), adds: 'Within the limit is relief enough, Sweet bottom-grass, and high delightful plain, Round rising hillocks' (*Venus*, vv. 235–237): where *relief* contains a double-meaning:—the features of hill and dale, plain and stream, such as are shown on a *relief*-map, i.e. *relief* in the sense of contrasts; and *relief*, a satisfaction for all the senses and of all amorous desires.

It. *relievo*: L. *relevare*, 'to raise; to lighten': *levis*, 'light' (not heavy).

relish, 'flavour', in T. & C., III ii 18–19, 'Th' imaginary relish is so sweet That it enchants my sense', refers to sensuous and sexual enjoyment of physical love; cf. **taste,** q.v.

Ex Old Fr. *relais* or *reles*, 'after-taste': L. *relaxare*.

rent. See the quotation at **revenue** for illustration and sense.

Via Old Fr. *rente*, ex Low L. *rendita* = Classical L. (*res*) *reddita*, 'a thing [that is] given back' (*re-dare* becomes *reddere*).

respect, v., is misused by Pompey and Elbow in *Measure*, II i 169–178, for 'to coït': e.g., 'I respected with her before I was married to her'.

revel in. Satiate oneself, sexually, in; enjoy (a woman) at ease. See second quotation at **strike.**

For etymology, see:—

revels. A joyous love-making; a **riot** of physical love. *Venus*, vv. 123–124, 'Love keeps his revels where they are but twain; Be bold to play, our sport is not in sight'.

Revel, n.; probably ex the v., which comes, via Old Fr., ex L. *rebellare*, 'to revolt'.

Cf. **disport, feast . . . , game, play, sport, toy,** which should adequately account for the semantics.

revenue. *Sonnets*, 142, vv. 5–8, (to his mistress) 'Those lips of thine, That have profaned their scarlet ornaments And seal'd false bonds of love as oft as mine, Robb'd others' beds' revenues of their rents': *revenues* = love-making, sexual intercourse; *rents* = either copulation, or, more probably, semen-expenditure paid as rent by a man to the woman legally his.

See **rent.**—*Revenue*: (*chose*) *revenue*, Fr. *revenir*, 'to return': L. *venire*, 'to come'.

ribald. Obscene, indecent, coarsely indelicate. There is perhaps an allusion to these senses in the quotation at **a-weary.**

Originally a noun, its earliest sense being 'a low-born retainer'. From French, its ultimate etymology is dubious: but its intermediaries were Teutonic, as, e.g., Old High Ger. *hriba*, 'a prostitute'.

ribaudred. Scarus refers to Cleopatra as 'yon ribaudred nag of Egypt' (*A. & C.*, III x 10), where the sense is 'sexually ribald; lascivious'. Literally: 'rendered ribald'.

ride; rider (Of a man) to mount sexually; a man super-incumbent in the sexual act. 'You rode, . . . your French hose off', *Henry V*, III vii 53–54; cf. lines 57–58 (quoted in the essay).—*A. & C.*, IV viii 15–17, Cleopatra to Antony, 'Leap thou, attire and all, Through proof of harness to my heart, and there Ride on the pants triumphing!'

Probably a Celtic ingredient (cf. Cymric *rhwydd*, 'a horse') in the common-Teutonic stock-pot.

riding on his ass. See **ass.**

riggish. Amorous; lecherous, lascivious. Of Cleopatra, Enobarbus says, 'Vilest things Become themselves in her; that the holy priests Bless her when she is riggish', *A. & C.*, II ii 242–244.

Ex **rig,** 'a trick, a game': cf. **full of game, play, sport, sportive, trick, toy,** qq.v. Love-making as a game ('the greatest of indoor sports', as some wit has called it), or as fun, is a conception fairly common except among the puritanical, the solemn—and the spiritual (for whom Love is not only Eros but also Psyche). Or it may derive ex *rig*, 'a wanton', itself perhaps ex **wriggle.**

ring. (Cf. Grose's *Carvel's ring*.) The pudend—for the semantics cf. **circle** and **O.** '*Gratiano*. But were the day come, I should wish it dark, That I were couching with the doctor's clerk. Well, while I live I'll fear no other thing, So sore as keeping safe Nerissa's ring', *The M. of V.*, v i 304–307.—See next entry (= *Hamlet* II ii 435).—See quotation at **strange fowl.**

Cf. **circle:** *ring* is of common-Teutonic origin, but cognate with Old Slavonic *kragu*, 'a circle'.

ring, crackt within the. See **crackt . . .**

riot, n. Dissolute living: see quotation at **blain;** cf. that at **melt.**

riot, v. To live dissolutely. Octavius to Antony, 'I wrote to you When rioting in Alexandria', *A. & C.*, II ii 76.

Cf. the n.—also **luxury,** q.v. The Old Fr. *riote*: r(u)*ihoter* 'to quarrel': L. *rugire*, 'to roar'. Therefore cognate with *rut* (see **rut-time**).

rioter. A dissolute wencher: *Timon*, III v 68.

Ex—and cf.—the preceding term.—Cf. the Biblical quotation at **chamberer.**

riotous. Given to drinking and wenching. 'Riotous youth, with dangerous sense', *Measure*, IV iv 30.—See quotation at **go to it.**

rise, v. Its application to the penis is seen in the second quotation at **O;** cf. **stand,** q.v.

rite of love. See **love.**

road. A low prostitute. 2 *Henry IV*, II ii 165–168, 'This Doll Tearsheet should be some road.—Pointz. I warrant you, as common as the way between Saint Alban's and London'. A road is trodden by many feet, as a hen may be trodden by many cocks.

The word stands in a gradational relation to **ride:** it is ridden-along and driven-along. Semantic comparables are **trade,** n., and **way;** cf. also **trot.**

roam. See at **flesh.**

Roger or **roger.** 'Both with an R.—Nurse. Ah, mocker! that's the dog's name; R. is for the—No; I know it begins with some other letter', R. & J., II iii 213–215. The 'R' is generally explained by the dog's *ar* (or growling: this is correct; but R is also short for *Roger*, a dog's name, and also a slang term (*Roger* or *roger*) for the penis—note the Nurse's 'it'.

root. Either penis or *penis erectus* or, as in modern slang, an erection or a copulation; the first sense is the most probable: see passage quoted at **fuck,** and *Pericles*, IV v 86–87.

Cognate with certain other Teutonic words that have the related meanings 'plant' and 'snout' or 'trunk': cf., therefore, **nose** and **trunk** in addition to **carrot.**

rose. Pudend; maidenhead. The rose with its velvet, fleshy leaves recurs in modern slang, in a slightly different sense (see *A Dictionary of Slang*, 2nd ed., 1938, and cf. the entry at **velvet leaves**). —'He that sweetest rose will find, Must find love's prick and Rosalind', *As You Like It*, III ii 112–113.—See quotation at **thorn** and the third at **prick,** v.—*Lucrece*, v. 492.

rotten. Infected with venereal disease and/or soiled and decayed with constant copulation. Bawd, in reference to her three whores, 'They can do no more than they can do; and they with continual action are even as good as rotten', *Pericles*, IV ii 7–9.

Cf. **sodden.**

rotten medlar. See **medlar.**

round. To grow big with child. 'The queen . . . rounds apace', *The W. Tale*, II i 15.

round-wombed. Synonymous with **great-bellied.** *Lear*, I i 14.

rubbing. A fricative sexual caress, especially of the male by the female. '*Costard*. She's too hard for you at pricks, sir: challenge her to bowl.—*Boyet*. I fear too much rubbing', where the ostensible allusion is of the same kind as that in 'There's the rub': L.L.L., IV i 138–139.

Perhaps the v. **rub** is echoic; it seems to be of Scandinavian origin.

rudder. Rump or pudend. Antony, to Cleopatra (who, in her ship, has fled the battle), 'Egypt, thou knew'st too well My heart was to thy rudder tied by the strings', III xi 56–57: cf. **wagtail,** q.v.

Rudder is very closely connected with 'to *row* (a boat)': probably the first rudder was an oar: the O.E. and M.E. *rother* = both 'oar' and 'rudder'.

ruff, 'a projecting frill on a woman's gown', is used in *2 Henry IV*, II iv 133 and 143 in the secondary—perhaps slang—sense, 'pudend' (cf. the C.18–19 cant *muff*). Pistol to Doll Tearsheet, 'I will murder your ruff for this'; Doll to Pistol, 'You a captain! you slave, for what? for tearing a poor whore's ruff in a bawdy-house.'

The dress *ruff* is also a *ruffle*, from a v. that means 'to rumple, to wrinkle'.

rump. Posteriors, especially with an erotic connotation. See quotation at **potato-finger.**

Of Scandinavian origin; anterior history, obscure.

running banquet. In reference to the ladies attending a banquet, Lord Sands remarks, 'Some of these Should find a running banquet ere they rested, I think would better please 'em', *Henry VIII*, I iii 11–13: amorous pursuit, followed by a feast of love-making: for the semantics of this, I think, plausible explication, cf. **eat** and **feed**. (Literally, a **running banquet** is a hastily eaten banquet or meal; a snack.)

rut-time and **rutting.** Rutting-season; (of animals) in heat. '*Falstaff.* I am here a Windsor stag, and the fattest, I think, i' th' forest.—Send me a cool rut-time, Jove, or who can blame me to piss my tallow?', *Merry Wives*, V v 13–16.—'I'll do anything now that is virtuous; but I am out of the road of rutting for ever', *Pericles*, IV iv 8–9.

Rut: heat—the period of sexual excitement in male deer, goat, ram and other animals. Via Fr., ex L. *rugitus*, 'bellowing, roaring'.

ruttish. Amorous; addicted to womanizing. 'A foolish idle boy, but, for all that, very ruttish', *All's Well*, IV iii 215–216.

Cf. origin of preceding term.

sack, in *Lucrece*, v. 1170. = **ransack** (q.v.) in its meaning.

salmon's tail. See **change the cod's head.**

salt, adj. Lewd, lascivious, obscene. 'Whose salt imagination yet hath wrong'd Your well-defended honour', *Measure*, V i 399–400.—'For the better compassing of his salt and most hidden loose affections' (passions, amorous desires), *Othello*, II i 242–244.—*Ibid.*, III iii 404, 'As salt as wolves in pride'.—'All the charms of love, Salt Cleopatra, soften the waned lip', *A. & C.*, II i 20–21.—*Timon*, IV iii 85.

Salt = salted, as *spicy* = spiced; a salt tale is a spicy story. The implication is: witty (cf. *Attic salt*) in a lewd way; and highly seasoned for jaded palates.—Cf. **saucy.**

salve, n. 'With this she seizeth on his sweating palm, The precedent of pith and livelihood, And, trembling in her passion, calls it balm, Earth's sovereign salve to do a goddess good', *Venus*, vv. 25–28.

As *salve* (L. *salvare*, 'to save') = an ointment for healing wounds or sores, *balm* (L. *balsamum*, 'balsam') = a medicinal ointment for soothing or healing. (Love-making as a drug.)

sate. To satisfy; especially to the point of exhaustion or disgust (the very word comes from an Old English verb that has been assimilated to L. *satis*, 'enough': cf. *satisfacere*, 'to do enough for'). 'Lust, though to a radiant angel linkt, Will sate itself in a celestial bed And prey on garbage', *Hamlet*, I v 55–57.—*Othello*, I iii 354, 'When she is sated with his body, she will find the error of her choice'.

satiate. Satiated. 'The cloyed will,—That satiate yet unsatisfied desires, that tub Both fill'd and running,—ravening first the lamb, Longs after for the garbage', *Cymbeline*, I vi 46–49.

See **sate;** L. *satis* + -are (first conjugation verb-ending).

satiety. Sexual satiety—weariness and distaste resulting from excessive or scheduled love-making. *Othello*, II i 230: see at **act,** second quotation.—'Not cloy thy lips with loath'd satiety', *Venus*, v. 19.

Via Fr., ex L.: see **sate.**

satisfaction. The sating of sexual desire; a yielding to, or compliance in, another's appetence. See quotation at **entreat.**— And that at **affect.**

satisfy. To satisfy one's sexual desire. *Titus Andronicus*, II iii 180: see at **fee.** Cf. **sate,** q.v.

saucy. Mostly, 'impudent' or 'insolent', but occasionally in sense 'love-intending; passion-meaning' as, e.g., in L.L.L., I i 85, 'saucy looks'. —*2 Henry IV*, II iv 128, (Doll Tearsheet to bawdy Pistol's bawdy speech) 'I'll thrust my knife in your mouldy chops, an you play the saucy cuttle with me'.—*All's Well*, IV iv 23.—*Measure*, II iv 46 (see next entry).—And elsewhere.

Semantics: seasoned with sauce—with wit—with bawdy wit or humour; some sauces are hot—cf. the slangy **hot stuff.**

saucy sweetness. 'Ha! fie, these filthy vices! It were as good To pardon him that hath from nature stol'n A man already made, as to remit Their saucy sweetness that do coin heaven's image In stamps that are forbid', *Measure,* II iv 43–47. The reference is to the piquancy of sexual desire and to the **sweetness** of its satisfaction.

scald. To **burn** (sense 1)—and to infect venereally. *Timon,* II ii 70.

scale. Tarquin to Lucrece, whom he is about to rape: ' . . . Am I come to scale Thy never conquer'd fort': vv. 481–482.

Cf. **climb** and **mount; and siege.**

scambling, n. Scrambling. 'If ever thou beest mine, Kate, . . . I get thee with scambling, and thou must therefore needs prove a good soldier-breeder', *Henry V,* v ii 207–210: not necessarily bawdy, yet probably so.

scratch, v.t. 'But none of us cared for Kate; For she had a tongue with a tang, Would cry to a sailor, Go hang! She loved not the savour of tar nor of pitch; Yet a tailor might scratch her where'er she did itch', *The Tempest,* II ii 51–55, where *scratch* possesses the further meaning, 'to caress manually'.

Of obscure etymology, *scratch* is probably echoic: as many Teutonic-stock *scr*-words are.

scut. Short tail—especially of a deer, a rabbit, a hare; hence, posteriors or pudend: *Merry Wives,* v v 18.

Probably from Old Norse *skott,* 'fox's brush' (Wyld).

secret-false, to be. To hide one's unfaithfulness from one's marriage-partner: *Com. of Errors,* III ii 15.

secret parts. *Pudenda muliebria,* particularly the pudend itself, as in 'Viola. What I am and what I would, are as secret as maidenhead', *Twelfth Night,* I v 204–205.—'Then you live about her waist, or in the middle of her favours? . . . In the secret parts of Fortune?', *Hamlet,* II ii 234–237.

Euphemistic; cf. **forfended place.** *Secret* comes, via Old Fr., ex L. *secretus*, 'set apart'; *secernere*, 'to set apart, to seclude; to separate'. Cf. the next three entries.

secret things. Clown to Shepherd, concerning Perdita, in *The W. Tale*, IV iii 682–683, 'Show those things you found about her' (a babe cast away); 'those secret things' (money and jewels), 'all but what she has with her' (in her physical form).

Secret things, in short, bears the same sense as **secret parts,** q.v.; see also **thing.**

secretly open. Cressida, flirting with Diomedes, 'What would you have me do?', on which Thersites comments in an aside, 'A juggling trick,—to be secretly open', T. & C., V ii 24–25.

Sexually open, in a secret part and in private, to his phallic ingression. Cf. the ulterior, the sexual, significance of the French proverb, *Une porte doit être ouverte ou fermée.*

secrets. Secrets of sex and love; secrets of the female body. 'If thou wilt deign this favour, for thy meed A thousand honey secrets shalt thou know', *Venus*, v. 16.

Cf. **secret parts, secret things,** and **honey.**

seduce. To overcome a woman's virtue, or rather, to ensure her effective compliance in its loss; fig., to lead astray or bewitch or enchant. *Richard III*, III vii 188.—'Thou subtle, perjured, false, disloyal man! Think'st thou I am so shallow, so conceitless, To be seduced by thy flattery?', *Two Gentlemen*, IV ii 92–94.—'Lady Falconbridge ... By long and vehement suit was I seduced To make room for him in my husband's bed', *King John*, I i 254–255.—'So to seduce! —won to his shameful lust The will of my most seeming-virtuous queen', *Hamlet*, I v 45–46.

Lit., 'to lead astray' (L. *ducere*, to lead; the privative L. prefix *se* = 'apart; away').

seducer. (Letter) ' ... I blush to say it, he won me ... I follow him for justice: grant it me, O king! ... ; otherwise, a seducer flourishes, and a poor maid is undone. DIANA CAPULET', *All's Well*, v iii 139–145.

seducing, adj. Sexually—or most sensously—attractive: R. & J., 1 i 212 (see at **siege**).—*Lucrece*, v. 639.

seed. Semen. This Biblical and literary term occurs several times in Shakespeare; e.g., 'the seed of Banquo kings' (*Macbeth*, III i 69); cf. *Pericles*, IV v 86–87.

A farming metaphor.

sell one's desires. Less 'to sell her own desires' than 'to sell her body to please a man—to sate his physical desire' is the sense in *Othello*, IV i 94–96, 'Bianca, A housewife that, by selling her desires, Buys herself bread and clothes'.

Semiramis. A type of luxury-loving, lustful queen: *Titus Andronicus*, II i 22 (see quotation at **siren**) and II iii 118. A mythical Assyrian queen, famed in legend, literature, opera.

sense, in *Measure*, IV iv 30, may = sensuality. ('His riotous youth, with dangerous sense'.)

sensual; sensual race. Voluptuous; carnal, licentious desires and actions. For *sensual*, see quotation at **libertine.**—'Now I give my sensual race the rein: Fit thy consent to my sharp appetite', *Measure*, II iv 160–161.

L. *sensualis*, ex *sensus*, 'feeling, sense, bodily sensation', ex *sentire*, 'to feel, to perceive'. (For the modern distinction between *sensual* and *sensuous*, see 'Murray' or 'Webster' or 'Wyld' or 'Fowler'.)

sensuality. Excessive addiction to sex; excessive fondness for love-making. 'You are more intemperate in your blood Than Venus, or these pamper'd animals That rage in savage sensuality', *Much Ado*, IV i 59–61.—*Othello*, I iii 329–330, 'One scale of reason to poise another of sensuality', *Othello*, I iii 329–330.

serpigo (or 'herpes') is only a skin-disease; nevertheless, in *T. & C.*, II iii 75, Thersites appears to relate it to venereal disease.

Commonly known as 'ring-worm': a creeping disease, *ser-*

pigo comes from L. *serpere*, 'to creep'; cf. *serpent*, lit. 'a creeping thing'.

serve. (Of a stallion) to serve a mare; hence a man, a woman. 'To serve bravely is to come halting off, you know', *2 Henry IV*, II iv 49–50.—See *Lear* quotation at **deed of darkness.**—*A. & C.*, III vii 9.

For other animal-copulation terms, see **cover, trend, tup.** *Serve*: Fr. *servir*, which, in meaning, owes something to L. *servare* as well as to L. *servire*, its etymological antecedent.

serve one's lust. To be the object of a man's lust. 'I would we had a thousand Roman dames At such a bay; by turn to serve our lust', *Titus Andronicus*, IV ii 41–42.

Cf. the sexual derivative sense of the It. *cavaliere servente*, lit., 'gentleman-in-waiting'.

service and **services.** Sexual attention to a woman; in *Lear*, IV ii 26–28, however, it = sexual attentions to a man. See quotation at **sword.** —'I would cozen the man and his wife, and do his service.—*Lafeu.* So you were a knave at his service, indeed.—*Clown.* And I would give his wife my bauble, sir, to do her service', *All's Well*, IV v 28–32.—See quotation at **sport,** n.

set on. To incite and excite (a man) to seek the satisfaction of his desire to coït: see at **provoke:** *Macbeth*, II iii 33.

Cf. *set*, 'the basal sense is to put, place, lay; hence, to bring into a specified position or condition' (Wyld).

set on horns. Falstaff, in *The Merry Wives*, V v 2–4, 'Now, the hot-blooded gods assist me!—Remember, Jove, thou wast a bull for thy Europa; love set on thy horns'; either, 'love sat on thy horns'; or, as an injunction, 'Love, give me strength!'

Cf. **horn,** q.v.: there may be an allusion to the 'penis' sense.

set to't. To render a person lustful; it being sexual intercourse, or the desire therefor. 'I dare not for my head fill my belly; one fruitful meal would set me to't,' *Measure*, IV iii 154–156.

Cf. **set on;** also **it.**

set up one's rest. Cf. the origin, *set lance in rest*, 'to set one's lance against the check that holds the butt of a tilter's lance when it is couched for the charge against the tilter's opponent', *R. & J.*, IV v 5–7, 'For the next night, I warrant, The County Paris hath set up his rest That you shall rest but little': cf. the entries at **stab** and **lay knife aboard.**

shake (a man's) **back.** To test his sexual horsemanship with propping and curvetting: *Henry V*, III 49–50, 'Methought yesterday your mistress shrewdly shook your back', where there is the further innuendo of ensuing back-ache.

shame, n. Source or cause of shameful (especially of sexual) behaviour: *All's Well*, II i 173 (see **impudence**).—*Measure*, III i 136 (see **incest**).—Several times in *Venus and Adonis*; frequently in *Lucrece*.—*Sonnet*, 129, 'The expense of spirit in a waste of shame Is lust in action'.

shameful. See the *Hamlet* quotation at **seduce.**

shameless. Without modesty. See quotation at **courtezan.**

sharpen appetite, to. To increase sexual desire (cf. 'my sharp appetite' in the quotation at **sensual**). (See quotation at **libertine** (*A. & C.*, II i 25).

Cf. **edge** (and contrast **disedge**) and **keen.**

sheet and **sheets.** In reference to a nuptial or any other love-making bed. 'Incestuous sheets' (see at **incestuous**).—See quotation at **do one's office** (*Othello*, I iii 389–390).—'Well, happiness to their sheets!', Iago in reference to Othello and Desdemona: II iii 27.—'Got 'tween my lawful sheets', *Lear*, IV vi 119.—Alexas to Charmian, 'You think none but your sheets are privy to your wishes' (amorous dreams, and masturbation): *A. & C.*, I ii 41–42.—See at **Diana** (the *Cymbeline* quotation).—And elsewhere.

Several C.17 dramatists use the phrase *the dance of the sheets* for 'sexual intercourse'; cf. the proud claim of the woman whose Ku Klux Klan husband was 'a wizard between the sheets (or under the sheet)'.

shift. Chemise. 'The ghostly father'—actually, King Edward in
close talk with Lady Grey—'now hath done his shrift', says
Gloster, and Clarence replies, 'When he was made a shriver,
'twas for shift', 3 *Henry VI*, III ii 107–108, where shift means
'stratagem, trick' but where, also, there is undoubtedly an
allusion to shift, 'chemise' (cf. first quotation at **smock**).

A basic sense of shift, n. and v., is 'a change' (cf. *Cymbeline*, I ii
1)—present both in the 'trick' and in the 'chemise' sense. It is
not irrelevant to recall the classical error committed by the
French translator of Cibber's play, *Love's Last Shift: La Dernière
Chemise de l'Amour*, and the Italian *mutande*.

shoe with a hole in it. See **hole.**

shoot, v. Vaguely yet indubitably this verb indicates or insinuates
the pointing of the male towards the female generative
organ—with or without a further allusion to the emission of
the seminal arrow or bullet. L.L.L., IV i 10–13.

short, in innuendo-reference to length of penis, occurs in R. & J.,
II iii 100, and in A. & C., II v 8; cf. the quotation at **nose.**

shrive (cf. shrift at **shift**) is used figuratively and with sexual
innuendo in the first **smock** quotation; cf. the entry at
confessor.

siege; wanton siege. 1, Wooing regarded as a siege laid by a
man to a woman (as though there were not enough Fifth
Columnists among the garrison!). 'She hath Dian's wit. . . .
She will not stay the siege of loving terms, Nor bide th'
encounter of assailing eyes, Nor ope her lap to saint-seducing
gold', R. & J., I i 207–212.—'Lays down his wanton siege
before her beauty, Resolved to carry her', *All's Well*, III vii 18–
19.—'This siege that hath engirt his marriage', Tarquin, pro-
posing to rape Lucrece (v. 221).

Siege, via Old Fr., comes from L. *sedere*, 'to sit': *sit down before a*
town is to beleaguer or besiege it.

2, Excrement (semantically cf. the medical *stool*): see second
quotation at **vent.**

sin, in *Measure*, II ii 183, is 'to have sexual intercourse': 'To sin in loving virtue'.

sinful fantasy. Amorous imaginings. 'Fie on sinful fantasy! Fie on lust and luxury! Lust is but a bloody fire, Kindled with unchaste desire, Fed in heart; whose flames aspire, As thoughts do blow them, higher and higher', *Merry Wives*, v v 96–101.

Cf. **hot thoughts.**

sing, v.t. (Of a woman) to allure, to make advances to; (of a man) to coït with (cf. later slang *strum* and *twang*). Troilus, watching Cressida whisper intimately to Diomedes, 'Yes, so familiar! *Ulysses*. She will sing any man at first sight.—*Thersites*. And any man may sing her; if he can take her cliff; she's noted', *T. & C.*, v ii 9–12.

sink in. To become ensheathed in, to penetrate, a woman in sexual intercourse. '*Romeo*. Under love's heavy burden do I sink.—*Mercutio*. And to sink in it, should you burden love', *R. & J.*, I iv 22–23.

siren. Sexually and dangerously attractive woman. 'This queen, This goddess, this Semiramis, this nymph, This siren, that will charm Rome's Saturnine, And see his shipwreck and his commonweal's', *Titus Andronicus*, II i 21–24.

In Greek mythology, a sea nymph (half woman and half bird) that, with her singing, lured sailors to destruction on the rock where she dwelt.

sirreverence and **sir-reverence.** A catch-phrase uttered when one comes upon a lump of (human) excrement; the lump itself (the impolite—yet Standard English—turd). 'Such a one'—a fat, greasy kitchen wench—'as a man may not speak of, without he say "sir-reverence"', *Com. of Errors*, III ii.—'We'll draw thee from the mire Of this sir-reverence love, wherein thou stick'st Up to the ears', *R. & J.*, I iv 40–42.

Ex *save your reverence!*, used apologetically before any unseemly expression—or incident.

sit down before (*All's Well*, I i 1·18) = **besiege,** and it implies an innuendo upon the idea in **lay one's arms** . . . ; cf. **siege,** q.v.

skains-mate. A ribald companion, with a connotation of sexual sport: R. & J., II iii 156 (see **flirt-gill**).

   ? for *skeins-mate*: skein being, perhaps, suggestive of the phallic-vulval similitude of the interweaving of web and warp on a loom (cf. the semantics of **amorously impleacht**).

slack one's duties. (Of a man) to withhold, or to participate grudgingly or rarely in, the marriage-rites. See the *Othello* quotation at **fall,** v., and cf. 'Then if your husband have stables enough, you'll see he shall slack no barns (punning 'bairns': *Much Ado*, III iv 43–45).

   Slack, 'to slacken', comes from the adj. *slack*, itself ex O.E. *slaec*, 'slow, sluggish': of common-Teutonic stock, it has the variant 'to *slake*'.

sleep occurs on several occasions in its euphemistic sense as a synonym of 'to lie (with a man or a woman)'.

   Cf. **lie,** v., and **lie with.**

   Of common-Teutonic stock, it has the basic sense, 'drowsiness, lethargy', and it is cognate with Slavonic words that mean 'weak' and 'to become weak' (Wyld).

sleep in. Of Lavinia's lopped-off arms, Andronicus says, 'Two branches . . . Whose circling shadows kings have sought to sleep in' (*Titus Andronicus*, II iv 18–19), where the sense is 'to lie in, during sexual intercourse'.

   Cf. preceding entry.

slippery. 'My wife is slippery?', Leontes (jealous of Polixenes) in *The W. Tale*, I ii 272.

   The semantics may perhaps be explained by *greasy* or by the fact that Leontes thinks that she is preparing to *slip* from virtue to infidelity.

sluice, v.t. To copulate with (a woman). 'Many a man there is, . . . holds his wife by th'arm, That little thinks she has been sluic'd in's absence, And his pond fisht by his next neighbour, by Sir Smile, his neighbour', The W. Tale, I ii 192–196.

Sluice, 'to pour water freely upon', comes from the n., ex Old Fr. escluse, 'a flood-gate' (itself ex L. (aqua) exclusa, 'water shut out'), hence 'body of water passing through a flood-gate'.

slut. A slovenly wench; a wanton girl or woman, especially if of low origin or of dirty habits and slatternly dress. See quotation at **apron mountant.**

The word is cognate with slattern and its basic etymological sense appears to be that of 'idleness'; it is also cognate with Old Norse slota, 'to droop', to 'flag' (Wyld).

sluttery. Wenching; the sexual attractiveness of, or sexual intercourse with, sluts (see preceding entry). 'Sluttery, to such neat excellence opposed, Should make desire vomit emptiness, Not so allured to feed', Cymbeline, I vi 43–45.

sluttish. Trollopy; impure, immodest; licentious. See quotation at **encounterer** and cf. **slut.**

sly. Sexually sly; cunning, secretive, furtive, stealthily artful in sexual matters. See the quotation at **lay down.**

M.E. sli, sleigh, ex Old Norse slaegr (or slogr), 'crafty'.

smack, v. 'My conscience . . . says very wisely to me, "My honest friend Launcelot, being an honest man's son,"—or rather an honest woman's son;—for, indeed, my father did something smack, something grow to,—he had a kind of taste', The M. of V., II ii 13–16. The innuendoes are obscure—but almost certainly sexual; the implication probably being that the father was a lusty, ardent fellow; something may imply the pudend, as he doubtless had a taste for amorous incident or adventure.

smock. A chemise. 'Doubtless he shrives this woman to her smock', 1 Henry VI, I i 119: cf. the quotation at **shift.**—Much Ado, II iii 135.

O.E. smoc(c), cognate with Old Norse smokkr and Old High Ger. smoccho, is connected with O.E. smugan, 'to creep into', e.g.

to don a garment by slipping it over one's head (Wyld).—Cf. **shift,** q.v.

sodden. Heavy and dull and stupefied. Bawd, in reference to her grossly overworked harlots: 'The stuff we have, a strong wind will blow it to pieces, they are so pitifully sodden', *Pericles*, IV ii 18–19.

Cf. **rotten.**—O.E. *soden*, ex *seothan* (whence our *seethe*), 'to boil; hence, to cook'.

soil, n. and v. Sexual defilement; to defile (a woman). 'Free from touch or soil', *Measure*, V i 140.

Via Old Fr. *soillier*, 'to defile'—perhaps ex L. *sus*, 'a pig'. A doublet of *sully*. (*The C.O.D.*)

soiled, in quotation **at go to it,** = in rut, in heat. Perhaps in reference to the 'hippomane'.

soilure. A soiling by lust; sexual defilement. 'Not making any scruple of her soilure', *T. & C.*, IV i 57.

Ex **soil.**

soldier to a lady, be a good. (Concerning Benedick) '*Messenger.* And a good soldier too, lady'—*Beatrice.* And a good soldier to a lady', *Much Ado*, I i 48–49. Not only courteous-manly, but also manly-virile. This phrase, taken along with such others as **siege, weapon, lance,** illustrates the C.16–17 convention of 'a woman and therefore to be won' by martial guile and warlike investment and attack, as though her virtue, conventionally seated, as honour, in her pudend (*quel drôle d'endroit de mettre son honneur*, as the French realist expressed it), were a fortress to be 'occupied'.

solicitation. An urging or enticement to unchastity or to infidelity: *Othello*, IV ii 202.—Cf. 'solicit' in *Cymbeline*, I vi 146.

Via Fr. ex L. *sollicitare*, 'to urge, to excite', ex *sollicitus*, 'violently agitated' (*ciere*, to arouse).

something. See quotation at **smack** and cf. **thing.**

sound. Free from venereal disease. *Measure for Measure*, I ii 53. O.E. *sund*, 'uninjured'.

source of all erection. See **erection**.

south. When, in *Troilus and Cressida*, v i 18–19, Thersites speaks of 'the rotten diseases of the south', he very probably uses *south* in the sense 'buttocks' or 'rump'.

Spain. 'A. of S. Where Spain?—D. of S. Faith, I saw it not; but I felt it hot in her breath.—A. Where America, the Indies?—D. O, sir, upon her nose, all o'er embellished with rubies, carbuncles, sapphires, declining their rich aspect [= *gaze*] to the hot breath of Spain, who sent whole armadoes of caracks to be ballast at her nose' (*Comedy*, III ii 128–134): *Spain* must be the pudend, to judge by the evidence of 'I saw it not'—**hot**— **whole**—and **carack**.

sparrows. These birds are often taken as symbolic of feathered lechery, as monkeys and goats are of animal lustfulness. Lucio, concerning the seemingly austere Angelo, 'Sparrows must not build in his house-eaves, because they are lecherous', *Measure*, III ii 177–178.

   Sparrow is of common-Teutonic origin, and it has cognates in Greek and Latin.

speaking looks; parling looks. Love-eloquent or lust-hinting glances. 'But she, that never coped with stranger eyes, Could pick no meaning from their parling looks, Nor read the subtle-shining secrecies Writ in the glassy margents of such looks', *Lucrece*, vv. 99–102.—'She gave strange œilliades and most speaking looks To noble Edmund', *Lear*, IV v 25–26.

   The two phrases are exactly synonymous. *Parling* comes from obsolete *parle*, 'to speak', ex Fr. *parler*.

speed, v.i. To be sexually potent. 'My flocks feed not, My ewes breed not, My rams speed not; All is amiss', *The Passionate Pilgrim: Sonnets to Music*, 3, vv. 1–4.

   Literally: to prosper, to succeed. Ultimately from an Aryan root, signifying 'increase'.

spend. To expend sexually; to discharge seminally. 'He wears his honour in a box unseen, That hugs his kicky-wicky here at home, Spending his manly marrow in her arms', *All's Well*, II iii 282–284.

In the language of venery, *spending* is an emission, or emissions collectively considered.—*Spend* is a shortening of *dispend*, ex L. *dispendere*, 'to weight out' (*pendere*, to pay out, to weigh).

spicery. See **nest of spicery.**

spin off. (Cf. **distaff.**) Belch to Aguecheek concerning the latter's 'excellent head of hair', 'Excellent; it hangs like flax on a distaff; and I hope to see a housewife take thee between her legs and spin it off', *Twelfth Night*, I iii 99–101: here, 'distaff' probably = penis; the hair ('flax') of the innuendo would therefore be the male pubic hair, but 'it' may refer, not to the flax but to the distaff; if the latter, then the sense is 'cause to have an emission'.

spirit. 'Mr Partridge ... completely omits ... "spirit" as a euphemism for "semen". The ... *Oxford English Dictionary* also fails to include the meaning. Yet the evidence for claiming that it carried this extra sense in Elizabethan times (compare "spunk" today) is undeniable. ... I see that Leslie Fielder ... makes the same point. This gives edge and bite to the famous "The expense of spirit in a waste of shame Is lust in action", especially if "waste" can also be read as "waist". And I have a clinching quotation to help Mr Fielder along—in Bacon's *Sylva Sylvarum* (1627), he writes, "It hath been observed by the ancients that much use of Venus doth dim the sight. ... The cause of dimness of sight is *the expense of spirits.*" ' Thus Mr Alan Brien in his witty essay 'Afterthought' contributed to *The Spectator* of 7 April, 1964. The reference is to *Sonnet* 129.

spit white. In 'I would I might never spit white again' (2 *Henry the Fourth*, I ii 218–219), Falstaff apparently refers to seminal emission.

splay. To excise the ovaries of (a female animal); hence, of a woman; occasionally, to castrate. See the quotation at **geld.**

Short for *display*, which, literally, has the meaning of the Latin original, *displicare*, 'to unfold'.

spoil, n. A woman as the spoils of a sexual conqueror; cf. the verb. See quotation at **encounterer** ('Sluttish spoils of opportunity'); see that at **flesh one's will.**—(Of women seduced by a deceiver) 'His amorous spoil', *A Lover's Complaint*, v. 155.

spoil, v. To despoil or violate (a woman); to defile (her body). See second quotation at **spot.**

L. *spoliare*, 'to plunder': here, to strip or plunder a woman of her honour.

sport. n. Amorous sport. 'Intercepted in your sport', which follows immediately on the **foul desire** quotation from *Titus Andronicus*, II iii 75–79; cf. v i 96.—*Measure*, III ii 120–121, in reference to womanizing and whoring, 'He had some feelings of the sport; he knew the service'.—'The act of sport', *Othello*, II i 228–229: see also **act.**—*Ibid.*, II iii 17–18, 'He hath not yet made wanton the night with her; and she is sport for Jove'.— 'A summer's day will seem an hour but short, Being wasted in such time-beguiling sport', *Venus*, vv. 23–24.—And elsewhere.

Cf. the v.; also *disport*, **play** and **toy;** cf. also **game,** q.v. And see:—

sport, v. To **toy** and **dally;** to **play** amorously (cf. the entry preceding this one). Venus, referring to Mars (her captive in love), 'Over my altars hath he hung his lance, His batter'd shield, his uncontrolled crest, And for my sake hath learnt to sport and dance; To toy, to wanton, dally, smile, and jest', *Venus*, vv. 103–106.

Short for *disport*: via Old Fr. *desporter*, ex L. (*se*) *disportare*, 'to carry (oneself' from the beaten track of routine and seriousness'.

sportive. Fond of, addicted to, the **sport** of love and libido. 'For why should others' false adulterate eyes Give salutation to my sportive blood?', *Sonnet*, 121, vv. 5–6.

Cf. **riggish.**

spot, v.t. To **pollute** or **stain** or **defile** (a woman, a woman's honour). 'Let fair humanity abhor the deed That spots and stains love's modest snow-white weed', *Lucrece*, vv. 195–196. —*Ibid.*, v. 1172, 'Her sacred temple spotted, spoil'd, corrupted'.

stab, v. To copulate with (a woman). '*Hostess*. He stabb'd me in mine own house, and that most beastly: in good faith, 'a cares not what mischief he doth, if his weapon be out: he will foin like any devil', *2 Henry IV*, II i 13–16; *Julius Caesar*, I ii 272–276 (*Caesar moechus*: see Oman's *Seven Roman Statesmen*).

stable. In *Much Ado*, III iv 41–45, Margaret exclaims, 'Clap's into'—let us attempt—'*Light o' love*; that goes without a burden: do you sing it, and I'll dance it' and Beatrice (43–45) replies, 'Ye light o' love, with your heels!—then, if your husband have stables enough, you'll see he shall lack no barns': if your husband have erections enough, you'll see he shall lack no bairns. By definition, a *stable*—Latin *stabulum*, from *stare*, to stand—is 'a *standing* place for horses'; this leads to the sexual sense of *standing*, the modern *stand* or, in full, *cock-stand*.

When, *The Winter's Tale*, II i 133–134, Antigonus, suspecting his wife of infidelity, swears that, if she is proved to be unfaithful, 'I'll keep my stables where I lodge my wife; I'll go in couples with her', the sense is extremely obscure unless, here too, *stable* means 'erection'. If that interpretation, made to me by a scholar (2 October 1955), be correct, Antigonus implies, 'I'll maintain a constant priapism wherever my wife may be, and I'll remain constantly coupled with her'—to quote that scholar, 'very much as the Devil advised Hans Carvel to do'.

stag is used allusively for a cuckold in *Titus Andronicus*, II iii 70–71, the reference being to the branched horns (i.e., antlers) of that animal.

See **horn** and **horned herd;** and cf. **buck.**

stain, n. Sexual defilement; pollution. 'Giving our holy virgins to the stain Of contumelious, beastly, mad-brain'd war', *Timon*, v i 173–174; *Cymbeline*, II iv 138–141.—*Lucrece*, v. 1701.

Cf. **violation** and **pollution**.

stain, v. To defile (a woman). See quotation at **enforce.**—See quotation at **uncleanness.**—*Lucrece*, v. 655.

Cf. **defile** and **pollute.**

stair-work. 'Dirty work' on the staircases; casual copulation. The Old Shepherd, finding the babe Perdita: 'This has been some stair-work, some trunk-work, some behind-door-work: they were warmer that got this than the poor thing is here', *The W. Tale*, III iii 74–77.

Cf. the four **work** entries.

stake, n. See the next entry and cf. the jealousy-mad Leontes's outburst to Camillo, in reference to the friendship between Hermione and Polixenes: 'A fool That seest a game play'd home, the rich stake drawn, And takest it all in jest'; *The W. Tale*, I ii 246–248. The only satisfactory explanation is that *stake* = penis; cf. **stalk** and especially **yard** (q.v.).

stake down. '*Bassanio*. We'll play them with the first boy for a thousand ducats.—*Nerissa*. What, and stake down.—*Gratiano*. No; we shall ne'er win at that sport, and stake down', *The M. of V.*, III ii 213–216. Stake (of money) down on the table: *penis dependens* (therefore impotent).

The exact sense is somewhat doubtful: the salacious intention is clear enough!

stale, adj. See **dull, stale, tired bed.**

This adj. is not anterior to M.E.; it probably derives ex *stale*, the urine of horses and cattle: cf. Middle Low Ger. *stal*, 'horse-urine'; both the English and the Ger. word are cognate with, perhaps originating in, Gr. *telma*, 'stagnant water'.

stale, n. Prostitute, as probably, in bitter irony, in *Com. of Errors*, II i 101—see quotation at **break the pale.**—Allusively: see quotation at **hare.**—'A contaminated stale', *Much Ado*, II ii 24; IV i 65, 'A common stale'.

Ex the preceding adj.: such a woman is no longer sexually fresh.

2, Horse-urine: *A. & C.,* I iv 62. (For etymology, see **stale, adj.**)

stale, v. See quotation at **variety,** where *stale* = to render stale: unpalatable to sexual appetite: uninteresting to sexual curiosity.

Ex **stale,** adj.

stalk. Allusively, 'the penis' in *Pericles.* IV v 39–40, where the Bawd, having called Marina 'a rose', says to Lysimachus, 'Here comes that which grows to the stalk,—never pluckt yet, I can assure you'. Obviously, also, there is an erotic innuendo in 'grows to'.—In *A Lover's Complaint* (see **flower**), it probably = trunk of, or entire, body.

Cf. **root.**—M.E. *stalke,* 'stalk, reed' (cf. **pipe**); O.E. *stalu;* perhaps cognate with L. *stilus,* 'a **stake**).

stamp, v.t. (Cf. the use of the n. in the quotation at **saucy sweetness.**) To engender. 'That most venerable man which I Did call my father, was I know not where When I was stampt; some coiner with his tools Made me a counterfeit', *Cymbeline,* II v 3–6.

Cf. **coin,** q.v. *Stamp* is of common-Teutonic stock; perhaps cognate with Gr. *stembein,* 'to crush with the feet'.

stand, v., is applied to *penis erectus.* '*Speed.* How stands the matter with them?—*Launcelot.* Marry, thus; when it stands well with him, it stands well with her.—*S.* What an ass art thou! I understand thee not.—*L.* What a block art thou, that thou canst not! My staff understands me', *Two Gentlemen,* II v 20–25, where *staff* may bear the equivoque, *staff of love,* literary euphemism for 'penis'.—*R. & J.,* 'Me they shall feel while I am able to stand' (see at **feel**); II i 25 (see **circle**); III iii 88 (see second quotation at **O**).—*The Taming,* Induction, ii 125, 'Ay, it stands so that I may hardly tarry so long'. Cf.:—

stand to; stand to it. To 'stand' (see preceding entry) to a woman. '*Clown*. The danger is in standing to't; that's the loss of men, though it be the getting of children', *All's Well*, III ii 40–41.—Drink, says the Porter in *Macbeth*, II iii 34–35, 'makes' a man 'stand to, and not stand to'.

To stand is to assume an upright position (*penis erectus*); to have a *cock-stand*.

standard. Penis. '*King*. Saint Cupid, then! and, soldiers, to the field! —*Berowne*. Advance your standards, and upon them, lords; Pell-mell, down with them! but be first advised, In conflict that ye get the sun of them.—*Longaville*. Now the plaindealing; lay these glozes by: Shall we resolve to woo these girls of France', *L.L.L.*, IV iii 363–367.

The reference, obviously, is to the shaft; cf. preceding pair of entries.

stark-naked. The *A. & C.* locus (v ii 57–59) is non-sexual: 'Rather on Nilus' mud Lay me stark-naked, and let the water-flies Blow me into abhorring!'—*The Passionate Pilgrim*, 6, vv. 9–14, 'Anon he comes, and throws his mantle by, And stood stark naked on the brook's green brim: The sun lookt on the world with glorious eye, Yet not so wistly as the queen on him. He, spying her, bounced in, whereas he stood: "O Jove", quoth she, "why was not I a flood?" '

Not 'stiff (or strong)-naked', but 'tail-naked' (O.E. *steort-naked*), i.e. 'bare-arsed'.

steal a shive of a cut loaf. To steal a slice from a loaf already cut, in reference to sexual intimacy with a married woman: 'Easy it is Of a cut loaf to steal a shive, we know', *Titus Andronicus*, II i 86–87.

stealth; by stealth. Secretly: especially as applied to sexual intercourse or delinquency. *The Comedy of Errors*, III ii 7 (see quotation at **do it**).—*Lear*, I ii 11, where Edmund speaks of his begetting 'in the lusty stealth of nature'.

Steal + abstract-noun suffix -th. M.E. *stelen* = 'to steal; to move furtively; to hide'.

stew; generally, **the stews.** A brothel. 'An I could get me but a wife in the stews, I were mann'd, horsed and wived', Falstaff in 2 *Henry IV*, at I ii 56–57.—*Measure*, v i 315–316, 'I have seen corruption boil and bubble Till it o'er-run the stew' (with pun on a stew being cooked).—*Cymbeline*, I vi 150–151, 'To mart As in a Romish stew'.

Original sense of *stew(s)* is 'bath'-room or -house, hence 'hot bath': cf. the sense-changes of *bagnio*, 'a Turkish bath; Turkish baths', later (e.g., see Grose) 'a (high-class) brothel'. 'Public baths were formerly, in many countries, the resort of persons of ill-fame' (Wyld).

sting. The sting of sensual desire: *As You Like It*, II vii 76: see quotation at **libertine.**

Ex the v., which may be the nasalized form of **stick.**

stir; stir up. To arouse or excite sexual desire (in, especially, a man). 'Never could the strumpet, With all her double vigour, art and nature, Once stir my temper', *Measure*, II ii 183–185.— 'Men must comfort you, men must feed you, men must stir you up', Bawd to Marina in *Pericles*, IV ii 91–92.—*Ibid.*, IV ii 146 (see at **eel**).

O.E. *styrian*, 'to arouse, agitate, set in action'; cf. Old High Ger. *storen*, 'to disturb'.

stoln hours. Illicit time; hours of clandestine infidelity. 'What sense had I of her stoln hours of lust? I saw 't not, thought it not, it harm'd not me . . . He that is robb'd, not wanting'— lacking or missing—'what is stoln, Let him not know't, and he's not robb'd at all', *Othello*, III iii 338–343.

Parallel to **stealth**, q.v.

stomach, n. In L.L.L., IV iii 291–292 (see at **abstemious**), *stomach* probably refers to sexual appetite and its organ of satisfaction.— In *Othello*, III iv 112–115, it certainly does: ''Tis not a year or two shows us a man: They are all but stomachs, and we all but food; They eat us hungrily, and when they are full, They belch us'.

Via Old Fr., ex L. *stomachus*, 'stomach; gullet; taste' (cf. *to have a taste for something*).—Cf. **dish, eat, feed.**

stone (and **stones**). A testicle. Perhaps equivocal in 'Give her no token but stones; for she's as hard as steel', *Two Gentlemen*, I i 134–135.—*The M. of V.*, II vii 20–22, 'And jewels,—two stones, two rich and precious stones, Stol'n by my daughter!—Justice, find the girl! She hath the stones upon her, and his ducats.—*Salarino*. Why, all the boys in Venice follow him, Crying—his stones, his daughter, and his ducats'.—*Henry V*, II 24–28.—*Merry Wives*, I iv 110.—'A philosopher, with two stones more than's artificial one', *Timon*, II ii 111–113.—And elsewhere.

Of common-Teutonic origin, it has an Aryan verb-base, meaning 'to stiffen; to become thick or compressed'. (Wyld.)

stoop one's body to pollution. (Of a woman) to yield to such sexual intercourse as brings shame. See quotation at **pollution** and cf. **yield one's body to shame.**

strain, v. To clasp; to embrace closely. 'Our king has all the Indies in his arms, And more and richer, when he strains that lady: I cannot blame his conscience', *Henry VIII*, IV i 46–48.

Via. Fr., ex L. *stringere*, 'to tighten'.

strange fowl. Iachimo, to Posthumus, in reference to the latter's virtuous wife and his much-prized finger-ring, 'You may wear her in title yours: but, you know, strange fowl light upon neighbouring ponds. Your ring may be stolen too', *Cymbeline*, I iv 87–89.

Strange fowl = strangers; see **pond** and **ring.**

strange love. Love hitherto strange; with an implication of 'foreign'—hence 'exotic'—hence 'warmly passionate and ingenious': *R. & J.*, III ii 15–16, ' . . . Till strange love, grown bold, Think true love acted simple modesty'.

stray one's affection. To allow, or cause, one's love to stray unlawfully. 'Hath not else his eye Stray'd his affection in unlawful love?', *Com. of Errors*, v. i 50–51.

strike. To copulate with. 'Single you thither, then, this dainty doe [i.e., Lavinia], And strike her home by force, if not by words', *Titus Andronicus*, II i 117–118;—cf. 129–131, 'There speak, and strike, brave boys, and take your turns; There serve your lust, shadow'd from Heaven's eye, And revel in Lavinia's treasury'.

For the sadistic semantics, cf. **clap, cope, fuck, hit, throw down, thump;** also cf. **stuprum,** q.v.

O.E. *strican*, 'to rub; to move or go'; M.E. *striken*, 'to rub or stroke; to strike'. Perhaps cf. L. *stringere*, 'to touch; to draw together'.

strive. To struggle amorously. 'Think women still to strive with men, To sin and never for to saint', *The Passionate Pilgrim: Sonnets to Music*, 4, vv. 43–44.

Cf. **wrestle** and the quotation at **it;** also cf. the exactly synonymous **contend.**

Old Fr. *estriver*, ex *estrif*, 'strife; effort', ex Old Norse *strith*, 'oppression; pain'.

strumpet, adj. 'Hugg'd and embraced by the strumpet wind', *The M. of V.* II 72. Ex:—

strumpet, n. A prostitute; a (very) wanton woman. 'Strumpet, thy words condemn thy brat and thee', *1 Henry VI*, V iv 84.— 'That strumpet, your unhallow'd dam', *Titus Andronicus*, V ii 191.— *Com. of Errors*, IV iv ('O most unhappy strumpet!').— *Hamlet*, II ii 238 (see at **privates**): cf. II ii 501, 'Out, out, thou strumpet, Fortune!' —'A strumpet's boldness', *All's Well*, II i 173.—*Measure*, II ii 183.—*Othello*, IV i 97–98, ''Tis the strumpet's plague To beguile many, and be beguiled by one'.—*Ibid.*, IV ii 81.—'Impudent strumpet!'—*A. & C.*, I i 14, Antony is called 'a strumpet's fool'.— And elsewhere.

Of obscure etymology; perhaps, as Professor Wyld suggests, ex Old Fr. *strupe* or *stupre* (the former, a metathesis of the latter): L. *stuprum*, 'rape, violation'.

strumpet, v. To make a strumpet or prostitute of. 'Strumpeted by thy contagion', *Com of Errors*, II ii 143.—'Maiden Virtue rudely strumpeted', *Sonnets*, 66, v. 6.

Ex the n. (Cf. **bewhore.**)

stuff, n. 1, **Marrow** or semen. ' . . . Thy father, . . . who, in spite, put stuff To some she-beggar, and compounded thee Poor rogue hereditary', *Timon*, IV iii 271–274.

Old Fr. *estoffe*, ex L. *stuppa*, 'the coarse part of flax'.

2, A pejorative collective noun for 'Whores': see quotation at **sodden.**—*Cymbeline*, I vi 124–125, Iachimo, concerning Posthumus's supposed female company, 'Such boil'd stuff As well might poison poison!' Cf. **trash.**

stuff, v. '*Hero.* These gloves the Count sent me; they are an excellent perfume.—*Beatrice.* I am stuft, cousin; I cannot smell.—*Margaret.* A maid, and stuft! there's goodly catching of cold', *Much Ado*, III v 56–60. In low slang, even now, *stuff* is 'to coït with (a woman)', the metaphor coming either from cooking or from upholstery: for an almost exact synonym, see **bolster.**

Ex the n.: significantly, *stuff* = to fill tightly.

stumble, v. To **fall** sexually; (to be persuaded) to have sexual intercourse with a man. '*Julia.* Wouldst thou, then, counsel me to fall in love. —*Lucetta.* Ay, madam; so you stumble not unheedfully', *Two Gentlemen*, I ii 2–3.

Cf. **trip** and **fall backward.**—Etymologically, *stumble* is cognate with **stammer.**

stump, n. '*Lord Chamberlain.* Well said, Lord Sands; Your colt's tooth is not cast yet' (you are still vigorous and virile).—'*Lord Sands.* No, my lord; Nor shall not, while I have a stump': *Henry VIII*, I iii 46–48. Ostensibly, **stump** is 'stump of a tooth'; ulteriorly it = penis.

Ex Old Norse *stumpr*; basically, in Aryan, it is cognate with a v. that means 'to push or strike'.

stuprum. Latin for 'a rape, a violation': *Titus Andronicus*, IV i 79, 'Stuprum, Chiron, Demetrius'.

Stuprum is cognate with Gr. *tupos*, 'a blow (struck)' and *tuptein*, 'to strike'; cf., therefore, *strike*.

sty. See quotation at **enseamed bed.** There is a connotation of pig-like, filthy addiction to or indulgence in sexuality; perhaps also an obscure reference to a trollopy pudend.

sully. To soil or defile sexually. 'Sully The purity of my sheets', *The W. Tale*, I ii 324–325.

A doublet of 'to soil' (see **soil**), it comes from O.E. *sylian*: cf. O.E. *sul*, 'dirty'.

sunburnt. 'The Grecian dames are sunburnt, and not worth the splinter of a lance', *T. & C.*, I iii 282–283; see **lance.**

There is a pun on '*son* [= man]-*burnt*' (see **burn,** sense 1): i.e., infected with venereal disease.

supply the place. To take the bed-place of a husband. 'His bed my goal; from the warmth loathed whereof deliver me, and supply the place of your labour', Goneril to Edmund: *Lear*, IV vi 6–8.

Perhaps with a reference to its etymological sense, 'to fill up'— cf. **stuff,** v.

surfeit, n. Excess of sexual indulgence. *Measure*, I ii 123.—*A. & C.*, I iv 25–28, 'If he fill'd His vacancy with his voluptuousness, Full surfeits, and the dryness of his bones, Call on him for't'.

Old Fr. *sorfait*, past participle of *sorfaire* (itself ex L *facere*, 'to do'): to overdo.

surfeit, v. To indulge excessively in physical love. 'Henry, surfeiting in joys of love, with his new bride', *2 Henry VI*, I i 251.— *Measure*, V i 102, 'His purpose surfeiting' (sating his lustful purpose).— *Coriolanus*, I iii 24–28, 'Had I a dozen sons, . . . I had rather had eleven die nobly for their country than one voluptuously surfeit out of action'.—'Love surfeits not, Lust like a glutton dies', *Venus*, vv. 803–804.

Ex the n.

surfeiter. An excessive indulger in the exercise of physical love. Pompey calls Antony 'this amorous surfeiter' (*A. & C.*, II i 33).

surgery. Venereal surgery: see quotation at **pike;** and cf. **powdering-tub** and **tub-fast.**

sweat, n.; **sweating,** adj. The sweat resulting from and during the physical acts of sexual caresses and intercourse. 'The rank sweat of an enseamed bed', *Hamlet*, III iv 93.—'Here's a young and sweating devil here, That commonly rebels', *Othello*, III iv 41–42.—'Call it not love, for Love to heaven is fled, Since sweating Lust on earth usurpt his name', *Venus*, vv. 793–794.

Sweat, v., coming from the n., which, of common-Teutonic origin, is cognate with L. *sudor* and, further back, with an Aryan word.

sweet, adj. and n. The sweet pleasure of sexual intimacy; filled with sexual pleasure. Allusively in *All's Well*, II iv 42 (the n.).— 'I'd make a journey twice as far, t'enjoy A second night of such sweet shortness which Was mine in Britain', Iachimo to Posthumus in reference to a night that the former pretendingly spent with Imogen: *Cymbeline*, II iv 42–44.

Cf. **honey,** q.v., the entry at **pluck,** and also the semantically equivalent **bliss.** See also **sweetness.**

sweet body. 'A woman's soft, delicate, sweet-smelling body' seems to be Othello's meaning in III iii 346 (see at **taste**).

sweetness. The sweetness of sexual love—or, indeed, of physical desire. See quotation at **saucy sweetness.**—'Your never-cloying sweetness', *Sonnets*, 118, v. 5.

Sweet, adj., + -*ness*.—O.E. *swete*, pleasant; sweet, cognate with L. *suavis*: Sanskrit *svadus*, 'pleasant to the taste'.

swell, v. To become pregnant: grow big with child. Cressida says, 'If I cannot ward what I would not have hit, I can watch you for telling how I took the blow; unless it swell past hiding, and then it's past watching', *T. & C.*, I ii 270–273.—*The W. Tale*, II i 61.

Of common-Teutonic origin and cognate with the *solens* part of L. *insolens*, 'immoderate, haughty'.

sword; swords and bucklers. Penis; penises and pudends. '*Maria*.

Dumaine was at my service, and his sword: No point, quoth I', L.L.L., v ii 276–277.—*Much Ado*, v ii 16–19, 'Benedick. Call Beatrice: I give thee the bucklers.—*Margaret*. Give us the swords; we have bucklers of our own.'—In *Twelfth Night*, iii iv 252–254, there is a remotely allusive pun on *sword*.—See quotation at **plough:** *A. & C.*, ii ii 241.

O.E. *sweord*; cf. Old Frisian *swerd* and High Ger. *swert*. Semantically cf. **knife** in **lay knife aboard—lance—pike.**

Buckler: Old Fr. *boclier*: L. *buccula* (diminutive of *bucca*, 'a cheek') 'that part of a helmet which covers the cheeks; hence, a boss on a shield', the boss on the *buckler* ('a large shield') perhaps evoking the boss of the *mons Veneris*.

tail. 1, Pudend. See *The Taming*, ii i 210–216, and sense 3 of this entry.—See **tale, 3**.—See **change the cod's head for the salmon's tail.**

This sense comes from Old Fr. *taille*, 'a notch, a nick, or a cut' (cf. **wound,** q.v.): Fr. *tailler*, 'to cut'. Appositely comparable are the slang *nock* and the printers' terms, *one nick* (a male baby) and *two nicks* (a female baby): see my *A Dict. of Slang*.

2, Penis. (Cf. **tale,** sense 1.) 'Clown. Are these . . . wind-instruments? —Musician. Ay, marry, are they, sir.—Clown. O, thereby hangs a tail.—Musician. Whereby hangs a tale, sir?—Clown. Marry, sir, by'—i.e., near—'many a wind-instrument that I know': *Othello*, iii i 6–11.

Ex the animal's tail: the semantics being the dangling dependency of *penis non erectus*.

3, Podex. 'Panthino. Why dost thou stop my mouth? *Launce*. For fear thou shouldst lose thy tongue. P. Where should I lose my tongue? L. In thy tale. P. In thy tail!', *Two Gentlemen*, ii iii 49–53.—Cf. *The Taming*, ii i 213–216, where either podex (more probably) or pudend may be intended.

(This is the predominant sense in C.20 usage.) An animal's tail covers its fundament.

take. To take carnal possession of—to copulate with—a woman. 'To take her in her heart's extremest hate', *Richard* III, I ii 232.— R. & J., IV v 10–11.—*Lear*, V i 57–59, Edmund, referring to Goneril and Regan, 'Which of them shall I take? . . . Neither can be enjoy'd, If both remain alive:'—See *Timon* quotation at **filthy.**—Cf. 'while she takes all she can, not all she listeth', *Venus*, v. 564.

Cf. **occupy** and see **take it.**

take down. To reduce a man's sexual turgidity. 'I'll take him down, an 'a were lustier than he is, and twenty such Jacks; and if I cannot, I'll find those that shall', R. & J., II iii 152–155.

The property of a poultice is to *take down* (or reduce) a swelling; cf. **take off.**

take it. To accept or agree to or submit to amorous advances. 'Play the maid's part,—still answer nay, and take it', *Richard III*, III vii 51, where a knowledge of Shakespeare inevitably leads one to understand that the meaning is even more precise: to admit penis to vagina.—R. & J.: see quotation at **feel.**

Late O.E. *tacan*, 'to touch; to seize'. Cf. the 1940–43 saying, *We can take it.*

take off. To reduce a man's amorousness, especially by causing him an orgasm. '*Ophelia.* You are keen'—witty, but cf. **sharpen** . . . —'my lord, you are keen.—*Hamlet*. It would cost you a groaning to take off my edge': III ii 267–268.—See quotation at **provoke.**

Cf. **take down,** q.v.

take the blow. See quotation at **swell,** and the entry at **blow.** Significantly comparable is **take it.**

take up a woman's gown. To embark upon the preliminaries to a bout of love-making. *The Taming*, IV iii 160–161, 'Take up my mistress' gown to his master's use! O, fie, fie, fie!'

take vantages. To 'take advantage of' a woman. 'I fear her not, unless she chance to fall.—God forbid that! for he'll take vantages', 3 *Henry VI*, III ii 24–25.

In short, take advantage of opportunity and, at any sign of yielding, to press home one's advantage. A part of the time-honoured myth of man the pursuer, woman the pursued.

take with a wench. To apprehend a man engaging in sexual intercourse: L.L.L., I ii 281, 'Taken with a wench'.

taking. The vbl. n. corresponding to **take,** q.v. For an example, see the *Timon* quotation at **filthy.** (Cf. **occupation.**)

tale. (Cf. **tail,** 2.) 1, Penis. R. & J., II iii 96–103, esp. 97–98, 'Thou desirest me to stop in my tale against the hair'. An erotic pun.

2, Podex. See quotation at **tail,** 3; cf. the *Othello* quotation at **tail,** 2.

Semantically cf. **wind-instrument:** with which, cf. the C.20 low catch-saying, *Oh! shut your mouth and give your arse a chance.*

3, Pudend. 'Conceives her tale' (pun on *tale,* 'story', and *tail,* 'pudend'): see *The Taming* quotation at **conceive.**—R. & J., II iii 101–103 (with pun also on sense 1).

For origin, see **tail,** sense 1.

talk greasily. (Cf. **obscenely** and **slippery.**) See the quotation at **greasily.**

Tarquin. *The Rape of Lucrece* has rendered Tarquin the archetype of cruel lust. 'With his stealthy pace, With Tarquin's ravishing strides, towards his design Moves like a ghost', *Macbeth,* II i 54–56.—*Cymbeline,* II ii 12–14, 'Our Tarquin thus Did softly press the rushes, Ere he waken'd The chastity he wounded'.—*Lucrece,* vv. 813–814, 'The nurse, to still her child, will tell my story, And fright her crying babe with Tarquin's name'.

taste, v.t. To have sexual enjoyment of (generally, a woman). A vague allusion occurs in *Twelfth Night,* III i 80–84.—T. & C., III ii 20–21 (remotely).—*Othello,* III iii 345–347, 'I had been happy, if the general camp . . . had tasted her sweet body, So I had nothing known'.—Bawd to Marina, 'Taste gentlemen of all fashions', *Pericles,* IV ii 77.—'If you can make't apparent That

you have tasted her in bed . . . ', *Cymbeline*, II iv 56–57.—See
unripe.

Cf. **relish,** q.v.

M.E. *tasten*, 'to take', ex Old Fr. *taster*, 'to handle or to feel
(Mod. Fr. *tâter*); to taste': ex a presumed Low L. *taxitare*, ex L.
taxare, 'to appraise or value; to handle or touch': itself probably
ex Gr. *tassein*, 'to arrange, put in order; hence, to impose; to fix
as payment' (Wyld).

Tear-Sheet, Doll. A prostitute in *2 Henry IV*. So called, either
because she tore the bed-sheets in her amorous tossings or
because her partners did so while consorting with her. See the
quotations at **pagan** and **road.**

teem. (Of a woman) to be fertile. *Lear*, I iv 287–288, 'If she must
teem, Create her child of spleen'.

temperance, 'sexual temperance', occurs in *A. & C.*, III xiii
121.—*Lucrece*, v. 884, 'Thou [i.e., Opportunity] blow'st the
fire when temperance is thaw'd'.

Its radical sense may be 'seasonableness' (L. *tempus*, 'time').

temple, 'the human body regarded as a holy mansion' enshrin-
ing both the soul and—twice in *Lucrece*—the bodily sanctuary
of female virtue localized in the pudend. In vv. 1172–1173 we
have 'Her sacred temple spotted, spoil'd, corrupted, Grossly
engirt with daring infamy': cf. **vessel** and to *violate a temple.*

tempt. To entice sexually. *Hamlet*, III iv 193, 'Let the bloat king
tempt you again to bed', *Othello*, IV i 8.

Old Fr. *tempter, tenter*, 'to try or attempt': L. *tentare*, 'to handle
or touch; to put to the test'. Cf. **attempt** and **try.**

tempt one's love. To attempt to gain a person's love; less probably, to tempt a person to participate in love-making. 'With
what persuasion did he tempt thy love?', *Com. of Errors*, IV ii 13.

tender a fool, to. To give birth to a bastard. Polonius to Ophelia,
in reference to Hamlet's courtship, 'Tender yourself more
dearly; Or . . . you'll tender me a fool', I iii 117–119.

Tereus. 'Some Tereus hath deflower'd thee, And, lest thou shouldst detect him, cut thy tongue', *Titus Andronicus*, II iv 26–27; *ibid.*, IV i 49, 'Tereus' treason and his rapes'.—'She hath been reading late The tale of Tereus: here the leaf's turn'd down Where Philomel gave up' (a delicate example of dramatic irony), *Cymbeline*, II ii 44–46.—*Lucrece*, vv. 1133–1134.

Tereus married and then put away Procne; he deprived Philomela of her tongue, but she contrived to convey a message (cf. Lavinia in *Titus*); later she became a nightingale (Philomel).

thaw, v. To melt, gentle-gradually, the coldness of (a woman). See *Timon* quotation at **Dian.**

O.E. *thawian* (cf. Old Norse *theyja*, 'to melt'); perhaps cognate with L. *tabere*, 'to melt' (v.i.).

thigh, quivering. 'I conjure thee by Rosaline's bright eyes, . . . By her fine foot, straight leg, and quivering thigh, And the demesnes that there adjacent lie', *R. & J.*, II 17–20, where both rippling health and tremulous innate ardour seem to be implied.

Quivering = shaking with a tremulous motion; *quiver* would seem to be imitative.—*Thigh*, of common-Teutonic origin, literally = the swollen—the thick—part of the body (especially in women).

thing. 1, Pudend. *Falstaff.* Go, you thing, go.—*Hostess.* Say, what thing? what thing?—*Falstaff.* What thing! Why, a thing to thank God on.—*Hostess.* I am no thing to thank God on . . . I am an honest man's wife', *1 Henry IV*, III iii 20–24.—Both this sense (implied by Sands) and the next (intended by Anne) are glanced at in the second quotation of:—

2, Penis. 'She that's a maid now, and laughed at my departure, shall not be a maid long, unless things be cut shorter', *Lear*, I v 51–52.—*Henry VIII*, I iv 46–50, 'Anne Bullen. You are a merry gamester, my Lord Sands.—*Sands*. Yes, if I make my play' (cf. **stake down**). 'Here's to your ladyship; and pledge it, madam, For 'tis such a thing,—*Anne.* You cannot show me.'

Both senses: partly euphemistic, partly materialistic ('the thing'). Thing exists in O.E., where it is cognate with *thingian*, 'to settle or to arrange'. It is 'one of the words most highly generalized in meaning' (Wyld).

thing, another. Pudend. *Two Gentlemen*, III i 342–346, '*Speed*. Item, "She is too liberal."—*Launce*. Of her tongue she cannot, for that's writ down she's slow of; of her purse she shall not, for that I'll keep shut: now, of another thing she may, and that cannot I help.'

thistle (penis): see second quotation at **prick,** v., and cf.:—

thorn. (Cf. **needle** and **prick.**) Penis. 'If we are nature's, these are ours; this thorn Doth to our rose of youth rightly belong; Our blood to us, this to our blood is born', *All's Well*, I iii 130–132; cf. IV ii 18–20 (see **prick,** v., third quotation).

O.E. **thorn,** 'a thorn; a prickle'; ultimately cognate with an Aryan word for 'a grass blade'.

those that bawl. See **bawl.**

three-inch fool. A short-penis'd man. '*Curtis*. Away, you three inch fool! I am no beast.—*Grumio*. Am I but three inches? why, thy horn is a foot; and so long am I at the least', *The Taming*, IV i 25–27. Opposed to this slighting reference is the old folklore proverb—*not* to be found in the dictionaries of proverbs!— 'Short and thick Does the trick'.

throbbing breast. Queen Margaret, of Suffolk's severed head, says, 'Here may his head lie on my throbbing breast: But where's the body that I should embrace?', *2 Henry VI*, IV iv 5–6. Ostensibly, the reference is to grief-stirred heart; implicatively, it is to responsive breasts and lap that are throbbing with passionate desire.

See **breast.**—*Throbbing*: 'to throb' occurs in M.E. as *throbben*, but its earlier history is obscure; the word may be cognate with L. *trepidare*, 'to move noisily and irregularly' (Wyld).

throw down, to. To 'throw' a woman (see next entry). 'Better would it fit Achilles much To throw down Hector than Polyxena', T. & C., III iii 209–210.

To be added to the list of sadistic synonyms: **clap, cope, fuck, hit, strike, thump.**

Throw: O.E. *thrawian*, 'to twist' (cf. R. L. Stevenson's *Thrawn Janet*); cognate with L. *terere*, 'to rub, or wear, away'.

thrown, be. To be 'tumbled' (see **tumble**); to be caused to **fall;** to be thrown sexually. Concerning women, 'They are burs . . . they'll stick where they are thrown', T. & C., III ii 112–113.

Cf. the preceding entry.

thrust, n. A fencing metaphor for a penis-thrust or, hence, a sexual bout. Immediately following the quotation at **stab,** come the words, 'He will spare neither man, woman, nor child.—*Fang*. If I can close with him, I care not for his thrust.—*Hostess*. No, nor I neither' (2 *Henry IV*, II i 16–19).

For the semantics, cf. **foin, prick** (v.), **stab.**

Thrust, n., ex the v.: M.E. *thrusten*, ex Old Norse *thrysta*; cognate with L. *trudere*, 'to push or thrust' (cf. *intrude* and *extrude*).

thrust to the wall. 'Women, being the weaker vessels, are ever thrust to the wall:—therefore I will push Montague's men to the wall, and thrust his maids to the wall', R. & J., I i 14–17: cf. 'Backward she pusht him, as she would be thrust', *Venus*, v. 43.

Unfastidious courtship and summary copulation.

thump, v.t. (Cf. **hit** and **strike, clap** and **cope** and **fuck,** and the modern slang term, *bang*: all sadistic—or perhaps merely would-be manly.) To copulate with (a woman); with a connotation of vigour. 'Delicate burdens of "dildos" and "fadings", "jump her and thump her"; and where some stretch-mouth'd [= loose-talking, *broad*] rascal would mean mischief, and break a foul jape into the matter, he makes the maid to answer, "Whoop, do me no harm, good man", puts him off, slights him, with "Whoop, do me no harm, good man" ', *The W. Tale*, IV iii 194–201.

An echoic word.

Tib. A woman or girl, especially if of lowly origin or low occupation. Marina to Boult (a pandar's servant), 'Thou art the damned doorkeeper to every coistrel that comes enquiring for his Tib', *Pericles*, IV v 165–166.

Tib is hypocoristic—an endearment—for *Isabel*; and there is an allusion to *tib-cat*, an 'Isabel' or female cat—the opposite to a tomcat.

tickle, v. See quotations at **concupy, potato-finger,** and the next entry: in all there is, either overtly or covertly, an allusion to amorous or sexual tickling or caressing; cf. **scratch.**

Perhaps a frequentative of *tick*, 'to make a reiterated, slight yet sharp, clicking or thin-tapping noise': with stress on that sort of movement which generates this noise. *Tick* is certainly echoic; *tickle* probably is.

tickle one's catastrophe. A punning reference to *arse*: 'catastrophe'. 'Falstaff. Away, you scullion! you rampallian! you fustilarian! I'll tickle your catastrophe', *2 Henry IV*, II ii 59–60.

See preceding entry.

ticklish. Amorous; licentious; skilled in sexual allusion and in reading the signs and portents of love and desire and lust. See the quotation at **game, daughters of the.**

Cf. 'a ticklish passage in an otherwise austere book' and other such references; especially 'a very ticklish girl', with its overtone of susceptibility to ordinary tickling and its undertone of compliant susceptibility to intimate tickling.

ticktack (or **tick-tack**). In *Measure for Measure*, I ii 187–188, Lucio says to Claudio (arrested for getting a maid with child), ' . . . Thy life, who I would be sorry should be thus foolishly lost at a game of tick-tack'. Literally a sort of backgammon, in which, to keep the score, pegs are inserted into holes; hence, copulation.

The metaphor is that of driving-in a tack or nail, the tick or light tap being quick-followed by the tack or harder tap. The semantics? Much the same as in *tooth-ache*, modern slang for a throbbing priapism; and cf. **tick-tack-man** in my *A Dictionary of Slang*.

tillage. (Cf. **crop, ear,** and **plough.**) Cultivation of fields: ploughing, raking, sowing, etc. See quotation at **unear'd**.

Of common-Teutonic origin; cf. Dutch *telen*, 'to breed'.

tilt with lips. See **lip**, n.

tilth. See **husbandry** and cf. **tillage.**

tire on. (Of a man) to fatigue oneself in sexual intercourse with (a woman): see quotation at **disedge.**

Cf. **please oneself upon.**

tomboy. A light wench; a woman **full of game;** a whore. Iachimo, maligning Posthumus to Imogen, says to the latter that he pities her for being 'Partner'd With tomboys, hired with that self-exhibition Which your own coffers yield!', *Cymbeline*, I vi 120–122.

In Shakespeare's day, *tomboy* was pejorative: a wild girl—especially a sexually wild girl. The semantics: much the same as for **ramp.**

tool, n. (Cf. **instrument** and **organ** and **weapon;** and **sword** and **poll-axe.**) Penis. 'Sampson. Me they'—the maids—'shall feel while I am able to stand: and 'tis known I am a pretty piece of flesh.—*Gregory* 'Tis well thou art not fish . . . Draw thy tool; here comes two of the house of the Montagues.—*Sampson*. My naked weapon is out . . . ', R. & J., I i 27–32.—See quotation at **stamp,** where 'tools' = a man's generative organs.—'Have we some strange Indian with the great tool come to court, the women so besiege us? Bless me, what a fry of fornication is at door!', *Henry VIII*, V iii 131–134.

'O.E. *tol*, not found in other Germanic languages; probably formed from the base seen in O.E. *towian*, "to prepare land for sowing"' (Wyld).

top, v. To coït with (a woman) in the commonest of all 'the figures of *Venus*', the semantics being analogous to those of **mount, ride** (especially), **leap, vault.** *Othello*, III iii 394–395,

'Would you, the supervisor, grossly gape on,—Behold her topt?' (Iago to Othello).

See also the etymological—or rather, the semantic—note at **tup.**

Ex. the n.: O.E. *topp*, 'summit'. It is of common-Teutonic stock.

to't. To (*go*) *to* it sexually; to indulge in sexual intercourse. See quotations at **geld** and **it.**

touch, n. A sexual caress; a copulation. The Duke to pimp Pompey, *Measure*, III ii 24–26, 'Say to thyself,—From their abominable and beastly touches I drink, I eat, array myself, and live'.—*Othello*, IV ii 84, 'Foul unlawful touch'.—*The Passionate Pilgrim*, 4, vv. 7–8, 'To win his heart, she toucht him here and there; Touches so soft still conquer chastity'.

Cf. the French proverb, *Pas d'attouchements avant le marriage*, and:—

touch forbiddenly, to. To coït illicitly with (a woman). Camillo, to Polixenes, concerning Leontes: 'He swears . . . that you have toucht his queen Forbiddenly', *The W. Tale*, I ii 412–415.

Cf. **touch** and **forfended place.**

The n. **touch** comes from the v.: ex Old Fr. *touchier*, it has the original meaning, 'to twitch, to tug' (Wyld).

town bull. The most notable fornicator and womanizer in a village or a township. See the quotation at **pagan** and the entry at **bull.**

toy, n. A toying, a love-trick; an amorous (especially if sexual) caress —cf. **toy in blood,** q.v. *Othello*, I iii 269–273, 'When light-wing'd toys Of feather'd Cupid seel with wanton dullness My speculative and officed instruments [= my mind and my sense of duty], That my disports corrupt and taint my business, Let housewives make a skillet of my helm'.

'Once in 1303, = amorous play' (C.O.D.); cognate with Dutch *tuig* (and Ger. *Zeug*), 'a tool; trash'.

Seems, in Feste's final song, to mean—as *bauble* does in *Romeo and Juliet*—'penis': 'When that I was a tiny little boy . . . A foolish thing was but a toy' (*Twelfth Night*, v, at end)— if, as is generally held, he throughout refers to his sexual experience.

Cf. **disport** and **sport, play** and **game.**

toy, v. To play, or disport oneself; especially, amorously: not merely to copulate but also, and predominantly, to kiss and caress playful-passionately. (Of Adonis, love-besieged by *Venus*) 'With leaden appetite, unapt to toy', v. 34.—'[He] hath learnt to sport and dance; To toy, to wanton, dally, smile, and jest', *ibid.*, vv. 105–106.

From the noun—q.v.

toy in blood, a. A passing, sportive manifestation of amorous desire (cf. **hot-blood, hot-blooded**). 'For Hamlet, and the trifling of his favour, Hold it a fashion, and a toy in blood; A violet in the youth of primy nature, Forward, not permanent, sweet, not lasting', *Hamlet*, i iii 5–8.

See **toy**, n., and **blood.**

trade, n. The trade of whore, bawd, pimp, pandar. 'I do find your hangman is a more penitent trade than your bawd',— here, pimp, —'he doth oftener ask forgiveness', *Measure*, iv ii 49–51; cf. quotation at **doer.**—*Pericles*, iv v 66–69.

In M.E. it = 'a path': *trade* is therefore cognate with *tread*: the beaten *path*, the customary *way*, of commerce. Semantically comparable are **road** and **trot.**

trade, v. 'Give me some music,—music, moody food Of us that trade in love', says Cleopatra in *A. & C.*, ii v 1–2.

From the noun.

trader; tradesman. For the latter, see quotation at **women's matters**.— Pandarus, 'O traders and bawds, how earnestly are you set a-work, and how ill requited!', *T. & C.*, v x 37–38; *ibid.*, 46, 'Good traders in the flesh'.

Trader: ex **trade,** v.; *tradesman*: ex **trade,** n.

trading. Sexual intercourse with prostitutes or with light wenches: see quotation at **mackerel.**

Ex **trade,** v.

traffic, n. Sexual commerce; (sexual) intercourse. (To a woman) 'Having traffic with thyself alone, Thou of thyself thy sweet self dost deceive', *Sonnets,* 4, vv. 9–10: ostensibly and primarily it = keeping yourself sexually to yourself, you deprive yourself of a second self (a child); secondarily, it = by masturbating, you wrong your true self.

Fr. *trafic;* Late L. *trafficum,* of which, says Wyld, the origin is unknown: could it be a telescoped derivation of a L. *transficere,* 'to make across'—to cause merchandise to go across country?

tread, v. (Mostly of birds) to copulate with (the female). 'When turtles tread', L.L.L., v ii 898.—See the quotation (from *The Passionate Pilgrim*) at **trick.**

Ex the sexual position and foot-motion of the male bird. (Cf. **cover** and **tup.**)

O.E. and Old Saxon *tredan;* possibly cognate with Gr. *dromos,* 'an act of running'.

treason of the blood. The revolt of youthful blood against its possessor's sexual continence or chastity. In reference to Desdemona, reported by Iago to be love-making with the Moor, Brabantio says, 'O heaven!—How got she out?—O treason of the blood!', *Othello,* I i 171.

See **blood** and cf. **youth.**

Via Old Fr., ex L. *traditio,* 'a delivering-up'.

treasure and **treasures.** (Cf. **chaste treasure,** q.v.) 1, A woman's breasts and, especially, her 'secret parts'. 'Either you must lay down the treasures of your body To this supposed [person], or else to let him'—the brother condemned to death— 'suffer', *Measure,* II iv 96–98. (Cf. the quotation at **jewel**)— 'The treasure of her honour' (see **pick the lock**).

2. Semen: see quotation at **fall,** v.

Treasure comes, via Old Fr., ex L. *thesaurus* (ex Gr. *thesauros*), 'a store, esp. of valuables, laid up; hence, a treasure-house'.

treasury. 'There serve your lust . . . And revel in Lavinia's treasury', *Titus Andronicus*, II i 130–131.

A woman's sexual parts, both primary and secondary; especially the pudend; cf. the preceding entry.

tree. See **fall,** n., and **plum;** and R. & J., II i 30, where the secondary meaning is 'female pubic hair'.

trick, n. A bout of love-making; a sexual stratagem. (The former nuance is paralleled in Dr. Ben Reitman's *The Second Oldest Profession*, 1936.) See **momentary trick:** *Measure*, III i 110–112.— (Of women) 'The tricks and toys that in them lurk, The cock that treads them shall not know', *The Passionate Pilgrim: Sonnets to Music*, 4, vv. 39–40.

For the semantics, cf. **pranks** and **toy,** n.

Cognate with Dutch *trek*, 'a trick', and Fr. *triche*, 'a swindle'.

trim, v., and **trimming,** vbl. n., are allusive to sexual intercourse (from a male point of view) in *Titus Andronicus*, v i 93–95.

Probably ex gardening *trim*: O.E. *tryman*, 'to fortify; to arrange', ex *trum*, 'strong; healthy'.

trip, v. (Cf. **stumble.**) To **fall;** to succumb sexually. Simonides, in reference to dancing, 'Here is a lady that wants breathing too: And I have heard, you knights of Tyre Are excellent in making ladies trip; And that their measures are as excellent', *Pericles*, II iii 101–104.

Probably cognate with Ger. *Treppe*, 'a flight of steps', and English *trap*, 'a snare' (Wyld).

Troilus, as type: see quotation at **pandar,** n.

trot. A common prostitute. 'Give him gold enough and marry him to . . . an old trot . . . , though she have as many diseases as two and fifty horses', *The Taming*, I ii 77–80.

For the semantics, cf. **hackney, hobby-horse, nag;** also **ride, rider,** and **road.** Perhaps one who trots along the pavements: a street-walker. Trot, ex Old Fr. *trotter*, is, however,

268 SHAKESPEARE'S BAWDY

probably of Teutonic origin; and probably it is cognate with
tread.

trout. See **groping . . .**

truant with one's bed, to. To be unfaithful to one's wife. ' 'Tis
double wrong, to truant with your bed, And let her read it in
thy looks at board', *Com. of Errors*, III ii 17–18.

> Cf. **break the pale.**
> Old Fr. *truand*, 'a vagrant'.

trull. A low prostitute; a slatternly light o' love. 'The Dauphin
and his trull', 1 *Henry VI*, II ii 28.—'An Amazonian trull', 3
Henry VI, I iv 114.—*Titus Andronicus* (see **deflower**).—Cleopatra
(elsewhere called 'whore') is by Maecenas called a 'trull': *A. &
C.*, III vi 95 (see at **potent regiment**).

> *Trull* is a variant of *troll*, a mischievous creature of Scandina-
> vian mythology and folk-lore. (Other low Shakespearean
> strumpets are **callet, commoner** and **doxy.**)

trunk-work. See the quotation at **stair-work.** Trunk-work is ostensibly: casual or furtive copulation in large clothes-trunks (or
perhaps in the closets that house them). But there is also a pun
on 'work performed by the body-trunks of the partners in the
act'; and there may even be an allusion to the penis: cf. the
entries at **nose** and **root;** cf., too, the modern slang *dingle-
dangle*, 'penis'.

try. To approach and court (a woman) with a view to sexual
intercourse. See quotation at **fall to.**

> Lit., 'to test': cf. **attempt** and **assay** and **tempt.** Basic sense:
> 'to sift; to select'; ex Late L. *tritare*, 'to separate grain from husk'.

try experiments. To engage in a sexual bout, especially in an
experimental or expert way. 'Your Moor and you Are singled
forth' —i.e., have wandered off alone—'to try experiments',
Titus Andronicus, II iii 68–69.

try with tongue. In the Cymbeline passage, quoted at **penetrate,** the ostensible sense of *fingering* is 'playing upon stringed
instruments', and *try with tongue* is 'appeal to with singing': but

Cloten's mind being a bestial one, he probably, in try with tongue, insinuates a pun on cunnilingism.

See **try.**

tub. A 'pickling-tub'—a tub used in the C.16–18 cure of venereal disease. See quotation at **beef.**—See that at **tub-fast.**

Perhaps ex. L. *tubus*, 'a tube, a pipe': most tubs somewhat resemble abbreviated cylinders with bottoms affixed.

tub-fast. That old treatment for venereal diseases which consisted in sweating in a tub of hot water and in fasting. *Timon*, IV iii 85–87, 'Season the slaves'—her customers—'For tubs and baths; bring down their rose-cheekt youth to The tub-fast and the diet', Timon to harlot Timandra.

tumble, v.t. 1, To copulate with (girl or woman); to cause to **fall backward.** 'Young men will do't, if they come to't; By cock, they are to blame, Quoth she, before you tumbled me, You promised me to wed', *Hamlet*, IV v 60–63.

'Apparently a frequentative form from O.E. *tumbian*, to dance' (Wyld).

2, v.i. To play amorously. 'Let us grant it is not Amiss to tumble on the bed of Ptolemy; To give a kingdom for a mirth' (Octavius, referring to Antony: I iv 16–18).—See quotation at **aunt.**

tun-dish. See **fill a bottle . . .**

tup, v. (Cf. **ram.**) (Of a ram) to serve (a ewe); hence, of human beings. Iago to Brabantio, 'Even now, now, very now, an old black ram' (Othello) 'is tupping your white ewe', *Othello*, I i 88–89.

Cf. **ram,** v. and **tread,** qq.v.

'M.E. **tope, tupe,** etym[ology] dub[ious]', says *The C.O.D.* But that *tope* may provide the key: the v. may precede the n. (*tup*, a ram), and *tup* may be merely a variant of *top*: see **top.**

turd. A piece of excrement. '*Doctor Caius.* If dere be one or two, I shall make-a de turd'—the third. 'Sir Hugh Evans. In your teeth: for shame!', Merry Wives, III iii 225–226.

O.E. tord. It is from, or cognate with, L. tordere, 'to twist': from the twisted or rope-like appearance?

turn i' the bed. Messenger to Cleopatra, concerning Antony, 'He's bound unto Octavia.—Cleopatra. For what good turn?—Messenger. For the best turn i' the bed' (II v 58–59). Relevant too is 'Never count the turns', in Cymbeline, II iv 142.

Cf. **trick,** q.v., and:—

turn to. To seek sexually; be ripe for breeding. 'The ewes, being rank, In th' end of autumn turned to the rams', The M. of V., I iii 79–80; III iv 78–80, 'Nerissa. Why, shall we turn to men [= become men]?—Portia. Fie, what a question's that, If thou wert near a lewd interpreter!'

turrets, 'the female breasts': see the Lucrece quotation at **breast.**

[**turtle-doves** are, in 1 Henry VI, II ii, and not wholly in accordance with ornithological facts, emblematic of 'married chastity'; cf. The Phoenix and the Turtle (Dove), and **turtles** in L.L.L., IV iii 210.]

two backs. See **make the beast . . .**

unchaste. Amorous; immodest, indelicate, passion-venturous. Merry Wives, V v 99 (see at **sinful fantasy**).—See second quotation at **violate.**

Opposite: **chaste,** q.v.

uncleanliness and **uncleanness.** Sexual uncleanliness, whether unmarried licentiousness or married infidelity. See quotation at **cardinally** (the former term).—'To redeem him, Give up your body to such sweet uncleanness As she that he hath stain'd', Measure, II iv 54–56.

Cf. **filthy, foul, greasy, nasty.**

uncropped. Not 'unharvested' (i.e., not having yet borne a child), but 'unplucked'—still a virgin. King to Diana, 'If thou be'st yet a fresh uncropped flower, Choose thou thy husband, and I'll pay the dower', *All's Well*, v iii 325–326.

Cf. the semantics of **pluck** and **crop**.

uncuckolded. With wife still faithful: quotation at **loose-wived.** (See **cuckold, v.**)

under refers to male superincumbency in the sexual act in 'Their sons are well tutor'd by you, and their daughters profit very greatly under you', *L.L.L.*, iv ii 30–31.

undermine. To undermine a woman's sexual resistance, with honeyed words and progressively intimate caresses (cf. the idea implicit in *undertake*). Parolles, in reply to Helena's demand, 'Unfold to us some warlike resistance', says, 'There is none: man, sitting down before you, will undermine you, and blow you up.—*Helena*. Bless our poor virginity from underminers and blowers-up!', *All's Well*, i i 116–121, where the metaphor comes from the mining done by sappers.

underminer. One who performs the action defined in the preceding entry.

undertake. To woo (a woman) briskly and amorously: *Twelfth Night*, i iii 59 (see at **accost**).

With the innuendo 'take under' (in reference to garments:? to take underneath). See **take.**

undo; undone. (Cf. **wrong.**) To coït with (a virgin or with another's wife). 'Thou hast undone our mother', *Titus Andronicus*, iv ii 75; cf. v. 77 and quotation at **do.**—See quotation at **seducer.**

Cf. **do,** q.v.

unear'd. 'For where is she so fair whose unear'd womb Disdains the tillage of thy husbandry?', *Sonnets*, 2, vv. 5–6: literally, 'unplanted' (cf. the entry at **ear**): hence, unfertilized by man's **seed.**

Cf. also **tillage** and **plough;** and see **ear.**

ungenerative. Lucio, referring to Angelo the austere (whose urine is congealed ice), says, 'And he is a motion ungenerative', *Measure*, III ii 112–113: he lacks sexual potency, he cannot *generate* a child; cf.:—

ungenitured. Lacking testicles. 'This ungenitured agent'— Angelo—'will unpeople the province with continency', *Measure*, III ii 175–177.

Cf. preceding entry.

union. Sexual congress. 'The union of your bed', *The Tempest*, IV i 21. Lit., a making-one (L. *unus*, one).

unknown to woman. (Of a man) virgin. 'I am yet Unknown to women', *Macbeth*, IV iii 125–126.

Cf. **know** and **know carnally**, qq.v.

unlace. To unlace—hence, to undress—a woman, in preparation for the sexual act. ' "Even thus", quoth she, "the warlike god unlaced me", As if the boy should use like loving charms', *The Passionate Pilgrim*, II vv. 7–8.

unlawful (love or bed or touch or purpose). Sexually illicit. 'By her, in his unlawful bed, he got This Edward', *Richard III*, II vii 190–191.—'Unlawful love', *Com. of Errors*, V i 51.—'May be the amorous count solicits her In the unlawful purpose.— *Widow*. He does indeed; And brokes with all that can in such a suit Corrupt the tender honour of a maid', *All's Well*, III v 70– 73; cf. III vii 46.—*Measure*, IV ii 15.—*Othello*, IV ii 84 (see **touch**); *ibid.*, V ii 72 (the adv., *unlawfully*).—'All the unlawful issue that their lust Since then hath made between them', *A. & C.*, III vi 7–8.

unlookt-for issue. Not necessarily bastards, but perhaps merely unforeseen. 'Is Clarence, Henry, and his young son Edward, And all the unlookt-for issue in their bodies, To take their rooms, ere I can place myself?', *3 Henry VI*, III ii 130–132.

unmann'd. See **man**.

unpaved eunuch. 'The voice of unpaved eunuch', *Cymbeline*, II iii 33. The *unpaved*, unnecessary to the sense and—the passage being in prose—to the sound, has been introduced for the pun: unpaved—uncobbled—unstoned, stoneless—without testicles.

Cf. **unseminar'd,** q.v.

unproper beds. 'There's millions now alive That nightly lie in those unproper beds Which they dare swear peculiar' (*Othello,* IV i 68–70): *unproper* = belonging to others; *peculiar* = belonging to themselves. 'Unproper', because their wives belong, sexually, as much to other men as to their husbands.

unprovoke. See **provoke.** It = to abate (a man's) ability to coït; therefore cf. **conjure down, take down, take off.**

unripe. (Cf. **raw.**) Venus to Adonis, 'The tender spring upon thy tempting lip Shows thee unripe; yet mayst thou well be tasted' (vv. 127–128).

Un + *ripe*, of which the basic meaning is 'ready to be harvested'; cf. O.E. *ripan,* 'to reap'.

unseduced. Posthumus to Iachimo, 'If she remain unseduced,—you not making it appear otherwise,—for your ill opinion, and the assault you have made to her chastity, you shall answer me with your sword', *Cymbeline,* I iv 162–165. (See **seduce.**)

unseminar'd. Deprived of semen—of male seed. Cleopatra to Mardian the eunuch, ' 'Tis well for thee, That being unseminar'd, thy freer thoughts May not fly forth of Egypt', *A. & C.,* I v 9–11.

Cf. the note at **germen** and that at **unpaved eunuch.**

unstanch'd. See the quotation at **leaky.**

untied. See the first quotation at **knot,** n.

untrimmed. Undevirginated; sexually undealt-with (woman). 'O, Louis, stand fast! the devil tempts thee here In likeness of a new untrimmed bride', *King John,* III i 208–209.

Cf. **trim,** q.v.

untrussing. A loosing of one's garments, preparatory to sexual congress. 'This Claudio is condemn'd for untrussing', *Measure,* III ii 181–182.

Truss (up) = to tie or tighten (one's garments).

unviolated. Still unbroken, still pure. *The Comedy of Errors*, II i 88, 'Th' unviolated honour of your wife'.

See **violate.**

upshoot, in 'Then will she get the upshoot' (L.L.L., IV i 136), clearly indicates a seminal ejaculation.

urinals. See **knog . . .** For etymology, see:—

urine. The pale yellow fluid discharged through the urethra. 'When he makes water, his urine is congeal'd ice', *Measure*, III ii 111–112. —*Othello*, II iii 28–37.

The medical term; via Old Fr., ex L. *urina*, ex Gr. *ouron*, ex— or cognate with—Sanskrit *vari*.

use, n. Sexual enjoyment. R. & J., III v 225–226, 'Nurse. Your first is dead; or 'twere as good he were, As living here, and you no use of him'—See **take up . . .** —'Made her serve your uses both in purse and in person', *2 Henry IV* II i 118–119.

use, v. (Of a man) to copulate with, to be sexually intimate with. 'Did you not use his daughter very friendly?', *Titus Andronicus*, IV ii 40.—R. & J., II iii 159.—There is a similar pun on *use*, 'to treat', in *All's Well*, I i 215–216, Parolles to Helena, 'Get thee a good husband, and use him as he uses thee'.—*Othello*, V ii 72.—'Be a whore still: they love thee not that use thee', *Timon*, IV iii 83.

A particularly materialistic and callous term; ex L. *uti*, past participle *usus*. 'Do you want to *use* me?' is a 'practical' and unspiritual feminine invitation to a 'bedding'.

usury. Sexual indulgence or intercourse. ' 'Twas never merry world since, of two usuries, the merriest was put down', Pompey the pimp, *Measure*, III ii 6–7.—In *Sonnets*, 6, 'forbidden usury' (cf. the quotation at **traffic**) may euphemize 'masturbation'.

For the semantics: there is a pun on **use,** n. and v., as well as one on *usury* itself: cf. 'Poor rogues, and usurers' men! bawds between gold and want', *Timon*, II iii 61–62.

vantage. See **take vantages.**

variable. Promiscuous, as in *Cymbeline*, I vi 133–134, 'Whiles he is vaulting variable ramps, In your despite'. Cf. **ramp** on p. 172 and **vault** on p. 211.

variety. Enobarbus, concerning Cleopatra (and her sexual hold over Antony), 'Age cannot wither her, nor custom stale Her infinite variety: other women cloy The appetites they feed; but she makes hungry Where most she satisfies: for vilest things Becomes themselves'—are becoming, are attractively suitable—'in her', *A. & C.*, II ii 239–243: Aretino could have taught nothing to a reincarnated Cleopatra, nor Forberg have told her anything she had not known—and done.

vault, v.t. (Cf. **jump** and **leap;** also **climb** and **mount** and **ride;** the comparison will make the semantics sufficiently obvious.) 'Whiles he is vaulting variable ramps', *Cymbeline*, I vi 133.

Ex Old Fr. *volter*, 'to leap': ex. L. *volvere*, 'to turn'.

velvet leaves. 'On a day—alack the day!—Love, whose month is ever May, Spied a blossom passing fair, Playing in the wanton air: Through the velvet leaves the wind, All unseen, can passage find; That her lover, sick to death, Wisht himself the heaven's breath', *L.L.L.*, IV iii 99–106: not, I fear, so lyrically innocent as it seems: cf. the entries at **rose** and **piled . . . ,** and remember the sense of 'tip the velvet' (see my *A Dictionary of Slang*, 2nd ed., 1938).

venereal signs. Signs of Venus: signs or tokens of love or lust. 'No, madam, these are no venereal signs: Vengeance is in my heart, death in my hand', *Titus Andronicus*, II iii 37–38.

This etymological sense has long been obsolete; the present sense is '(of disease) caused by sexual intercourse'. Contrast *venery*, 'hunting', with *venery*, 'the art of love; love-making'.

And see **Venus.**

vent, v. To emit from the anus. 'Where air comes out, air comes in: there's none abroad so wholesome as that you vent', *Cymbeline*, I ii 3–7.—*The Tempest*, II ii 110–112, 'How camest thou to be the siege of this man-chief? Can he vent Trinculos?'

Probably from the n., which comes ex L. *ventus*, 'wind': cf. therefore, **break wind.**

Venus. *L.L.L.*, II i 256.—*R. & J.*, II i 11–12, 'Speak to my gossip Venus one fair word, One nickname for her purblind son and heir'.—*M.N. Dream*, I i 171, 'The simplicity of Venus' doves'; cf. 'Venus' pigeons', *The M. of V.*, II v 61.—'Saturn and Venus this year in conjunction', in reference to Falstaff and Doll Tearsheet: *2 Henry IV*, II iv 263.—*Much Ado*: several times.—'His heart Inflamed with Venus', *T. & C.*, v ii 165–166.—'What Venus did with Mars', *A. & C.*, I v 17.—*Venus and Adonis*: on the theme of female desire and lust. 'In *The Passionate Pilgrim* we get a fascinating variation of the theme; and there, by the way, Venus is 'sweet Cytherea'.

Venus, the Roman goddess of love and beauty, is a personification of *venus*, 'desire; love in its sexual aspects', as Psyche was love in its spiritual;—and also, beauty. It comes from the same base as that which has given us O.E. *wynn*, 'delight, joy'.

Venus' glove. Hector, concerning Helen, to Menelaus, *T. & C.*, IV v 179, 'Your *quondam* wife swears still by Venus' glove'. 'By Venus' glove,' may actually have been an oath; nevertheless, the implication is that *Venus' glove* = the female pudend: Helen is still a devotee of physical love.

vessel. 'If to preserve this vessel for my lord From any other foul unlawful touch, Be not to be a strumpet, I am none', Desdemona in *Othello*, IV ii 83–85.

This body, housing her pure spirit and her chastity: cf. **temple,** q.v.

vice. Pudend and closed thighs. '*Margaret*. Give us the swords; we have bucklers of our own.—*Benedick*. If you use them,

Margaret, you must put in the pikes with a vice; and they are dangerous weapons for maids.—*Margaret*. Well, I will call Beatrice to you, who I think hath legs', *Much Ado*, v ii 18–24.

Ex Old Fr. *vis*, 'a screw; a winding stair': L. *vitis*, 'a vine'.

vigour. Virility; proof or fruit of virility. Aaron, in reference to his illegitimate baby by Tamora, 'My mistress is my mistress: this, myself,—The vigour and the picture of my youth', *Titus Andronicus*, iv ii 107–108.

Via Old Fr., ex the base of L. *vigere*, 'to be lively, vigorous'.

violate; violation. Rape. *Henry V*, iii iii 20–21, ' . . . If your pure maidens fall into the hands Of hot and forcing violation'.— 'With unchaste purpose, and with oath to violate My lady's honour', *Cymbeline*, v v 284–285; almost the same phrase occurs in *The Tempest*, i ii 347–348.

Lit., 'to force': L. *violare*, ex *vis*, 'force, strength'.

virgin. A woman still undeflowered. 'A virgin pure', 1 *Henry VI*, v ii 83; cf. first quotation at **chaste**.—*L.L.L.*, i i 285.—'A maid yet rosed-over with the virgin crimson of modesty', *Henry V*, v ii 304–305.—'And on her virgin honour will not break it', *Pericles*, ii v 12.

Via Old Fr., ex L. *virgo*—probably cognate with *virga*, 'a young shoot, a pliant twig', which has yielded the literary Fr. *verge*, 'the penis'. It was a Frenchman who coined the term *demi-vierge*, 'a girl or woman still undevirginated, yet far from innocent with her compliance in vulval digitation and *mamma*-caresses': fear-held from frankness, they may be habitual *c.t.*'s (see *A Dict. of Slang*).

virgin knot. See **knot**.

virgin patent. Patent (or guarantee) of virginity; maidenhead. '*Theseus*. . . . In single blessedness.—*Hermia*. So will I grow, so live, so die, my lord, Ere I will yield my virgin patent up Unto his lordship', *M.N. Dream*, i i 78–81.

Cf. **chaste treasure** and **bond of chastity**.

virgin-violator. A violator or defiler of a virgin. 'Angelo is an adulterous thief, An hypocrite, a virgin-violator', *Measure*, v i 40–41.

See **violate.**

virginal, v. In reference to Hermione (conversing with Polixenes), jealous Leontes: 'Still virginalling Upon his palm?', *The W. Tale*, i ii 125–126, probably with an ironic pun on Hermione's *virginal* purity (see **virgin**).

To play the virginal (a square, legless spinet): to play with her fingers upon his palm as though upon the notes of that musical instrument. For other musico-sexual metaphors, see quotations at **fingering** and **penetrate.**

virginity. A woman's physiological state—and estate—before she has carnally known a man. 'I deny her virginity', *L.L.L.*, i i 287.—'The rich worth of your virginity', *M.N. Dream*, ii i 219.—*All's Well*, i i 110–116: the Shakespearean *locus classicus* on the subject.—*Timon*, iv i 7.—*Pericles*, iv ii 58.

Ex **virgin**, q.v.

virtue. Female chastity: *King John*, ii i 98 (see at **rape**); *Othello*, iv i 8. Ex L. *vir*, 'a man': the L. *virtus* = manliness, courage.

virtuous. (Sexually) pure: 'Virtuous, chaste intents', 1 *Henry VI*, v v 20.

voluptuously. See *Coriolanus* quotation at **surfeit**, v.

voluptuousness. 'There's no bottom, none, In my voluptuousness: your wives, your daughters, Your matrons, and your maids, could not fill up The cistern of my lust', *Macbeth*, iv iii 60–63.—*A. & C.*, i iv 26 (see **surfeit**, n.).

Ex L. *voluptas*, 'pleasure, especially if sensual'; the second u is on the analogy of 'virtuous' and 'sensuous'. The base is that of *volo*, 'I wish' (infinitive *velle*: cf. **will**).

wag; wag one's tail. The former is short for the latter. Here, *tail* is the pudend; hence, *to wag one's tail* is to employ one's sex in a wanton manner, to be light of love. 'Well I wot the empress never wags But in her company there is a Moor', *Titus Androni-cus*, v ii 87–88.

See **tail,** 1.—*Wag*: probably ex Middle Swedish *wagga*, 'to oscillate'; cognate with O.E. *wagian*, 'to move'.

wagtail. A loose woman; a dissolute man. Kent calls Oswald a wagtail: *Lear*, ii ii 68.

Cf. preceding entry.

The one wags her **tail,** 1; the other his **tail,** 2.

wanton, adj. Lewd; sexually light; amorously playful. 'Wanton dalliance with a paramour', *1 Henry VI*, v i 23.—Cf. first quotation at **lascivious.**—See quotation at **nymph.**—'Prize and purchase of his wanton eye', *Richard III*, iii vii 187.—*Two Gentlemen*, i ii 42.—And elsewhere—especially *T. & C.*, iv v 56.—See at **motions.**

Etymologically it means 'unrestrained'. Prefix *wan*, 'without; lacking' + M.E. *towen* (O.E. *togen*), 'to pull; hence to educate'.

wanton, n. A light woman. 'Nay, then, the wanton lies', *Two Gentlemen*, v ii 10.—See quotation at **eye.**—*M.N. Dream*, 'Oberon. Tarry, rash wanton: am I not thy king?', ii i 63.—In *Hamlet*, iii iv 193–194, 'Let the bloat king tempt you again to bed; Pinch wanton on your cheek', *wanton* may be a noun—or it may be an adverb.—See **lip,** q.v.

Ex the adj.

wanton, v. To be wanton; to sport amorously. 'To wanton with this queen', *Titus Andronicus*, ii i 21.—See second quotation at **toy,** v.

Ex the noun; cf. **play, sport, toy** as verbs.

wantonness. Sexual lightness or excess: see first quotation at **blood.**—*Sonnets*, 96.

warm. (As **warm** is to **hot,** so is **cool** to **cold.**) Sexually ardent; cosily warm in a sexual environment. *The Taming*, ii i 259–260, '*Katharina* . . . Keep you warm.—*Petruchio.* Marry, so I mean, sweet Katharine, in thy bed.'—*Merry Wives*, iv ii 194.—'The warm effects which she in him finds missing

She seeks to kindle with continual kissing', *Venus*, vv. 605–606.

Of common-Teutonic stock, ex an Aryan base, whence comes also Gr. *thermos*, 'warm'.

warmth has a sexual connotation in the quotation at **supply the place.**

wasp. 'Who knows not where a wasp does wear his sting? In his tail', *The Taming*, II i 213–214: Petruchio to Katharina, whom he thus indirectly declares to be waspish; he implies also that she is amorous.

Cognate with L. *vespa*, it comes from an Aryan word for 'to weave'—in reference to the appearance of a wasp's nest (Wyld).

water. Urine. *Twelfth Night*, III iv 103, 'Carry his water to th' wise woman'.—And see **make water.**

Note also what a valued correspondent has called 'Falstaff's magnificent remark to his Page when the latter returns from an errand to the V.D. specialist: "Sirrah, you giant, what says the doctor to my water?" in *2 Henry the Fourth*, I ii 2'.

watering. Urination. 'When you breathe in your watering, they cry "hem!" and bid you play it off', *1 Henry IV*, II iv 16–18.

way. Old Lady to Anne Bullen, 'I would not be a young count in your way, For more than blushing comes to' (*Henry VIII*, II iii 45–46): ostensibly, 'I should not, if I were a young count, like to meet you in any such manner as would raise more than a blush'. Perhaps, however, 'in your way' = *in coitu cum te*; a comparison with **road** might be relevant.

way of women-kind. Bawd to Marina (refusing to act the whore in the former's brothel), 'Will you not go the way of women-kind? Marry, come up, my dish of chastity . . . !', *Pericles*, IV v 150–152. Perhaps with pun on **way.**

weak. Sexually weak; easily tempted. *All's Well*, I i 116 (of woman's frailty); see the quotation at **function** (man's sexual **ability**).

Cf. **frailty.**

weakness and debility, the means of. Masturbation: *As You Like It*, II iii 51.

weapon. (Cf. **instrument, organ, tool**; also **sword, poll-axe, lance.**) Penis. 'My naked weapon is out', R. & J., I i 32 (see quotation at **tool**).—*Ibid.*, II iii 162 (see quotation at **pleasure**).—See quotation at **stab.**—See quotation at **vice.**—*Hamlet*, V ii 145.

O.E. *waepen*, with corresponding forms in Old Norse, Old Frisian, Old High Ger.

wear away. To wear away in sexual intercourse: see quotation at **lag end.**

Wear: O.E. *werian*, 'to clothe; to wear clothes': 'Apparently a specialized use of *werian*, "to protect, defend" ' (Wyld).

wedding-bed. 'Come, cords; come, nurse; I'll to my wedding-bed; And death, not Romeo, take my maidenhead', R. & J., III ii 136–137.

Wed: O.E. *weddian*, 'to promise, to pledge', ex *wedd*, 'an agreement, a pledge'.

weight, used bawdily: see quotation at **on** and cf. **load** and **burden.**—'O happy horse, to bear the weight of Antony!', *A. & C.*, I v 20.

wench. A girl or young woman, especially if of low birth and frequently with the connotation of low morals. 'A giglot wench', 1 *Henry VI*, IV vii 41.—'I know a wench of excellent discourse, Pretty and witty; wild, and yet, too, gentle', in reference to a courtesan: *Com. of Errors*, III i 109–110.—See quotation at **light.**—1 *Henry IV*, I ii 42–43, '*Falstaff.* . . . Is not my hostess of the tavern a most sweet wench?'

M.E. *wenche(l)*: O.E. *wenchel*, 'a child', and, as adj., 'weak' (cf. O.E. *wancol*, 'feeble'): remotely cognate with a Sanskrit v. for 'to limp'.

wenching, adj. Addicted to wenching or womanizing. Thersites, referring to Troilus's and Diomed's passion for Cressida, asks,

'What's become of the wenching rogues?'; *T. & C.*, v iv 34–35.
Ex v. *wench*, itself ex the n. (see preceding entry).

wenchless. Without—lacking—girls fit to serve as whores in a brothel: 'We lost too much money this mart by being too wenchless', *Pericles*, iv ii 4–5.

Cf. **wench.**

whale to virginity, a. A womanizer, specializing in the seduction of virgins. 'I knew this young count to be a dangerous and lascivious boy, who is a whale to virginity, and devours up all the fry it finds', *All's Well*, iv iii 219–222.

Whale: O.E. *hwael* (cf. Old Norse *hvalr*), cognate with L. *squalus*, 'large fish'. Formerly a type symbolizing voracity.

what, by itself or, in an indelicate context, in combination: pudend. 'What upward lies The street should see as she walkt overhead', *L.L.L.*, iv iii 277–278.—*T. & C.*: see quotation at **swell,** where it may = maidenhead.

whole. See the first quotation at **occupy** and the quotation at **Spain,** where obviously ('as every schoolboy knows') **hole** (cf. **wholly** and **holy**) is implied.

wholly. For the sexual pun in *A. & C.*, i ii 178, see quotation at **broach** and entries at **holy** and **whole.**

whore, n. A prostitute; hence, occasionally, a very loose woman; hence, as an insult. 'Thou that givest whores indulgences to sin', *1 Henry VI*, i iii 23.—*Titus Andronicus*, iv ii 71.—*R. & J.*, ii i 32; ii iii (see **hare**), in punning allusion as 'hoar'.—*2 Henry IV*, several times.—See quotation at **case.**—*T. & C.*, v ii 115, 'My mind is now turned whore' (Cressida *loquitur*).—And elsewhere. (In *Timon*, iv iii 141, 'Be strong in whore', it = whoring).

O.E. *hore*, probably from Old Norse *hora*, 'adulteress'; of common-Teutonic stock, *whore* is probably cognate with L. *carus*, 'dear'.

whore, v. To be a whore, to act like a whore; to make a whore of. *R. & J.*, ii iii 142, punningly in form *hoar* (see quotation at

hare).—'He that hath kill'd my king, and whored my mother', Hamlet in reference to Claudius: v ii 64.—Intransitive in Timon, IV iii 146.

Ex the n.

whoremaster. A whoremonger, a womanizer. 1 Henry IV, II iv 483.—See quotation at **whoremonger.**—As adj.: see quotation at **goatish.**—Timon, II ii 108–116: a witty definition.

Not a master of whores, i.e. a brothel-keeper or -owner, but a master in whores or whoring (a **fleshmonger.**)

whoremasterly. Womanizing. 'That same young Trojan ass, that loves the whore there, might send that Greekish whoremasterly villain, with the sleeve, back to the dissembling luxurious drab of a sleeveless errand', T. & C., v iv 5–9.—Ex preceding term.

whoremonger. A frequenter of whores. 'The deputy cannot abide a whoremaster: if he be a whoremonger, and comes before him, he were as good go a mile on his errand', Measure, III ii 36–38.

Cf. **whoremaster, fleshmonger**, and **trader.**

whoreson. (Cf. **Abhorson.**) From whore's son, this is usually an abusive adjective: cf. the pejorative use of bastard (n. and adj.). 'Why, thou whoreson ass, thou mistakest me', Two Gentlemen, II v 44.—Ibid., IV iv 46, 'You whoreson peasant!'—L.L.L., IV iii 202, 'Ah, you whoreson loggerhead!'—The Taming, IV i 148, 'You whoreson villain!'—'Whoreson caterpillars!', 1 Henry IV, II ii 85.—(To Falstaff) 'You whoreson round man', ibid., II iv 143; and after.—2 Henry IV, I ii, thrice in a single one of Falstaff's speeches; elsewhere in the same play.—'A whoreson mad fellow', Hamlet, v i 181, where it may be an adverb (cf. **devilish**).—'You whoreson cur!', T. & C., II i 42, and elsewhere in the play.—Lear, I i 24 (as noun: see **making**).—A. & C., v ii 275.—Cymbeline, II i 3–4, 'A whoreson jackanapes', and 1. 12, 'whoreson dog!'—appositely comparable with You son of a bitch!—And elsewhere.

whoring, n. Addiction to wenching or womanizing (ex **whore,** v.). Iago, speaking at Bianca, 'This is the fruit of whoring', *Othello*, v i 116.

whorish. Pertaining to—or characteristic of—a **whore.** 'You, like a lecher, out of whorish loins Are pleased to breed out your inheritors', T. & C., iv i 64–65.

whorum. See quotation at **case.**

will, n. A passionate, or a powerful, sexual desire. On several occasions; e.g., *Lucrece*, v. 243, where Tarquin, preparing to rape her, says, 'My will is strong, past reason's weak reproving';—and v. 247, ' 'Tween frozen conscience and hot burning will'.—Cf. quotation at **flesh one's will.**

In *Sonnets* 135 and 136, will does, as I have said, mean 'sexual desire; lust', but it also means, now the male, now the female, sexual organ, as a number of scholars have, ever since the book first appeared in 1947, hastened to tell me and as Mr. Alan Brien, in *The Spectator* of 17 April 1964, emphasizes. (Yet even they missed the adumbration visible in the final couplet of *Sonnet* 57.)

> Whoever hath her wish, thou hast thy *Will*,'
> And *Will*' to boot, and *Will*' in overplus,
> More than enough am I that vex thee still,
> To thy sweet will [pudend] making addition thus.
> Wilt thou, whose will [pudend] is large and spacious,
> Not once vouchsafe to hide my will [penis] in thine?
> Shall will [desire] in others seem right gracious,
> And in my will [desire] no fair acceptance shine?
> The sea, all water, yet receives rain still,
> And in abundance addeth to his store;
> So thou, being rich in *Will* [desire] add to thy *Will* [pudend]
> One will [penis] of mine, to make thy large *Will* [pudend] more.
> Let no unkind, no fair beseechers kill;
>   Think all but one, and me in that one *Will* [pudend].

References[1],[1],[1], are to *Will* Shakespeare himself and to lust and to the sexual organs; compare the punning in the last four lines of the sonnet. In these four lines, the word-play becomes so intricate that one may easily lose the thread—unless one remembers that Shakespeare delights in investing a significant word not merely with two meanings but often with three and perhaps even, as in the final *Will*, with four.

In the next, the complementary, sonnet we read:

> If thy soul check thee that I come so near,
> Swear to thy blind soul that I was thy *Will*,
> And will [penis], thy soul knows, is admitted there [pudend];
> Thus far for love my love-suit, sweet, fulfil.
> *Will* [desire] will fulfil the treasure [treasure-house, pudend]
>   of thy love,
> Ay, fill it full with wills [penises], and my will [penis] one.
> In things [pudends] of great receipt with ease we prove
> Among a number one is reckon'd none:
> Then in the number let me pass untold,
> Though in thy store's [pudend's] account I one must be;
> For nothing hold me, so it please thee hold
> That nothing me, a something, sweet, to thee:
>   Make but my name thy love, and love that still,
>   And then thou lovest me, for my name is *Will*.

The last four lines, superficially univocal, are yet, on a closer examination, equivocal enough. I have, however, refrained from pointing out every word or phrase that is possibly sexual.

In Shakespeare, the *nexus* between the sexual act and literary creation is closer, more potent, more subtly psychosomatic than in any other writer, whether of verse or of prose. In the *Sonnets*, this fact emerges more clearly, and much more persistently, than in the plays: and no one has so fearlessly and brilliantly treated this predominant Shake-spearean quality as Anthony Burgess has done in his very remarkable novel, *Nothing Like the Sun. A Story of Shakespeare's Love-Life*, 1964. ('My mistress' eyes are nothing like the sun': *Sonnet* 130.)

Will: O.E. *willa*, ex *willan*, 'to wish, to desire', which is cognate with L. *velle*, 'to wish'.

willing, adj. Sexually willing. *Macbeth*, IV iii 73, 'We have willing dames enough'. (Cf. preceding entry.)

Winchester goose. The Duke of Gloster to the Bishop of Winchester (1 *Henry VI*, I ii 53), 'Winchester goose! . . . Thee I'll chase hence, thou wolf in sheep's array! . . . out, scarlet hypocrite!' A little earlier in this scene, Gloster has taunted Winchester with the words. 'Thou that givest whore's indulgences to sin'.—'It should be now, but my fear is this,—Some galled goose of Winchester would hiss', T. & C., v x 53–54.

'The Bishop of Winchester had his Palace between London Bridge and the Globe Theatre and owned most of the land in that district, fattening himself on the rents of sin; for it was the region of brothels, the women of which were known as Winchester geese', Hesketh Pearson, *A Life of Shakespeare*, 1942 (p. 94).

Cf. **green goose.**

wind-instrument. Podex—or *ars musica*, as Grose records in his *A Classical Dictionary of the Vulgar Tongue*. See the quotation at **tail,** 2, and cf. **break wind** and **tail,** 3, and **tale,** 2.

winded in the forehead, a recheat. See quotation at **hang one's bugle . . . :** a recheat is a set of notes sounded to recall the hounds from a false scent: there is, I think, an allusion to the **horns** of cuckoldry; and **bugle** is the key-note of that supposition.

winning match. See **match.**

with child. See **child . . .**

withered pear. 'Your virginity, your old virginity [i.e., long retained], is like one of our French wither'd pears,—it looks ill, it eats dryly; marry, 'tis a wither'd pear', *All's Well*, I i 161–164. Her virginity is localized in, and made synonymous with, the pudend, which, unused, becomes dry and atrophied, with certain parts (e.g., the clitoris) recessive and increasingly latent.

wittol; wittolly. (Pertaining to) a husband complaisantly permitting his wife's unfaithfulness; an accommodating **cuckold**. 'The jealous wittolly knave': Falstaff, concerning Ford, whom he intends to cuckold: *Merry Wives*, II ii 276–277.— *Ibid.*, II ii 299–300, Ford, thinking he is about to be cuckolded by Falstaff, 'Cuckold! wittol! Cuckold! the devil himself hath not such a name.'

Ex M.E. *wodewale*, 'green woodpecker' (a simple and amiable bird).

wived. Provided with a wife: see quotation at **stew.**—*Othello*, II i 60, 'But, good lieutenant, is your general wived?'

Cf. slang *molled up*, 'in company—or living—with a woman': so, too, **woman'd.**

wiving. Iachimo, repentant, describes Imogen as 'A shop of all the qualities that man Loves woman for; besides, that hook'— lure, incitement—'of wiving, Fairness which strikes the eye', *Cymbeline*, V v 166–168: marriage with a woman: cf. preceding entry.

woman, as generic for 'women regarded as the aim and the gratification of man's sexual pleasure': see quotation at **out-paramour.**

woman'd. (Cf. wived.) To be accompanied by, and in conversation with, a woman. 'I do attend here on the general; And think it no addition, nor my wish, To have him see me woman'd', *Othello*, III iv 192–194, where there is an undertone of 'under the domination of a woman'.

And cf. **man.**

womb. 1, the uterus: 'The fruit within my womb', 1 *Henry VI*, v
iv 63.—*Richard III*, IV iv 54.

2, Belly: 'Thou detestable maw, thou womb of death!', R. &
J., v iii 45.

O.E. *wamb*, belly, womb. Of common-Germanic origin.

women, detected for. Known to be a womanizer. 'I never heard
the absent duke much detected for women; he was not
inclined that way', *Measure*, III ii 123–124.

Cf. the entry at **woman.**

women's matters. (Cf. **country matters.**) Women's intimacies;
intercourse with men; *pudenda muliebria*. '*Second Citizen.* Truly, sir,
all that I live by is with the awl: I meddle with no tradesman's
matters, nor women's matters', *Julius Caesar*, I i 24–26.

woo. To pay court, especially of a man paying amorous court to
a woman, as in *Richard III*, I ii.—*Two Gentlemen*, II i 141, 'She
woos you by a figure'.—*As You Like It*, V ii 1–5.—*Venus*, v. 6.

M.E. *wowian*, O.E. *wogian*, lit., 'to bend—or incline—in a certain direction', cognate with Sanskrit *vakras*, 'bent'.

woodman, in *Measure*, IV iii 163, 'He's a better woodman than
thou takest him for', means wencher or **doer.**

Cf. **husbandry** for the semantics.

wooer. One who woos a woman; especially if briskly or amorously. 'He is the bluntest wooer in Christendom', 3 *Henry VI*,
III ii 83.—'A jolly, thriving wooer', *Richard III*, IV iii 44; cf. IV
iv 228, 'a wooer's tale'.

work, n. See **go to work** and cf. *dirty work at the cross roads* (origin
in highwaymanry).

'She did gratify his amorous works' (caresses and con-
gresses): *Othello*, v ii 213.

Cf. **act** and **deed** and **performance.**

work, v. To 'do the deed', to 'perform', i.e. to copulate. Iago,
satirizing women, says, 'You rise to play, and go to bed to
work', *Othello*, II i 116.

'The present verb is a new formation from the n.', Wyld.

Work, n.: O.E. *weorc*, 'work—whether the act or the result; action; a building'. Of common-Teutonic stock, it is cognate with Gr. *ergon* 'action, work', and Gr. *organon*, 'instrument'.

work of generation. See generation, work of.

workman. A male copulator: see quotation at **fitness.**

world. Figuratively of a single female breast, the World consisting of two hemispheres,—a fact on which Shakespeare characteristically embroiders. *Lucrece*, vv. 407–411. 'Her breasts, like ivory globes circled with blue, A pair of maiden worlds unconquered, Save of their lord no bearing yoke they knew; And him by oath they duly honoured. These worlds in Tarquin new ambition bred.'

wound, n. A gash. (For a perhaps corresponding use of the v., see the *Cymbeline* quotation at **Tarquin.**) ' "See, in my thigh", quoth she, "here was the sore." She showed hers: he saw more wounds than one, And blushing fled, and left her all alone', *The Passionate Pilgrim*, 9, vv. 12–14, where, clearly, the pudend is implied.

O.E. *wund*, probably cognate with O.E. *winnan*, "to fight" (Wyld).

wrack, v.t. To deflower; to 'ruin'. Polonius to Ophelia, in reference to Hamlet, 'I fear'd he did but trifle, And meant to wrack thee', II i 112–113: cf. the use of the n. to = 'sexual dishonour' in Lucrece's self-reproach (apostrophic of her absent husband, Collatine), 'Yet am I guilty of thy honour's wrack' (v. 841).

Cognate, at least in sense, with *wreck*. *Wrack*: M.E. *wrac*, probably ex Old Norse *wrack*, 'a wreck; refuse, trash'; cognate with O.E. *wraecu*, 'vengeance; misery' (Wyld).

wrack of maidenhood. 'Ruin'; loss of virginity before marriage. *All's Well*, III v 23.

Cf. **wrack** and **maiden loss.**

wrestle. To be one of the two contenders in a love-bout. See **wrestler** and cf. **contend** and **strive.**

O.E. *wraestlian*: *wrest* + frequentative suffix *-le*; *wrest* comes from a Teutonic stem that means 'to turn, to twist' (cf. therefore, **turn i' the bed**).

wrestler. A contender in a bout of love; an exponent of amorous catch-as-catch-can. *As You Like It*, I iii 20–24, '*Celia*. Come, come, wrestle with thy affections.—*Rosalind*. O, they take the part of a better wrestler than myself.—*Celia*. O, a good wish upon you! you will try in time, despite of a fall.'

wrong, v. To get (a woman) with child outside wedlock; to rape (a married woman). 'Ravisht and wrong'd, as Philomela was', *Titus Andronicus*, IV i 53.

Ex the n.: a *wrong* comes from O.E. *wrang*, itself ex Scandinavian; cognates, O.E. *wringan*, 'to turn, to twist'—Old High Ger. *ringan*, 'to twist'—and Gothic *wruggo*, 'a snare, a noose': ultimately cognate with a Sanskrit word for 'crooked'. (Wyld.)

yard. Penis, usually with implication of *penis erectus*. '*Armado*. I do adore thy sweet Grace's slipper.—*Boyet*. Loves her by the foot.— *Dumaine*. He may not by the yard', L.L.L., V ii 661–663.

It is the same word as *yard*, 'a measure of length—3 feet'; *yard*, in the sense of 'a measure', comes from M.E. *yarde*, O.E. *gerd*, 'a rod, a staff', which is cognate with L. *hasta*, 'a staff; a shaft; hence, a spear': cf. the Biblical and literary Fr. *verge*, 'the penis', and **stake,** n., and **stalk.**

In the approximate period 1590–1780, *yard* was perhaps the most generally used literary term for 'penis'; and, obsolete by ca. 1850, it never suffered the social declension of **cock** and **prick** and **tool.**

yield one's body to shame. (Of a woman) to yield to a man that she does not love. 'Were I under the terms of death Th' impression of keen whips I'ld wear as rubies, And strip myself to death, as to a bed That longing have been sick for, ere I'ld yield My body up to shame', *Measure*, II iv 101–105.

A euphemism rather less mild than **yield one's virginity** (*Measure*, III i 95).

M.E. *yeelden*, O.E. *gelden*, 'to pay' (cf. Gothic *-gildan*, 'to requite'): hence, to pay the price of one's body and its **treasures**.

yield to. See **yield unto.**

yield to one's will; yield one's body to (another's) **will.** To yield sexually to a man (whether beloved or not). Angelo to Isabella, 'Redeem thy brother By yielding up thy body to my will', *Measure*, II iv 163–164.

yield unto; yield to. To yield to a man's sexual desire. *Measure*, v i 101 (the latter).

yield up one's body. See **yield to one's will.**

yielding. A woman's surrender of her chastity. 'I should get ground of your fair mistress; make her go back, even to the yielding, had I admittance, and opportunity to friend', *Cymbeline*, I iv 103–106.

Cf. the five entries preceding this one.

yoke. 'Her breasts, . . . A pair of maiden worlds unconquered, Save of their lord no bearing yoke they knew', *Lucrece*, vv. 407–409: the significance springs from the sense of 'bearing' (see **bear).**

Of common-Teutonic origin, it is cognate with L. *jugum*, itself cognate with *jungere*, 'to join'; cf. Sanskrit *yugain*, 'a yoke; a pair'.

youth is often used by Shakespeare to mean 'youth with its sexual curiosity and amorous ardour', as in *Measure*, II iii 10–12, 'A gentlewoman . . . , Who, falling in the flaws of her youth, Hath blister'd her report: she is with child'.

In English, ultimately O.E. *geong*, 'young' + -th, suffix of 'state, condition, quality'. *Young* is cognate with L. *juvenis*.

Routledge Classics
Get inside a great mind

The Wheel of Fire
Interpretations of Shakespearian Tragedy
G. Wilson Knight

'I confess that reading his essays seems to me to have enlarged my understanding of the Shakespearean pattern, which, after all, is quite the main thing.'
T. S. Eliot

Originally published in 1930, this classic of modern Shakespeare criticism proves both enlightening and innovative. Standing head and shoulders over all other Shakespearian interpretations, *The Wheel of Fire* is the masterwork of the brilliant English scholar G. Wilson Knight. Founding a new and influential school of Shakespearian criticism, *The Wheel of Fire* was Knight's first venture in the field – his writing sparkles with insight and wit, and his analyses are key to contemporary understandings of Shakespeare.

Hb: 0–415–25561–9   Pb: 0–415–25395–0

Romantic Image
with a new epilogue by the author
Frank Kermode

'In this extremely important book of speculative and scholarly criticism Mr Kermode is setting out to redefine the notion of the Romantic tradition, especially in relation to English poetry and criticism ... a rich, packed, suggestive book.'
Times Literary Supplement

One of our most brilliant and accomplished critics, Frank Kermode here redefines our conception of the Romantic movement, questioning both society's harsh perception of the artist as well as poking fun at the artist's occasionally inflated self-image. Written with characteristic wit and style, this ingeniously argued and hugely enjoyable book is a classic of its kind.

Hb: 0–415–26186–4   Pb: 0–415–26817–2

For these and other classic titles from Routledge, visit
www.routledgeclassics.com